THE MEDIATOR'S HANDBOOK
SKILLS AND STRATEGIES FOR PRACTITIONERS

HEAD OFFICE: 100 Harris Street PYRMONT NSW 2009
Tel: (02) 8587 7000 Fax: (02) 8587 7100
For all sales inquiries please ring 1800 650 522
(for calls within Australia only)

INTERNATIONAL AGENTS & DISTRIBUTORS

CANADA
Carswell Co
Ontario, Montreal,
Vancouver, Calgary

HONG KONG
Sweet & Maxwell Asia
Hennessy Road, Wanchai

Bloomsbury Books Ltd
Chater Road, Central

MALAYSIA
Sweet & Maxwell Asia
Petaling Jaya, Selangor

NEW ZEALAND
Brooker's Ltd
Wellington

SINGAPORE
Sweet & Maxwell Asia
Albert Street

UNITED KINGDOM & EUROPE
Sweet & Maxwell Ltd
London

UNITED STATES
Wm W Gaunt & Sons, Inc
Holmes Beach, Florida

William S Hein Co Inc
Buffalo, New York

JAPAN
Maruzen Company Ltd
Tokyo

THE MEDIATOR'S HANDBOOK
SKILLS AND STRATEGIES FOR PRACTITIONERS

2ND EDITION

by

RUTH CHARLTON
LLB
Solicitor, Supreme Court of New South Wales,
Lawyer Mediator

and

MICHELINE DEWDNEY
BA, Dip Soc Stud, Dip Crim, MA (Hons), Dip Laws
Solicitor, Supreme Court of New South Wales,
Lawyer Mediator

Foreword by
PROFESSOR JOHN WADE

LAWBOOK CO.
2004

Published in Sydney by

Lawbook Co.
100 Harris Street, Pyrmont, NSW

First edition... 1995
Second edition 2004

National Library of Australia
Cataloguing-in-Publication entry

Charlton, ruth.
The mediator's handbook: skills and strategies for
practitioners.

2nd ed.
Includes index.
ISBN 0 455 21982 6.

1. Mediation – Handbooks, manuals, etc. 2. Dispute
resolution (Law) – Australia – Handbooks, manuals, etc. 3.
Mediation – Australia – Case studies. I. Dewdney, M. S.
II. Wade, John H. (John Harington), 1948- . III. Title.

Editor: Evonne Irwin
Senior Project Editor: Merilyn Shields
Product Developer: Shelagh Coleman

Typeset in Stone Sans and Stone Serif, 9.5 on 11.5 point, by
Midland Typesetters Pty Ltd, Maryborough, Victoria

*We dedicate this book to our families, for whom "mediation"
is a household word*

For our respective husbands Geoff Charlton and John Dewdney

*For our children Tom Dewdney, Natasha and Chris Charlton,
and also for Brooke*

And in loving memory of David Dewdney

Foreword to the first edition

The mediation and conflict management movement has grown dramatically over the last ten years. There continues to emerge a proliferation of theories, diverse practices, literature, organisations, training and legislation dealing with the diagnosis, evolution and management of conflict. These activities seem unlikely to abate. Happily, this interest in conflict management and mediation is an interdisciplinary venture. Reflective practitioners and theories come from management, psychological, communication, sociological, economic, legal and hybrid sources. Reflective practitioners constantly swap horror and wonder stories, practical hints, adapted 12-step processes, statistics true and not so true, grand visions and reworked theories.

This book represents an outstanding contribution to this tradition. Two pioneering mediators in Australia, Ruth Charlton and Micheline Dewdney, have chalked up many thousands of hours of mediation experience – often together as co-mediators. They have systematised this practice by years of leadership at training courses, speaking at conferences, supervising surveys of mediation schemes and jointly editing the ground-breaking *Australian Dispute Resolution Journal.*

Now in the pages of *The Mediator's Handbook* you will find a step-by-step description of a mediation process which has been adapted over the years. Helpfully, the authors identify where they have changed their own theory or practice due to the crucible of experience.

The authors have set out systematically in each section of the book a chart of recommended "Dos and Don'ts" for the novice or experienced mediator. My copy of the work is already highlighted and circled on many pages identifying new strategies which will be added to my repertoire or "tool box". All mediators, no matter what school they are from, will find practical wisdom to incorporate and test in their own laboratories. The authors are to be congratulated for this outstanding contribution to the tradition of reflective mediator practitioners who theorise, practise, critique, adapt theory and adapt practice cyclically.

Professor John Wade
School of Law, Bond University

Queensland
1995

Foreword to the second edition

Nine years after the first edition of *The Mediator's Handbook*, the authors have expanded their words of wisdom.

Ruth Charlton and Micheline Dewdney have again distilled thousands of hours of mediation practice into a practical toolbox. Their recommended process reflects a classical problem-solving or facilitative model of mediation. Yet they exhibit humility about the many possible variations to this foundational model.

Each chapter is summarised in a helpful fashion with a list of "Dos and Don'ts". Most importantly, each chapter tackles the difficult task of translating a *concept* (for example, creating doubt; asking questions; summarising) into actual *language* with a list of examples.

The authors are fearless in addressing controversial topics such as the role of legal representatives, mediator drafting, using shuttle meetings, using visuals and note-taking. They commend their own preferences, but are again open to alternatives. There is an excellent section (Chapter 20) in the book on subtle and not-so-subtle loss of impartiality. All this is done in very readable language, reinforced for concrete learners by case studies and illustrations. Occasional Australian colloquialisms will also attract foreign readers.

From two pioneer practitioners, teachers and writers in the field of mediation in Australia, it is a delight that such wisdom has been refined and expanded on this second occasion.

Professor John Wade
School of Law, Bond University

Queensland
January 2004

About the Authors

RUTH CHARLTON LLB is a solicitor in private practice. She is an accredited specialist in mediation under the New South Wales Law Society's Specialist Accreditation Scheme and is an arbitrator with the Workers' Compensation Commission. She works as an ADR consultant and is involved in the design of mediation courses and in the design and facilitation of workshops in complaint management and customer contact. Ruth has completed over 2,000 mediations (but has stopped counting) and is experienced as a course leader, trainer, coach, assessor and speaker both in Australia and overseas. She is editor of the *Australian Dispute Resolution Journal*.

MICHELINE DEWDNEY BA, Dip Soc Stud, Dip Crim (Melb), MA (Hons)(NSW), Dip Law (BAB), is a solicitor of the Supreme Court of New South Wales and a part-time presiding lawyer on the Mental Health Review Tribunal. She has designed and conducted mediation and conciliation workshops and training courses for universities, other training institutions and government organisations. Micheline has carried out over 1,000 mediations, conciliations and facilitations for a number of agencies as well as privately. She continues to mediate privately as well as for a number of mediation organisations and is also an arbitrator for the Workers' Compensation Commission.

Preface

As in the first edition of *The Mediators Handbook*, this second edition continues to be a "how to do it" book. Basically it focuses on the practical aspects of processes, practices and working dynamics of mediation and is designed to reflect the realities of mediation.

In the preface to the first edition, we expressed the hope that the book would remove many concerns, answer some questions, provide an easy reference and checklist to guide practitioners through the session and assist them in deciding what to do or say next. The feedback received from both experienced and less experienced practitioners over the eight years since the first publication has been gratifying to say the least. This feedback has encouraged us to believe that the book achieved what we set out to achieve – to cut to the heart of what actually happens at the "coal face". To quote one of our readers – *"The Mediators Handbook is my co-mediator."*

But the world moves on. So, too, with mediation. New ideas emerge; technological advances influence mediation practice or achieve greater prominence; new enthusiastic practitioners enter the field; the number of advisers trained in mediation and negotiation expands; and organisations adapt basic processes to meet their own particular terms of reference.

Because of these factors, we were enthusiastic when our publisher suggested that the time was ripe for a second edition of the *Handbook*. All mediators continue to be on a learning curve, no matter how extensive their years of practice or frequency of cases. Ideally, clients, advisers and mediators work as a team. Just as practitioners hope the mediation experience has some positive influence on the people participating in the forum, this is not a one-way street. New insights continue to be provided to us by our clients and their advisers – insights which can be put to practical effect and which have provided invaluable material for the second edition. We acknowledged these anonymous contributions in the first edition of the book. We do so again with this second edition.

We have learnt and applied the skills and processes outlined in this book from disputes dealing with all subject matters including personal injury, commercial, workplace, community, environmental, professional negligence, banking, wills, family and parenting matters. In addition, experienced mediators have had to grapple with new dynamics that apply because of technological advances. Since the first edition, telephone conferences have become commonplace. This change of scene is addressed in one of the new chapters in the book. What does not change is the successful formula of focusing on what happens at the "coal face". The aim of the book is to discuss not only what should or might be done from a theoretical stance but, importantly, to provide practical information on that vital ingredient of how to do it.

As well as acknowledging the enormous contribution by the users of mediation services, we would also like to acknowledge the input of the publication team at Lawbook Co., of whom there were many. Special thanks also go to Geoff Charlton who read almost every word, made constructive suggestions and sorted out any technological problems.

Readers have advised that the case notes in the first edition were of great value and enormous interest and "rang bells" of familiarity. Once again, we would stress that both the original and the new case notes are a composite of disputes and parties encountered in the mediation context and do not relate to one particular dispute or one particular set of participants.

Ruth Charlton
Micheline Dewdney

Sydney
January 2004

Table of Contents

PART 1
The Mediation Process and its Practical Application

PART 2
Procedural Variations to the Mediation Process

PART 3
Pre-mediation

PART 4
Mediation Skills and Strategies

PART 5
Special Mediation Issues

APPENDIX

Part 1

The Mediation Process and its Practical Application

Introduction to the mediation process

There is no universally accepted model of mediation. The process applied may depend on whether mediators are involved in the intake work required to bring the parties to the table. It may also depend on whether it is a dispute between two parties or whether it is a multi-party dispute; whether legal representatives are present at the mediation; whether third party representatives take an active role in the mediation as in personal injury disputes or whether the mediation is conducted on a solo mediation or co-mediation basis.

In certain circumstances and especially when legal representatives are present, preliminary conferences are held where an "agreement to mediate" is executed. A major purpose of holding a preliminary conference is for the mediator to ensure that each party has all the necessary information and documentation for effective mediation. During the preliminary conference, the mediator informs the parties and the lawyers of the features of mediation, explains the mediation process and the role of the mediator. Plans are made for relevant documents to be exchanged prior to the next session when the actual mediation is conducted. Individual private mediators may also have their personal preferences as may organisations employing mediators. A variety of models have also emerged from different training courses.

The stages in mediation depend on the particular model of mediation applied. The following seven-stage model is one which can be applied to a wide range of disputes. With minor variations, it has been applied and modified by a number of organisations and private mediators.

Variations to it will be referred to from time to time. The broad rationale for each stage of the mediation is identified and described briefly. A more detailed analysis will be provided in subsequent chapters, each focusing on individual stages.

Table 1.1: Mediation Model

STAGE 1	MEDIATOR'S OPENING STATEMENT	RATIONALE
	• Introductions. • Features of mediation: voluntary, confidential. • Role of mediators: neutral and impartial facilitator. • Status of agreement. • Process of mediation explained: parties in control of content and outcome. • Authority to settle established. • Parties' endorsement of ground rules. • Parties' agreement to proceed with the mediation.	To explain mediation and the role of mediators and to set the scene for constructive use of the mediation session and a satisfying resolution for the parties, after they have given informed consent to the mediation.
STAGE 2	**PARTIES' STATEMENTS AND MEDIATOR'S SUMMARIES**	**RATIONALE**
	• Mediator takes notes during each party's statement. • Second party's statement is not made in response to first party's statement. • Summaries of both statements are read out at end of second party's statement and checked for inaccuracies.	To help mediators understand the parties' perspectives, to encourage the parties to listen to each other's issues and gain an appreciation of each other's perspective.
STAGE 3	**ISSUE IDENTIFICATION AND AGENDA SETTING**	**RATIONALE**
	• Issues and discussion points are identified from the parties' statements. • Listed issues are expressed in neutral and mutual terms, endorsed by parties. • Agreement is reached on first item for discussion.	To set the scene for clarification, exploration and discussion of issues. To give mediator a "road map" for managing the early discussion.

STAGE 4	CLARIFICATION AND EXPLORATION OF ISSUES	RATIONALE
	• Parties discuss the agenda topics. They exchange feelings and perspectives about the dispute without pressure for premature resolution.	To clarify issues, eliciting underlying needs and interests. To identify options.

STAGE 5	PRIVATE SESSIONS	RATIONALE
	• A private and confidential session is held with each party. (More than one session may be held.) • Development of options and mutually satisfying outcomes facilitated.	To explore mutually satisfying outcomes, raise doubts re entrenched positions and rehearse negotiations.

STAGE 6	FACILITATING NEGOTIATIONS	RATIONALE
	• Development of further options are facilitated. • Options are evaluated and mutually satisfying agreement facilitated.	To help parties move from entrenched positions, encourage creativity for mutual benefit and help them own the final outcome.

STAGE 7	MEDIATION OUTCOME: AGREEMENT, ADJOURNMENT OR TERMINATION	RATIONALE
	• Terms of agreement are reality tested. • Parties congratulated on reaching agreement. • Parties are assisted to decide on future action if a partial or no agreement is reached.	To ensure lasting and realistic agreement. To ensure a positive conclusion of the mediation and enhance the parties' sense of achievement.

Figure 1 represents a summary of the stages of mediation. Pre-mediation in the diagram refers to arrangements made for getting the parties to the mediation table, for example, agreeing on the venue, who will attend the mediation and who the mediator will be. Post-mediation refers to arrangements which may be required based on the outcome of the mediation. For example, if the outcome was satisfactory and led to an agreement, the parties may wish to convert it into a legally enforceable outcome and perhaps file it in court. The outcome may, on the other hand, be a partial agreement or no agreement, in which case the parties may wish to have the unresolved issues or all the issues dealt with by litigation or any other dispute resolution process, including arbitration. Alternatively, the parties may wish to adjourn and implement under-takings agreed upon at the mediation.

The parties may prefer to have an interim agreement, if they wish to test whether an arrangement will work, especially in mediations relating to ongoing relationships. The mediator could invite them to return to mediation after a trial period of a few weeks or months to finalise or fine tune the terms of settlement.

OTHER PROCESS MODELS

Another popular process model, recommended by quite a few training providers, features the two triangles (see Figure 2). The stages are not dissimilar to those set out in the "Egg" diagram (Figure 1).

With the Egg, it is seen that the broadest and deepest space is allocated to "Stage 4 — Joint Session. Clarification and Exploration of Issues" — on the basis that this stage is vital to generating mutual understanding (whether acknowledged at the time or not) before moving to problem solving.

A similar philosophy applies with the triangles. Stage 4 is included in the top triangle as is, usually, the first private session. In other versions, the first private session does not feature in the top triangle, but appears between the two halves, to signify that it is considered to be a transition stage.

A further variation is where the triangles are not of equal proportion, the top one being allocated the most importance.

However the diagram is formatted, trainees are taught to allocate a fair amount of time to working in the top triangle before moving to the second one. This recommended sojourn in the top triangle is to discourage, among other things, the temptation to rush to solutions too early. In most cases such an exercise is considered to be counter-productive. This is because a rush to solutions carries the danger of locking parties into their opening positions at an early stage before they have had time to provide, and gain, some understanding of why an opposing position is being taken or before doubt has been created about maintaining their own position. Thus, both the Egg and Triangle diagrams illustrate a recommended time focus.

INTRODUCTION TO THE MEDIATION PROCESS

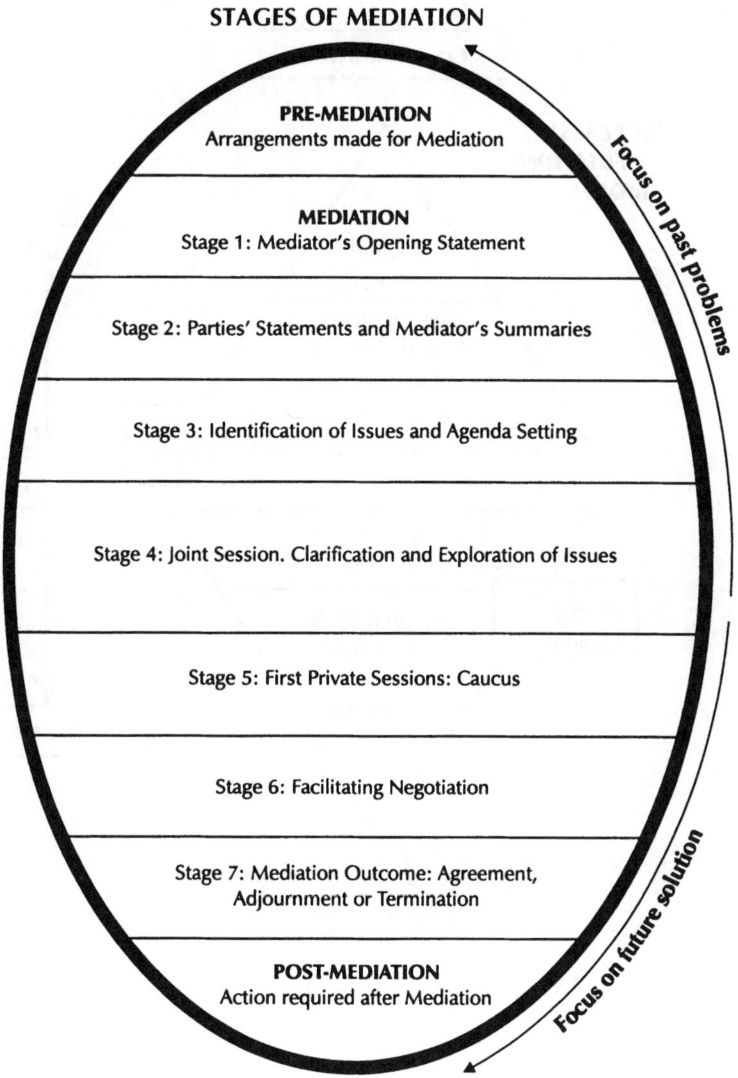

STAGES OF MEDIATION

PRE-MEDIATION
Arrangements made for Mediation

Focus on past problems

MEDIATION
Stage 1: Mediator's Opening Statement

Stage 2: Parties' Statements and Mediator's Summaries

Stage 3: Identification of Issues and Agenda Setting

Stage 4: Joint Session. Clarification and Exploration of Issues

Stage 5: First Private Sessions: Caucus

Stage 6: Facilitating Negotiation

Stage 7: Mediation Outcome: Agreement,
Adjournment or Termination

Focus on future solution

POST-MEDIATION
Action required after Mediation

Figure 1

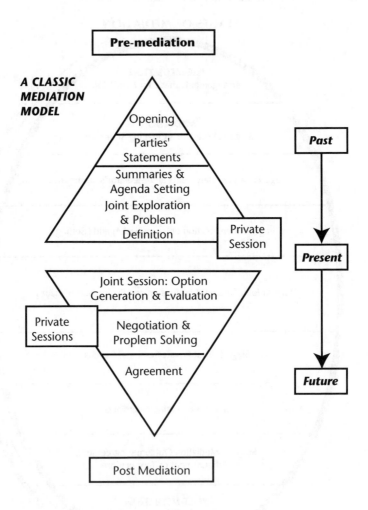

Figure 2

Case Note

A rare exception to this is when a mediation has been scheduled by a service provider with insufficient time to devote to intake and the dispute has not been defined clearly enough. Many years ago one of us was involved in such a mediation, which only lasted 35 minutes, but the outcome satisfied both parties. After both parties had delivered their opening statements, and after the mediator had summarised them, but before the agenda had been formulated, the first party said:

"Is that all you want — $500 for all the trouble I've caused you and that's fair enough?"

He then produced his cheque book, wrote out a cheque for $500 and handed it to the second party. The first party was delighted. Both parties shook hands and left highly satisfied with the outcome.

This is just one illustration of where slavishly following the process is unproductive. Experienced mediators can offer other examples where a "quick-fix" solution has been achieved simply by cutting across unnecessary process "protocol".

Both the Egg and Triangle diagrams convey a process which discourages early private sessions on the basis that the information conveyed often turns out to be a mere repetition of what parties have said in their opening statements and so the session is no further advanced. It has been observed that very early private sessions also tend to reinforce opening positions in common with the rush to solutions already discussed. (See "Timing of private sessions" in Chapter 6). Some mediators feel more comfortable in private than in joint sessions and may prematurely encourage the former.

Why use a process?

Following a formula in a flexible way brings structure to the session, discourages the confusion and lack of focus that occurs when participants are verbally and mentally jumping around all over the place, and encourages forward movement. Outlining a plan for the session at the outset promotes confidence in the participants that the mediator, at least, knows where he or she is headed. Parties appreciate a sense of order and predictability in the session knowing what will happen next and why.

The arguments against a stereotyped process include the basic philosophy that mediation is "flexible". It is said that mediators should not become "process bound" as this inhibits creativity. Mediators and parties should be able to conduct or partake in a mediation in such a way that the particular case demands. Clearly, there is merit in this argument, particularly where a process model is employed in a totally inflexible manner, no matter what the circumstances are. Where, for example, there is a statutory three-hour time limit on the proceedings, any preferred formula simply has to be adapted to the realities of the situation.

In being taught a process, trainees are provided with a road map to follow as one of the tools of the trade. Once this is mastered, they then go on to acquire other skills and strategies using the model as a springboard for these. Experienced mediators will often adapt the model they have been taught to accord with their own philosophy and working experience, having become aware of what works best for them. Some, for example, may choose not to summarise parties' opening statements and go straight to agenda setting. When mediators have a clear understanding of the purposes of the various stages of the process they can adapt the process to meet the particular circumstances in a knowledgeable way. It is important, however, for flexibility to be applied for purposes other than the mediator's own comfort zone.

Many mediation agencies have their own process models, which have been fashioned to suit their particular purposes. Generally, these models are variations on, or adaptations of, the common models discussed.

Perhaps the best case to be put for having reference to a road map is that the map appears to work well in the majority of cases. As with any suggested "travel arrangements", there is value and security in having a recommended route as a reference point even though the driver may choose to divert to a secondary road or take a short cut as circumstances demand. Again, with knowledge and experience, there is the ability to revert to the main route when and if necessary.

A process model provides a comforting reference point or fall-back for the mediator. How often is it said: "If in doubt, trust the process"? When the format is explained to the parties in the mediator's opening statement or at the preliminary conference, it provides reassurance that a standard, well-worked formula will prevail as far as possible; that the process is neutral in its application; and that, as a pure process, it does not favour or discriminate against any particular party. This is important for parties, most of whom are meeting the mediator for the first, and probably the only, time.

Stage 1 — The mediator's opening statement: what is it and what purpose does it serve?

There is no need for mediators to feel that they need to produce an Academy Award-winning speech out of their opening statement in order to impress the parties, who are generally restless and anxious to proceed with the mediation. Often the parties are only able to absorb a limited amount of monologue.

The mediator's statement should be brief and concise and should take no longer than five minutes. Where mediators elect to mention their mediation experiences and relevant qualifications, this should not be more than a one-liner. The content of the statement should include the features of mediation, the role of the mediator and an explanation of the mediation process: that is, the stages of mediation and the reasons for each stage.

The importance of the mediator's opening statement and its impact on the mediation should not be underestimated. Anxious parties need to be put at ease and trust in both the mediator and the process needs to be developed. The mediator needs to create a positive atmosphere. The parties also need reassurance about having selected mediation as an appropriate forum for their dispute.

Both the content of the statement and the style of delivery can enhance the prospects of a productive mediation. On the other hand, if from the outset the parties feel ill at ease and uncertain or confused about the process, the mediator faces unnecessary obstacles to facilitating communication and negotiation between them.

As previously mentioned, there may be minor variations in the content of the mediator's opening statement. For example, some models make sparing use of private sessions whilst others regard them as an integral part of the process. Some mediators like to congratulate parties for choosing mediation to settle their dispute whilst others prefer merely to thank them for coming. Some mediators like to refer to the high success rate of mediation to encourage the parties and to create an air of optimism. Rather than emphasise the high success rate in mediation, we like to create realistic expectations and say, for example: "No one gets 100% of what they want but you can still achieve a satisfactory outcome."

Mediators also vary in the emphasis they place on ground rules. We have a preference for understating the ground rules and making use of strategies in the course of the mediation to deal with difficult situations. We avoid a "contempt of mediation" situation by not constantly reminding the parties of the ground rules they have agreed to. We also avoid defining the ground rules in terms of behaviour that will not be tolerated. For example, we do not say: "There will be no interruptions, put-downs or personal attacks." This approach can sound negative and patronising. We prefer to refer to basic courtesy rules and to what works best in mediation. We also like to add that, especially during the parties' statements, it makes it easier for us to take notes if interruptions are kept to a minimum. Even if the parties are not inclined to listen to each other, they may be prepared to help the mediator do her or his job.

WHAT SHOULD THE MEDIATOR'S OPENING STATEMENT COVER?

The mediator's opening statement should include the features of mediation, the role of the mediator and an explanation of the mediation process. The mediator should then establish the parties' authority to settle, their endorsement of basic courtesy rules and their agreement to proceed with the mediation. (Depending on the mediation model, an Agreement to Mediate may be signed either at the preliminary conference or prior to the commencement of the mediation session. Agreements to Mediate are becoming prevalent and contain much of what the mediator includes as part of the opening statement. A copy of an Agreement to Mediate is included in the Appendix.)

Some mediators, even experienced ones, find it useful to have an aide-memoire in the form of a small plastic card to which they can refer just before making their opening statement in order to refresh their memory, for example.

Content of the mediator's opening statement

Normal introductions and welcoming remarks precede the mediator's opening statement. Agreement is sought on how the parties wish to be addressed: "Are first names okay by you?" The mediator also needs to reassure them on their choice of mediation. The parties should also be asked whether they have any other commitments or any parking problems that might affect the amount of time they can devote to the mediation. The mediator then proceeds with the opening statement (details of which are outlined below).

1. The Features of Mediation

   (a) Mediation is voluntary and can be terminated at any time by the mediator or the parties without the need to give reasons. Some mediation schemes are mandatory, and therefore the mediator's opening statement needs to take this into account and the statement should be varied accordingly.

   (b) Mediation is confidential unless otherwise required by law. Mediators cannot be called as witnesses in any ensuing court proceeding.

   (c) Form of agreement: oral or written, final or interim. If they wish, the parties can ask their lawyers to convert the agreement into one that can be filed in court.

   (d) Courtesy ground rules: respect for everyone present and allowing each person to speak uninterrupted.

   (e) Flexible process.

2. The Role of the Mediator

   (a) The mediator is a facilitator of communication, negotiation and decision-making between the parties.

   (b) The mediator does not give legal advice, professional or otherwise, or suggest solutions to the parties.

   (c) The mediator aims to be neutral and impartial, does not establish facts or decide which of the parties is right or wrong.

   (d) The mediator has nothing to gain in any way from the outcome of the mediation, whether agreement is reached or not.

3. Explanation of the Mediation Process

  (a) Parties' statements: to identify their own perception of the situation and how they have been affected by it.

  (b) Mediator's summary of the parties' statements: to elicit the issues as perceived by the parties.

  (c) Agenda setting: list of issues and concerns as perceived by the parties. Parties' endorsement of the agenda.

  (d) Exploration of issues in joint session: mediator facilitates the parties' discussion and clarification of the issues each in turn prior to the development of options.

  (e) Private and confidential sessions with each party: to explore options and mutually satisfying outcomes and to prepare for final negotiations.

  (f) Final or further negotiation, developing and evaluating options in joint session: facilitate the building up of the agreement and reality test it.

  (g) Concluding the mediation: reaching partial or total agreement, or terminating the mediation.

4. Establishing Parties' Authority to Settle.

5. Discussing the Option of Signing an Agreement to Mediate.

6. Proposed Courtesy Rules and Parties' Endorsement.

7. Parties' Commitment to Proceed with the Mediation.

FEATURES OF AN EFFECTIVE MEDIATOR'S OPENING STATEMENT

The opening statement should be brief but comprehensive and explicit. Mediators indulging in lengthy monologues risk losing the parties' attention. Parties often can only absorb about one-third of what they hear, at least at that early stage, especially if they are not familiar with the mediation process. Feedback from parties indicates that an over-detailed opening statement overwhelms them to the extent that when the mediator finally asks "Any questions?", they have difficulty recalling anything but the concluding sentences. Information overload can be self-defeating.

The dos and don'ts which are set out for each of the mediation stages have been developed over our several years of mediation practice and observation of difficulties experienced by mediators in training.

Table 2.1: Dos and Don'ts for the Mediator's Opening Statement

Dos	Don'ts
1. LENGTH OF THE STATEMENT	
• Keep it brief, no longer than three to five minutes or you risk losing the parties' attention. You can go into more detail at various stages of the mediation.	• Don't indulge in a long monologue.
2. MEMORISING THE STATEMENT	
• Practise your opening statement to ensure it is kept as brief as possible.	• Don't refer frequently to a prepared script. At the end of your statement, you can, however, refer to a brief checklist saying: "I just want to make sure I haven't missed anything." Be as natural and informal as possible.
3. LANGUAGE USED	
• Use simple everyday language devoid of jargon. Use the language you feel comfortable with. • Ensure parties feel free to ask questions at any stage of the mediation.	• Don't use such terms as "disputees" or "heads of agreement" or "without prejudice" or any other technical language. Parties who are not lawyers may feel they should know their meaning and be reluctant to ask for explanations.
4. MEDIATOR'S CONTROL OF THE PROCESS	
• Adopt a confident and business-like but relaxed and positive approach when explaining your role as a mediator and the mediation process.	• Don't keep asking for the parties' approval of the process in the course of making your opening statement, eg, don't keep asking "Is that okay by you?" at each stage of the statement. The parties expect you to be in control.
5. BACKGROUND INFORMATION ABOUT THE MEDIATOR	
• Give minimum details about your background. If you qualified recently as a mediator, say: "I'm a mediator and my role is to ..." If you're an experienced mediator, you could say: "I've been mediating for several years and my role is to ..."	• Don't refer to your lack of experience if you've only recently qualified as a mediator, eg: "I've only just become interested in mediation." This may cause the parties to lose confidence in you.
6. LEVEL OF DETAIL IN EXPLAINING THE PROCESS	
• Give a very brief outline of the stages in mediation. Additional, more detailed explanations, including underlying rationale, can be provided at each stage of the mediation.	• Don't explain the process in minute detail as parties will be unable to grasp it fully. It takes trainee mediators a four-day course to do so.

Dos	Don'ts
7. THE NEUTRAL AND IMPARTIAL MEDIATOR • Enable the parties to own the issues, eg, when explaining the process, you could say: "I'll be summarising your statements to identify the issues as you see them." • Stress the parties' ownership of the outcome of the mediation, eg: "You both need to decide what is the best outcome for you. I'm not here to tell you what your agreement should be. I'm only here to facilitate your negotiations."	• Don't give parties the idea that you will be identifying the real issues as this may give them the impression that you will be deciding what the important issues are. • Don't make the parties feel that you know best what outcome they should aim for.

HOW IS THE MEDIATOR'S OPENING STATEMENT DELIVERED IF CO-MEDIATION IS APPLIED?

How can the mediator's opening statement be shared by two mediators?

There is no hierarchical relationship between the two mediators. Their roles as mediators are identical as facilitators of communication, negotiation, development and evaluation of options, and reaching agreement. The only difference between solo mediation and co-mediation becomes evident during the mediator's opening statement, the parties' statements and the agenda setting. In co-mediation, tasks are divided between the mediators as equally as possible to avoid giving the impression that one of the mediators is the senior mediator and the other an assistant mediator. From the exploration of issues to the conclusion of the mediation, mediators work together. A more detailed account is set out in Chapter 9 — "Co-mediation".

The following sample statement (which assumes that the parties' legal representatives are not present at the mediation and that a preliminary conference has not been held) should not be treated as a script to be adopted by all mediators. It merely serves as an illustration. The content of the statement will, of course, depend on the particular model of mediation adopted. It is most important that mediators use language that they feel comfortable with.

SAMPLE MEDIATOR'S OPENING STATEMENT BASED ON SOLO MEDIATION IN THE ABSENCE OF THE PARTIES' LEGAL REPRESENTATIVES

Welcome to the mediation. My name is Jo Bloggs. Please call me Jo. How would you like to be addressed (or are first names okay by you)?

I don't know how familiar you are with mediation. Perhaps I could start by saying a few words about it. You might be aware that it has a high success rate, about 80%.

It's a voluntary process so that you can feel free to leave at any stage of the mediation. Naturally I'm encouraging you to stay and work through it together. I can also terminate the mediation at any time and neither of us needs to give reasons for doing so.

It is also confidential unless the law requires otherwise. I'm bound by confidentiality and would ask you also to keep what is said during mediation confidential. The confidentiality of the session enhances the prospects of settlement.

If you don't resolve the dispute and take the matter to court, you won't be able to call me as a witness. If you do reach agreement and it's reduced to writing, it serves as a useful record of what you have decided for the future. If you want your agreement to be filed in court, your lawyers can help you convert it into a document appropriate for the purpose. However, your agreement can be enforceable whether or not it is filed in court.

My role as mediator is not to establish facts or to take sides and decide who is right or wrong. I have nothing to gain from any particular outcome of the mediation. I try to be neutral and impartial. If either of you feels at any stage that I am not, please let me know.

Are there any questions at this stage? It's a lot to absorb in one go.

Perhaps I could now talk about the way we'll proceed. I do follow a particular process, which I've found to be very helpful, but I'm happy to be flexible and if either of us feels that any changes would be helpful, we can discuss that at any stage.

What I'll do first is ask each of you in turn to tell me what brought you to mediation, how you see the situation and how you've been affected by it. While you're doing that I'll be taking notes. I'll then read back a summary of my notes at the end of both statements to make sure I've got it right. I'll then be making a list on the whiteboard of the main issues you've raised in your statements. I'll then ask you to let me know whether you want any changes made to the list or whether you want any additions to it. The list will act as a guide to your discussions and the negotiations which follow.

At some stage during the mediation I will probably have a private and confidential session with each of you in turn. This will give you an opportunity to have a cup of coffee and to explore options for agreement in more detail and to assess any progress achieved. This should take about 10 to15 minutes with each of you.

When we get together again in a joint session, we should be moving towards an agreement. I will be asking questions to ensure that both of you agree that the agreement reached is fair and realistic, an agreement that you both feel you can live with.

Could I ask you both whether you have full authority to settle today?

These types of mediations usually last at least [three] hours. Do you have any time constraints?

I'd just like to mention ground rules for the mediation. They're really basic courtesy rules. Mediation works best when people respect each other and give each other the opportunity to speak without interruptions. Do you have any problems with that? I think I've covered everything, but just let me make sure. Yes I have. Any questions? Please feel free to ask any questions at any stage.

It makes no difference to me who starts. Do we have a volunteer? [PAUSE] If we do not, Mary, as you brought the matter to mediation first, would you like to start? And Bob, rather than make comments during Mary's statement, why don't you make notes of any points you'd like to bring up later during the discussion period? And Mary, I'll ask you to do the same when Bob is making his statement. Bob, when you make your statement, could you do so as though I had asked you first — in other words, don't respond to Mary's statement at this stage.

Shall we start?

Stage 2 — Parties' opening statements and mediator's summaries

The parties' opening statements are ostensibly made for the mediator to hear and note the concerns of each party without interruption from the other side. The mediator takes written notes of what each party says and then feeds back these statements in summary form. From those usually different versions the mediator then identifies and extracts the common and individual issues and concerns. This stage reinforces the impartiality of the mediator, who gives equal attention and acknowledgment to each side.

WHAT ARE THE PURPOSES OF THE PARTIES' OPENING STATEMENTS?

Apart from leading to the procedural function of setting the agenda, the purposes of the parties' opening statements are as follows:

1. To encourage and initiate the parties' active participation by allowing them to have their say.

2. To set the scene for the creation of doubt in their current perspectives by:

   (a) ensuring that they listen to each other without interruption; and

   (b) ensuring that each side has the advantage of hearing the other's statement twice, first from the other party and then when the mediator summarises.

3. To enable the mediator to get the wider picture but not the intricate details at this time.

1. Encouraging parties' active participation by allowing them to have their say

The invitation to the parties to make an opening statement is a clear indication to them that the role they are expected to play in mediation is one of active participation rather than one of depending on others. If the dispute had continued on the court path the lawyers would have been charged with the main responsibility of handling the parties' case. Even when the lawyers are present at a mediation, we always request the parties to make the opening statements. However, if parties prefer to delegate that function to their lawyers, we would of course respect their wishes. The role the lawyers play at a mediation is discussed later.

The parties are asked by the mediator to outline what the dispute means to them, not just in terms of identifying the issues, but in terms of how they have been affected by them. It is important that the parties are encouraged to share their feelings about what has happened rather than just give a factual or legalistic account.

2. Setting the scene for doubt creation

It has been observed that both parties come to mediation with a problem. They also come with a solution. The solution is usually a change of attitude or behaviour on the part of the other side! This observation is rather simplistic. Parties generally come with the expectation that the result may well involve some sort of compromise, that a 100% win is not realistic in mediation. However, parties naturally want to achieve the best result for themselves in the circumstances. This may involve a determination to concede as little as possible. Others may come believing that their perception of the total rightness of their case will be equally convincing to the other side, once the other side has heard it.

However, a characteristic of mediation is its ability to create doubt. New information emerges. The other point of view is given an equal airing as each party gives an opening statement. The doubt creating begins at this stage in quite a subtle manner as each party hears the other side directly, perhaps for the first time.

3. Enabling the mediator to get the wider picture but not the intricate details

Ideally each party's opening statement should take no more than five minutes. We encourage the parties to be brief and request "just an overview at this stage as you will have the opportunity to get into detail later". We do not want to hear a party quoting a lengthy section of the *Trade Practices Act* verbatim or relating every minute detail of a 12-year business arrangement. The opening statements are analogous to an abstract or the synopsis of a book before we plunge into the story that is to follow. The whole phase, including the mediator's summary of each opening statement, should be completed in approximately 20 minutes with the identified purposes being readily fulfilled in that time. A mediator might say:

> I would just like you to briefly outline what brought you here today and what you hope to achieve from this meeting. I will be making some notes of what you are saying which will be checked back with you when you have both made your statements.

or more succinctly:

> Can you tell me about this matter as you see it? Just give an overview at this stage so I can get the general picture. We can fill in the detail shortly.

The other drawback from a party's overly-detailed opening statement is the same as that outlined when the mediator's opening statement is too long. One of the purposes, that of doubt creation, may not be fulfilled because the non-speaker may have switched off from an information overload.

Where a preliminary conference has been held the mediator may write a follow-up letter confirming what has been discussed. It can be useful to include: "Would you please prepare a brief (five-minute) opening statement from which we will compile a list of topics for discussion in as much detail as the parties wish."

However, it does sometimes happen that a party cannot be discouraged from relating all the ins and outs of what happened or, more often, what should have happened. They are anxious that the mediator should understand their position absolutely. They do not need to convince the mediator of the rightness of their case and sometimes it can be timely to remind them of this. Our role does not require that we be convinced; we just want to get the general picture. Also, unlike a solicitor representing a client, a mediator need not know all the facts to be able to mediate a solution.

The difficulty for the mediator is that it is not always possible immediately to distinguish important points from less important points and, in the interests of fairness, there is a tendency to allow a detailed monologue to drag on until it becomes obvious that the party is going to dominate the phase unless they are curtailed.

Note: An over-detailed opening statement can sometimes alert a mediator to the speaker's state of mind. Later in the session it may become obvious that the speaker is a person who has become so obsessed with the dispute that he or she is unable to prioritise (see "Prioritising" in Chapter 17). Thus, every little dynamic has taken on equal importance. Forgetting to water the flowers 12 years ago ranks equally with fire-bombing the car last month.

When and how should a mediator intervene?

It is certainly appropriate to intervene when parties start repeating themselves or reframing something that has already been said. In response, a mediator might say:

> Mary, I heard you mention that earlier and have made a note of it. I will be reading it back in a minute.

Intervention is also appropriate where legal precedents or statutes are being interpreted in great detail, or architects' or builders' plans are being tabled accompanied by in-depth explanations, or numerous dates with their corresponding events are rolling off the tongue. In the latter case, where a matter is complex or has a long, convoluted history, the parties might be asked to prepare beforehand a simple chronology of events (see "Chronology of events" in Chapter 14). Where a party tables architect's plans with accompanying detail, they can be assured that the plans can be the subject of an agenda item, which will allow for far more detail to be raised.

What can the mediator do if the statement is too long?

If a statement seems to be proceeding past one page of notes with no end in sight, it is in order for the mediator to intervene and remind the party of the purpose of the statement, but in such a way that the speaker does not feel squashed or that her or his statement is considered unimportant. The mediator might say:

> I wonder if we might pause here for a minute. I seem to be hearing some detail that might be more useful to get into when we are having our joint discussion rather than now. Just an overview would fill me in at this stage. Is there anything you need to add briefly to what you have already said?

If this does not work, the mediator may have to be more direct and either point out to the first speaker that the other person is waiting for their turn to speak so it is important to keep it brief or, with the second speaker, emphasise the mediator's role by saying:

> As I explained, part of my role is to be as even-handed as possible. I need to ensure that each side has roughly equal time for their opening statement.

Some mediators have difficulty in intervening because of the need to get the parties' confidence and endorsement. However, allowing one party significantly more time than the other encourages the early development of a power imbalance. If the lengthy speaker is the second speaker, the first speaker, who has been brief, may then demand the right of reply and so we are well and truly into the accuser–defendant mode. A way of redressing any imbalance is for the mediator, when reading back the statements, to put more detail into one and less into the longer version.

It may become obvious to the mediator that the speaker who is making a prolonged statement may have an emotional need to ventilate. It may be counter-productive to frustrate the party and the mediator may need to be flexible.

What can the mediator do if the statement is too short?

It may be that an opening statement is so short that scarcely any useful picture at all is gleaned. This sometimes occurs when a party imagines that the mediator has detailed advance knowledge of the dispute or if the party's normal method of communicating is vague, imprecise or abrupt. A party may be inarticulate or shy.

In such a case, the mediator may need to ask some clarifying questions in order to draw the person out. These should be kept to a minimum and should not take the form of an inquisition, which has the potential to drive some parties further into their shell. A mediator might say:

> Jane, you started your statement by talking about the second doctor's opinion but didn't mention what led you to seek this. Would you like to briefly fill us in on what led up to this action?

Some mediators, for their own security, feel they need to know all the details of a dispute. They do not. Acquiring detailed knowledge is the role of a solicitor when interviewing clients. Details emerge as the session develops. It is irritating to the party who is excluded if the mediator engages in prolonged questioning with one party for a considerable time, solely for the mediator's edification.

It should be kept in mind at all times that we are trying to create a perception of balance.

Case Note

An anecdote fed back to one of the authors was from a first speaker in a mediation. The second speaker's opening statement was twice as long as that of this first party. The first speaker related how he felt dis-empowered by the double-length statement and then by the mediator delving into more detail at the end of it.

HOW TO PROCEED WITH THE OPENING STATEMENTS

Who should begin?

Rather than nominating the first speaker, it is a good idea for the mediator to ask the parties who would like to begin. By issuing an open invitation, the mediator is reinforcing her or his impartiality and is not perceived as placing any priority on one party's position. If the mediator feels that this might lead to stalling, arguments or indecision (usually it does not), then the mediator can nominate which party should begin.

Traditionally the person who initiated the mediation, the action or the complaint is invited to begin if no one has volunteered. It seems quite logical that the initiator should be given the opportunity to say what prompted the action in the first place. In cases where the invitation is thrown open, the respondent party often nominates the initiator of the action as the "beginner", or the initiator will volunteer. However, when inviting a particular party to speak first, it is a good idea for the mediator to imply a personal indifference with regard to who begins and give a reason (which need not be elaborate) for the nomination. For example:

> Joe, I understand you brought this to mediation (initiated the action in this case) so perhaps you would like the courtesy of kicking off (or giving your outline first).

When giving a reason for the nomination, some mediators will preface this by saying that it makes no difference to them who begins but that, as somebody has to, then Joe, who initiated the mediation, might like to start. This is not, as it may seem, being overly cautious. While most parties do not appear to mind a nomination, it has been noted that a particularly sensitive or nervous person might see an ulterior motive in a mediator nomination and feel disempowered. It is a safeguard that pays off with particular people.

Are there advantages/disadvantages in being the first or second speaker?

The relative advantage of being the first or second speaker obviously depends on the perception of the parties. At first glance it would seem that the first speaker has the advantage because that person takes the offensive. However, the second speaker may feel it is in their interests to let the other go first and hear what that person has to say before showing their own hand. Generally though, it is perceived that the first speaker has the advantage of the initiative. However, if both show a reluctance to be the first speaker, the mediator might assure them that "in my experience, there is no advantage or disadvantage in going first".

The second speaker should not respond to the first

Parties who are the second speaker should be encouraged to give their statement as if they were the first speaker. They should not be made to feel that their statement is merely a response to what the first speaker has said. The mediator might say:

> Thank you, Mary. And Bob, thank you for listening without interrupting. Bob, we would really like to hear from you now. Can you tell us how you see things? Please give us your views as you would have if you had been speaking first.

It is totally inappropriate to say (as some trainees are apt to do), "Bob, would you like to respond to Mary?" Bob should not be disadvantaged by being put into a position of having to "respond" to Mary. An invitation to "respond" brings in an accuser–defendant dynamic and carries the danger of the insinuation of a mediator bias.

The realities are that Bob may find a response irresistible in any case. This could be an argument for the second speaker having the advantage, not only because of the opportunity to give their unilateral view of events but also because of the chance to knock down some of the other party's arguments. A mediator may, quite appropriately, invite a party to respond to something the other has said during the joint dialogue session, particularly if that person is fairly reticent. It is not, however, appropriate to do so during the opening statements.

Why a request by the first party for a right of reply should be discouraged

When the second speaker has concluded, the first speaker will sometimes ask for a right of reply, particularly if the second party has not only given their version but also responded to the first speaker's statement. This sometimes occurs where the second statement has been out of proportion to the first; where the second speaker has included some accusation against the other; or where the second speaker's statement has reminded the first party of an issue or concern they overlooked initially. The "right of reply" should be discouraged, otherwise this phase has the potential to take on the open-ended accuser–defendant characteristic already discussed, with each party demanding ongoing rights of reply. This could plunge the whole session into unstructured turmoil. The mediator can handle this by saying:

> Mary, could you please save what you have to say for the moment. You will shortly have the opportunity to say more on that issue. It is important that we get on to the stage where you can talk to each other about all the issues as soon as possible.

Why should interruptions and discussion be discouraged during the parties' opening statements?

The mediator's opening statement will have outlined the process and what happens during each stage. Before the parties give their opening statements, it may be useful to remind them that their opening statements are for the mediator's benefit (even though they do serve other purposes) and thus it would help if there are no interruptions.

> While one person is speaking I'd like to ask the other not to interrupt even if you do not agree with what is being said. It would be surprising if there were no disagreement. Fortunately, a mediator has no interest in who is right or wrong, but it would benefit me to get a clear idea of how each of you sees things. Just make a note of any points you may wish to raise and these can be clarified shortly when we get into a general discussion.

Even though the mediator may already have heard the parties' views at an intake session; a preliminary conference; via legal documents and submissions; or through a telephone co-ordination of the meeting, this step should not be omitted. As we have outlined, there are good reasons for the parties to be given the opportunity to say things in their own words and to hear the other side "from the horse's mouth", so to speak.

Although the emphasis on the opening statements being for the mediator's benefit is to discourage interjections, the statements have a wider purpose. This is perhaps the first time that each party has been in a position of actually having to listen to the other or listen without interrupting. And this occurs twice, the second time being when the mediator summarises each opening statement.

Although we will actively encourage the parties to talk to each other shortly, we do not want them getting into dialogue or arguments at this stage because this defeats the purpose of the mediator getting the individual pictures and of each one getting the other's picture without interruption. We are trying to set the scene for doubt creation, not defensiveness, about positions.

Discouraging discussion during opening statements

Some mediators hold the view that any dialogue between the parties is good and may allow it at this stage "because at least they are talking to each other". Our experience has been that the "talking to each other" during opening statements generally takes the form of denials and arguments and is not particularly constructive. Cross-table discussion is far more constructive during the first joint exploration session when the issues have been listed and the mediator is in a much better position to direct the traffic.

Dialogue at this stage can also be unfair to the second speaker who has allowed the other party to proceed without interruption. It can put the mediator in the position of having to deal with a scrambled egg, rather than steering the parties to an ultimately more productive session by separating the white, the yolk and the shell.

Dealing with interruptions

Of course parties will sometimes interrupt. If the interruption is brief and only results in a short exchange it is best to ignore it, rather than to read the riot act straight away, which makes the mediator appear as a disciplinarian. Sometimes the other side may only interject to make a minor correction, "No, that happened in 1992". However, if an interjection is disruptive or occurs more than once, the interjector should be reminded that the opening statements are for the mediator's benefit and there will be plenty of opportunity for clarification and round table talk later. If it continues you can be more direct:

> Mary, I had the benefit of hearing you without interruption which was really helpful to me. It would be good if I can get Bob's picture in the same way.

If sniping continues to occur, again remind them that they agreed to talk just to you at this stage.

Non-verbal interruptions

Interruptions can take the form of snorting derisively, paper shuffling, or delving noisily into briefcases (legal representatives are often guilty of the latter two actions). These are discourtesies. Where the table is strewn with papers before the opening statements commence, ask parties and representatives if they can put the papers aside for the present so that the speakers may proceed without distraction. You can pre-empt this behaviour at the beginning by stating:

> We will begin once everybody has settled and got their papers in order.

During the statement the mediator might say:

> A, could you just pause for a minute. B, I was wondering if you could leave your papers for a moment. It's really important that we all hear each other at this stage.

What happens when there are joint parties or where parties are legally represented at the mediation?

In some cases there are joint parties at the mediation, such as a husband and wife. The joint parties should be requested to nominate a spokesperson to make the opening statement on their behalf. The others should only be requested to contribute if the spokesperson has omitted something. The mediator might say:

> Do you have anything to add to what Mary has said that she has not already covered?

This does not mean that the other parties cannot all contribute during the exploration phase, but it is neither efficient nor effective to have several parties going over the same ground in the opening statement.

The role of legal representatives is discussed in Part 5, Chapter 20. For now it is sufficient to mention the desirability of encouraging the party to make the opening statement and, as with joint parties, to invite the lawyer to contribute any additional information a client may have omitted.

Some dos and don'ts for the parties' opening statements are set out below.

Table 3.1: Dos and Don'ts for the Parties' Opening Statements

Dos	Don'ts
1. ENCOURAGING PARTIES' ACTIVE PARTICIPATION	
• Ask parties to make opening statement even in the presence of their representatives. • Ask parties to include how they have been affected by the dispute.	• Don't ask parties to specify just the main issues of the dispute.
2. SETTING THE SCENE FOR DOUBT CREATION	
• Encourage parties to listen carefully to each other's statements and to the mediator's summaries.	
3. AVOID PROBLEMS EARLY IN THE MEDIATION	
• Explain the need for brief opening statements: five minutes each. • Let parties decide who the first speaker will be. • Explain why it is insignificant who goes first in making their opening statement. • Indicate indifference as to who begins. • Let second speaker make statement as though he or she has been first to do so. • Ignore minor interjections.	• Don't let the parties give too many details in their statement. • Don't help parties decide who the first speaker will be unless they disagree. • Don't invite or allow second speaker to respond to first opening statement. • Don't encourage potentially disruptive interjections or prolonged discussions. • Don't invite or allow first speaker a right of reply to second opening statement.
4. GETTING THE GENERAL PICTURE, NOT THE DETAILS	
• Request opening statement as overview only, as a basis for formulating the agenda. • Ask clarifying questions if statement is too short.	• Don't let party persevere with minute details before intervening. • Don't conduct inquisition or cross-examination when asking clarifying questions.

THE MEDIATOR'S SUMMARIES OF THE PARTIES' OPENING STATEMENTS

The purposes of the mediator's summaries of the parties' opening statements are:

1. To assure the parties that the mediator has heard, noted and summarised their individual issues and concerns.

2. To give each party the opportunity to hear, through the mediator, the other side's version a second time.

3. To act as a guide for formulating the agenda in order to facilitate the exploration and discussion of the issues which either one or both parties have raised in their opening statements.

Reinforcing that parties have been heard

The mediator should convey to the parties that they have been heard. The parties' concerns should be noted and summarised in a way that reinforces the mediator's neutrality and impartiality.

The mediator will summarise what each party has said. This will be what it implies: a summary, not a verbatim report even though the note-taking may have been quite detailed. It is useful to take comprehensive notes while people are speaking because these can be used for reference later. However, the mediator should develop the art of *précising*, that is, selecting the important issues and incorporating both the facts and feelings.

It is important for the mediator to check the summaries back with each party to ensure their accuracy.

How does the mediator record the statements?

(a) Advantages of note-taking skills

There are good reasons to develop note-taking skills, not just for reading back purposes. It can be useful for reinforcement purposes to refer to one's notes later and to use the notes as a tool to facilitate direct communication during the joint dialogue by saying:

> Bob, I remember you touched on that in your opening statement. Perhaps you can elaborate on that point now that Mary has raised it.

Using parties' statements down the track[1]

Many mediators give no more thought to the parties' opening statements other than these being just one more discrete stage of the generic mediation model which begins the process and has been completed. This is why some choose not to take comprehensive notes of what the parties have said, on the basis that these statements are merely to kick-start the meeting or that making notes is impossible during a fast delivery.

As discussed, a principal purpose for the parties' statements is to use these statements as the springboard to identify issues and set the agenda. However, once this task has been completed some practitioners may not consider referring to the statements again.

---

[1] See "Using process to best advantage", Charlton, R, *Dispute Resolution Guidebook* (LBC Information Services, 2000), p 33–5.

The use of parties' opening statements should not end when the mediator summarises these and then identifies the issues. As well as these being of ongoing use to the mediator, it should be borne in mind that parties have often put considerable preparation into their statements. It is the one part of the process that they clearly understand and feel they have some control over prior to their embarkation into what may be for them a "mysterious" forum. They may feel somewhat disappointed if this thoughtful input is neglected once the mediation is underway.

In order to exploit the opening statements, and to give the parties the acknowledgment for their efforts, mediators *do* need to take comprehensive notes. Note-taking is, in itself, an important acknowledgment. Asking a fast speaker to slow down emphasises the importance to the mediator of having a record of what they are saying. This is further enhanced by the assurance that the mediator will be consulting those notes throughout the mediation and may be raising what has been said. The mediator might say:

> Thank you for preparing these statements. They are very useful to me and I will be referring to them from time to time throughout the day.

It is pleasing to the parties when the mediator refers to something they have said perhaps three hours previously. Such later reference also imparts an acknowledgment of the importance of those statements to the parties and to the efforts that went into preparing them.

The opening statements are the main tools for opening up the discussion during the issue exploration phase. Each topic can be introduced by reference to the opening statement of one or both parties. To encourage discussion on a particular agenda item, the mediator might say:

> In your opening statements you both mentioned this particular topic. Tim, you said you were annoyed that this situation had arisen. Joe, could you say something to Tim about how you saw it.

The mediator's notes can also be used as a reference point in the private session. It may encourage a party to open up if the mediator makes reference to the opening statement:

> I remember in your opening statement you said X. In what way do you feel this was clarified with Joe during your discussions on that point?

Opening statements have further uses. Even at the time the parties are making their statements, an alert mediator can identify possible options for later use, or begin to decode what they are saying in order to identify underlying needs. Opening statements often include demands and assertions. Even negative statements can be converted into options later by a mediator who has been listening constructively.

> Party A: (in opening statement) Paying her $X would amount to unjust enrichment and I am certainly not going to be contributing to her flashy lifestyle.

When parties are in the option generating mode, it can be productive to refer to the initial notes and assist the parties by contributing an option that you have identified. Option identification, which involves active listening, is different from option generation. Option identification can be the mediator's unique contribution.

> Mediator: (at option stage) Also, from what you said in your opening statement it seems that one of your options is to consider some form of payment, and that may need to be related to what you feel is reasonable.

Even at the final stages, when an agreement is being formulated, the mediator can still refer to the parties' opening statements in order to emphasise that any needs identified from the statements have been addressed as far as possible.

(b) How much note-taking should occur?

It is obviously not necessary or possible to take down a verbatim report. If this was the case we would all have to be shorthand writers. If parties are getting into the "On 6 June 1994 in the afternoon he said to her and she said to him" kind of detail it may only be necessary to note something like "1994 — A denied B's claim". When the whole context becomes clearer, it may be even less necessary to read this back.

(c) A useful note-taking method

One note-taking method is to draw a line down the middle of the paper and write A's summary on the left side and B's on the right. This assists in cross-checking when extracting the issues for the agenda. This could work as follows:

A	B
Accident June 1992. Car cut across lane. Caused collision. Upset and shaken.	No police report. Witness A driving too close to car in front.
Cuts and bruising. Nightmares since accident.	Accept A's pain and suffering. Last medical report no lasting traumas.

These notes can be fed back in narrative form such as:

You also mentioned how upset and shaken you were and that you have suffered nightmares since the accident.

This method of recording assists with agenda setting because it makes it easier to cross-reference the concerns that each has spoken about and to mutualise the agenda.

(d) Maintaining eye contact

It is emphasised in the training of some mediators that they should keep eye contact with parties during the parties' statements. The trainees complain that they cannot take notes and keep up the appropriate body language. Of course they can't. Trainers should avoid over-emphasising this requirement. But opportunities do occur when mediators can look up from their notes at the speaker or nod to indicate that they are hearing what is being said. In order to prevent a perception of bias, some mediators make a practice of saying:

> You may see me nodding while I am taking notes. This does not mean that I agree or disagree. It only means that I have heard what you said.

(e) What if the speaker's delivery is too fast?

If speakers are going too fast, simply request them to slow down by saying:

> I'm having a bit of trouble keeping up here Mary. Could you slow down (repeat what you just said) as it is important for me to get the gist of what you are saying.

Fast delivery most often occurs when parties have prepared a written opening statement. While point form notes can help parties to remember their issues, a prepared "script" can present a difficulty. In such a case it is useful to invite them to speak spontaneously or "in your own words" and discourage the reading out of a prepared statement. Most will remember their points because they have been thinking about them for quite a while.

How does the mediator deliver the summary?

(a) How brief should it be?

Although the summary should be briefer than the statement it should not be so short that it is an issue extraction exercise. Issue extraction is done at the agenda setting stage. The stages are quite different. It is not sufficient to say: "Well, Mary, your issues are your clients, office management and compensation." This sort of summary defeats the purpose of assuring the parties that the mediator has heard their issues and concerns as individuals. The mediator's summary is also important in terms of doubt creating since it has been found that parties are far more likely to listen carefully to a mediator's summary of a speaker's statement, than they are to listen to the original speaker. This is particularly so in the case of the second speaker who has probably spent time during the first party's statement thinking about what he or she needs to say, or has focused on an early point of the first speaker and thus not listened productively to other points of the statement. In fact, a "listener" is sometimes observed to appear to be deliberately refraining from listening to the other's statement by fiddling with a briefcase or rattling papers. Dealing with this discourtesy has already been discussed.

(b) What form should the summary take?

The summary itself can be a mixture of mediator's paraphrasing and *précising*, but it is always good to use a couple of direct quotations in the following way:

> You talked about the effect of the accident at that point. In fact "the accident has given me nightmares" were the words you actually used.

Let the parties know that you have heard their statement by using "You" language: "You told us that ...", "You made the point that ...", "The other thing you said was ...", and so on. This not only emphasises that you have heard them, but reinforces your neutrality by demonstrating that it is the speaker's version, not yours, and that you are not endorsing a particular person's version of events.

Parties generally like to hear the "feeling" components of their statements fed back, such as:

> You talked about how upset your husband was when he heard the contract had been terminated.

A mediator should avoid such expressions as "Now the way I see your issues is ...". What should be emphasised is the way the parties see things, not the mediator's view of their statements. Paraphrasing is an efficient way of summarising. More drastic reframing should be avoided at this stage and should only occur to minimise the effect of pointed insults or particularly provocative statements. In the interests of the lay person, it is useful to reframe into plain English legal expressions sometimes used by lawyers/mediators such as "time is of the essence", "discovery", "third party notice" and so on. The same comment applies to technical jargon used by other professionals unless all participants are knowledgeable in this regard.

(c) When should the summaries be read?

Should summaries be read immediately after each party's statement or at the end of both statements? Our preferred method is for each party to speak in turn before we summarise for each of them at the end of the second speaker's statement. In our view this helps to create the neutrality and balance we are aiming for. Some mediators summarise the first speaker's statement before inviting the other party to speak. Thus, the first speaker gets instant validation. However, this method carries the danger of concentrating on one person and leaving the other person "out in the cold" for too long at this vital initial stage. Unless the statements are very brief, this method can create feelings of power-lessness and frustration in the second party.

Excessive clarifying questions directed to one party can also promote these feelings, whether at this stage or during joint session exploration. It has been observed that where the first speaker's statement is quite long and is then instantly summarised, the second speaker is far more likely to attack the first person's statement rather than speaking first of their individual issues. Thus, the accuser–defendant syndrome is promoted.

The immediate individual feedback that results from summarising directly after a statement may assist a mediator who is not a good note-taker, and of course provides instant gratification to the particular speaker. This method may not be harmful when the statement is short, but the length of a statement can never be anticipated. On the other hand, if the first party's statement is long and is followed by the mediator's summary, the second speaker may feel frustrated and neglected.

Some mediation models include the step of reading back the summary immediately following the individual statement and then merging them. The idea of merging the summaries is to identify common ground or reinforce common problem solving. Where this step is included, it might make more sense to give instant individual feedback after each speaker's statement so as to clearly separate the individual summary from the joint one. This merging step has been noted to be particularly problematic for trainees.

To do full justice to the parties' statements, feelings expressed should always be included in the summary, preferably in the form of a direct quote to avoid any misinterpretation. It is also important not to quote the statement in an emotive way in order to avoid any perception of bias by the other party.

(d) Should common ground be elicited at this stage?

The idea of identifying common ground either by the merging method or a pro-active identification at the issue clarification stage may be an idealistic one. In reality, parties generally have very little common ground during the early stages and, in fact, may want or need to argue.

That is not to say that some mutual principles cannot be extracted from the parties' statements such as "fair result", "don't want to go to court" or "best interests of the child". If such mutual principles can be extracted, the mediator should seize them and put them under a heading of "Common ground" on the whiteboard. Another useful technique, where a mutual intention is identified, is to say:

> You both said you didn't want to go to court. Why don't we make "out of court settlement" a principle of our negotiation today?

But the mediator should not artificially force common ground. The parties will see through the mediator's attempts and this will lower their regard for the process. It is also important to recognise the need parties might have to express their hostile or negative feelings towards each other. Therefore, during the early stages of a mediation session parties are not interested in identifying common ground.

(e) What is common ground for the purposes of mediation?

Common ground for mediation purposes is not agreement on facts that are not in dispute, such as the date of a marriage, the date of an accident, or agreement that certain issues should be listed on the agenda. Common ground is where, for example, there is agreement that a contract or a lease should be terminated, rather than renewed, and the parties need to mediate on the ways and means to achieve this. Other examples are where there is an early acknowledgment that a property needs to be sold to effect a property division, but not agreement on the means of dividing the property; where payment of compensation is agreed upon, but not the amount; where it is agreed a child will reside with a particular parent, but an arrangement needs to be made for the child's contact with the non-residence parent; where liability is not in issue; and so on.

(f) How does the mediator ensure that each summary is relevant?

At the end of the summary, the mediator can clarify its relevance with the parties by asking "Is this a fair summary of what you said?" Generally it will be confirmed that the summary is fair, but most parties are quick to point out when the mediator has missed what to them was a cogent point. This is where over-editing their statement or just picking out issues can work against the mediator's credibility. The mediator may then be put in a position of standing corrected or having to apologise for a glaring omission or repeated omissions. This may be insignificant in the whole scheme of things but obviously a mediator should avoid the appearance of incompetence or lack of interest.

There are indications that parties do feel rather dissatisfied if a mediator has picked out only the issues and ignored the feelings generated by the issues. It is an interesting exercise to ask role players in a training simulation what they would like to have heard back. Quite often the response will be something like: "Well, the mediator didn't say anything about how X's building work had affected my customers" or "The mediator used none of my words".

Because of the thought that parties have often put into their opening statements, it can be useful for a mediator to mentally change hats and think "If I were the speaker, what would I like to hear summarised?" Such an exercise can highlight the fact that a person might like the summary to include that "You told us that you felt very shocked when the matter first came to your notice".

Some dos and don'ts for the mediator's summaries of the parties' opening statements are set out below.

Table 3.2: Dos and Don'ts for Mediator's Summaries of the Parties' Opening Statements

Dos	Don'ts
ENSURING PARTIES' ISSUES AND CONCERNS HAVE BEEN DEALT WITH IN A NEUTRAL AND IMPARTIAL WAY	
• Take summary notes of parties' statements.	• Don't take down a verbatim report of parties' statements.
• Let the parties own the statements and the related issues.	• Don't convey the impression that the statement and the related issues are the way you see them.
• Present the issues in terms of how the parties see them, eg, "you felt that ..." and quote from parties' statements to avoid impression of endorsing the statements.	• Don't give your opinion or make value judgments. • Don't extract just the bare issues from the statements.
• Extract facts as well as feelings from the statements.	• Don't concentrate on note-taking at the expense of failing to observe the parties reacting to each other.
• Keep the summaries brief but comprehensive.	• Don't record on the board common ground extracted as facts that are not in dispute.
• Maintain eye contact with the parties from time to time while note-taking.	
• Ask a fast speaker to slow down.	

- Summarise at the end of the second
  speaker's statement.

- At end of your summaries, record on the
  board common ground extracted as
  principles or intentions for the future.

The following case study, with its background facts, illustrates how the parties might deliver their opening statements and how the mediator might summarise them.

WORKPLACE DISPUTE: MARY AND BOB

Background facts

Bob Ainsworth and Mary White are solicitors who have been in partnership for eight years since they graduated in law. Bob has remained single as he wished to build up the practice before taking on family commitments. He has almost paid off his apartment overlooking the ocean worth $180,000. His parents have lent him $30,000 towards the purchase of the office. He still owes them $15,000. The office cost $120,000.

Mary has contributed $10,000 towards the office premises and she owes her parents $5,000; her parents had paid the original $10,000. Bob and Mary still owe the Bank $80,000.

Six months ago Mary became engaged to Bob's best friend, Matthew Lightfoot, an economist who is studying for his doctorate. He has no prospects of earning his living for another three years. They have plans to marry in three months' time, and Mathew will be financially dependent on Mary for at least the next three years.

Bob and Mary's legal practice has, in the last three years, been most successful. Bob has concentrated on conveyancing and commercial law and Mary on family and criminal law, much of the latter through Legal Aid Commission referrals. Much of the profit for the practice has been generated by Mary's family law matters. They have worked together harmoniously until recently when some tensions have developed, especially since Mary's engagement. She has been spending far less time at the office. Last week Bob and Mary had their first serious disagreement since they started working together and Mary has taken two weeks' stress leave, and threatened to leave the partnership. Her clients are constantly ringing up Bob and complaining about her absence.

Bob and Mary have agreed to try to settle their differences through mediation before the situation deteriorates any further. They have asked for two mediators, one male and one female.

Mary's opening statement to the mediator

I don't know where to start. Bob and I have been partners for eight years since we graduated. We decided that we had got on so well at university that we would try to build up a practice together.

Neither of us had any ready cash to put into the practice. Bob's parents did lend him money and he still owes them $15,000. My parents also helped by advancing $10,000 and I still owe them $5,000. We both owe the Bank about $80,000.

I feel that if it wasn't for my efforts in attracting family law clients to the practice we would have been in serious difficulties. I've also attracted a lot of criminal law business through Legal Aid. Bob can't stand all the emotional stuff that comes with family and criminal law matters. I, on the other hand, have got all the patience it takes.

Yet, do you think he's ever thanked me or acknowledged my contribution? And another thing, although he claimed to be sympathetic to the feminist cause at university, he just expected me to take over the responsibility for office management and even financial management. He always says women are much better than men at that sort of thing. His father always gave his pay packet to his mother who then paid all the bills and just gave him and his father spending money.

I don't really mind doing it. In fact I enjoy it. It's a challenge. What I really resent is that there's no recognition for my efforts. He doesn't seem to realise how much money I've saved the practice. Because of what I do we don't have to employ a full-time legal secretary. I don't like being taken for granted. I'm really sick of it. I admit one thing, though. He hasn't pressured me into making a greater financial contribution towards the cost of the office premises.

Bob knows I'm getting married soon. I haven't actually talked it over with him — he's always so busy — never mind how busy I am! What I've been wanting to tell him is that I don't intend to spend as much time in the office once I'm married. I want to give my marriage a go. I don't want to face the prospect of a divorce like my parents did because my father was never at home, he was so busy running the family business.

I'm really hoping we can discuss the future arrangements at the mediation and I hope you can help him see reason so that he doesn't expect me to pay 50% of the money still owed to the Bank when I've put in so many extra hours, attracted so much business and saved us the need to pay for the services of a full-time secretary.

Bob's opening statement to the mediator

You know Mary, I wish you had had the decency to talk to me about all this. You always keep things to yourself, don't you? And then you complain that I don't understand you.

Before we went into partnership, you agreed never to let personal commitments affect the interests of the partnership. And yet here you are getting married and saying you won't have as much time to devote to it.

[To the mediator] I'm really annoyed that her relationship with Matthew is taking top priority over her work commitments. We had such a harmonious working relationship before that. And now she's going to spoil it all. I think it's very selfish of her.

I didn't want to tell her about this and worry her but I've been getting a number of complaints from our regular clients who are thinking of going elsewhere because they never seem to be able to make an appointment to see Mary at a time convenient to them. She just doesn't have her heart in the partnership any more.

She used to be able to arrange her appointments so that the tattooed and ear-ringed bikies were not in the same waiting room as our middle class and more conservative clients. I've had a number of complaints from that group saying they don't feel safe. Some of the women objected to the whistle calls and vulgar language used in the waiting room. In fact they are openly scared of the bikies. Mary used to be able to keep them apart. It's obvious to me that she doesn't give a damn any more.

[Interruption from Mary who reminds Bob of his undertaking to bear most of the share of the repayment of the $80,000 by way of compensating her for her efforts.]

I really don't remember giving you that undertaking. I need to talk about that in more detail.

Mediator's summary of Mary's statement

Mary, you began by explaining that because you and Bob got on so well at university you decided to practise together, which you have done for eight years.

You spoke of the loans from both sets of parents. Bob's parents are still owed $15,000 by him and you owe $5,000 to yours. You jointly owe $80,000 to the Bank.

A point you made was that the partnership would be in difficulties if it were not for your individual efforts in attracting your family and criminal law clients. The point was made that Bob has never acknowledged this special contribution.

You also said that you didn't mind assuming the responsibility for office and financial management. However, you "resent", that was the word you used, Bob's lack of recognition for your efforts and the financial saving to the practice.

You did give Bob acknowledgment for not pressing you for a greater contribution to the cost of the premises.

Due to your busy schedules, you have not been able to discuss with Bob your intention to spend less time at the office once you are married. You do want to give your marriage a go, and stressed that you do not want to repeat your parents' experience.

In your view, Bob should not expect a 50% contribution from you to repay the bank loan because of your extra input and the saving of the cost of a secretary. You want to discuss future arrangements today.

Mary, is that a fair summary of what you told us?

Mary: Yes, very fair.

Mediator: Could I just clarify the amount of the original contributions from your respective parents?

Mary: Bob's parents lent him $30,000 and mine lent me $10,000.

Mediator: Thank you, Mary. And Bob, thank you for listening to what Mary had to say. I'll now summarise what you told us.

Mediator's summary of Bob's opening statement

Bob, you began by saying that you wish Mary had spoken to you beforehand about her concerns.

You mentioned the pre-partnership agreement that personal commitments would not affect the partnership, and you emphasised the previous working harmony. However, you are now concerned that work is not Mary's priority. In your own words, she "doesn't have her heart in the partnership".

To avoid worrying Mary, you have not previously raised the issue that some regular clients are thinking of going elsewhere because of her unavailability.

At that point, you spoke about the different sets of clients. Previously Mary's appointments were arranged so that they would not meet in the waiting room. The more conservative clients have expressed concerns about safety, harassment and bad language. It's obvious, in your view, that Mary is no longer concerned about this aspect.

You have no recollection of giving Mary any undertaking that you would repay most of the bank loan by way of compensating her. You particularly wish to discuss this today.

Bob, have I fairly summarised what you said?

Bob: Yes, that's it.

Mediator: Can I just clarify whether you were saying that the bikies and the other clients are now meeting in the waiting room?

Bob: Er, yes, they are starting to.

Mediator: Thank you for that. And Mary, thank you for listening to Bob.

Note: In summarising, the mediator mainly used paraphrasing but included a couple of direct quotations. The mediator combined good notes with active listening. The clarifying questions were kept to a minimum. The summaries included facts, concerns and feelings. It is not usually necessary to neutralise the content of opening statements, as this can defeat the purpose of capturing the individual concerns and allowing the other party to gain some understanding. Mary's statement was longer than Bob's because of her more elaborate expression. The mediator summarised about 50% of what Mary actually said and more of Bob's statement was retained. Referring to the parties directly as "you" made it possible to emphasise that the summaries were not the mediator's view of events. To include the other party as one of the listeners the mediator asked Mary if the mediator had summarised fairly what she had told "us".

ARE THERE ANY ALTERNATIVE METHODS OF COMMENCING A MEDIATION?

Some mediation models do not include individual opening statements. It is common not to include them where the model involves conducting individual preliminary interviews. At the joint session, the mediator often begins by asking one party a question or questions, and then invites both parties to contribute and feeds back each one's thoughts or opinions on an ongoing basis. An agenda is compiled progressively.

Where there have been no individual intake interviews and the parties attend the first meeting together, this method seems to take on the character of an intake interview in itself and thus rolls the opening statements, issue extraction and joint dialogue session into one stage. The advantages may be to establish instant rapport. This model also places the mediator in a much more central role than other models in which the mediator is ultimately aiming to hand the responsibility over to the parties. It is probably a technique derived from the counselling discipline and does seem to be more widely used in the family mediation area.

This method is also commonly used by agencies where the mediation takes the form of a series of short one-hour or 90-minute meetings, conducted over several weeks, again analogous to counselling methods. It has the advantages of being more "folksy", relaxed and less structured. A disadvantage would be that the other side may be waiting much longer for their "turn" of the mediator's attention and it probably would not encourage doubt creating where each side listens to the other without interrupting. This method is not efficient where the aim is for a same-day resolution.

There is some rather sparse evidence, reinforced by anecdotal information, that mediators tend to "carry" the first speaker's, or the initiator's statement with them more strongly through the session. If this is the case, then this "counselling" method of proceeding may not carry this danger.

Stage 3 — Issue identification and agenda setting

WHAT IS MEANT BY ISSUE IDENTIFICATION AND AGENDA SETTING?

All meetings, if they are to proceed in a constructive manner and be concluded in a reasonable time, have agendas, that is, a list of topics to be discussed. A mediation is simply another form of meeting with the mediator as a specialist chairperson.

A mediation agenda is a list of the issues and concerns which the parties agree need to be discussed (but not necessarily resolved) before a final agreement is possible. These issues and concerns are mainly isolated from the parties' opening statements. The agenda is not inflexible and can be added to as more issues emerge from subsequent dialogue or expanded information. Items can also be eliminated or amalgamated if the focus changes. It can be a very versatile tool but sometimes there is no need to refer to it at all because progress flows smoothly. In other cases, a topic may be listed for strategic reasons, usually to give recognition to something said in the opening statement. It may be unnecessary to explore this topic because of the comprehensive manner in which it was covered in the party's statement. For simplicity, when discussing "agenda setting" we are including the two-step process of (i) issue identification, and (ii) clarification and listing of issues.

In summary, an agenda is (a) a snapshot summary of the parties' opening statements; (b) a list of topics for discussion (not simply issues requiring settlement); (c) a management plan; and (d) an indicator of direction.

Some mediators, particularly trainees, find issue extraction and therefore the subsequent agenda setting one of the most difficult of the procedural steps. A survey conducted of participants prior to an advanced mediation course revealed that agenda setting was the most problematic area for these reasonably experienced practitioners. Several things contribute to this difficulty and create pressure. These include the tasks of:

▌ identifying topics from two differently expressed opening statements;

▌ converting toxic statements into neutral language and then melding them into mutual topics as far as possible;

▌ recording topics in succinct written wording which also needs to be meaningful (in the sense that, when a particular item is reached, this wording triggers a recognition of the scenario(s) it was intended to represent).

Another pressure experienced by solo mediators is the perceived need to quickly identify the issues from their notes. This is discussed below in "Overcoming difficulties".

An experienced mediator will sometimes declare "I never set an agenda". This omission may be because their basic training did not include this step or, if it did, it presented difficulties that the practitioner has preferred to avoid. A mediation can, of course, be successfully concluded without an agenda. It has been observed, however, that mediations seem to last longer and get more bogged down when there is no agenda or no effective use of an agenda. For the uninitiated or the discouraged, we would encourage persistence with mastering this most useful technique. Our purpose is to provide the mediator with as comprehensive a repertoire as possible.

WHAT ARE THE PURPOSES OF ISSUE IDENTIFICATION AND AGENDA SETTING?

1. To identify, clarify and validate the parties' issues and assure parties their topics will be addressed.

2. To provide an early opportunity to co-operate on an action plan.

3. To encourage co-operative problem solving by converting individual issues into mutual items as far as possible.

4. To break the dispute into manageable segments for the benefit of both mediator and parties.

5. To provide an opportunity to clarify/expand on points in opening statements.

6. To set the scene for mutual discussion, detailed exploration, negotiation and problem solving.
7. To reinforce the mediator's impartiality by listing issues in neutral terms.
8. To bring structure to the discussion and provide a focus.
9. To encourage an objective "focus on the problem", not on the people.
10. To encourage and maintain focus on one specific item at a time.
11. To encourage appropriate flexibility.
12. To break an impasse.
13. To highlight progress and move the session along.
14. To avoid later backtracking.

HOW TO MAKE THE MOST EFFECTIVE USE OF ISSUE IDENTIFICATION AND AGENDA SETTING

Identifying, clarifying and validating the parties' issues as their own

Identifying issues and discussion topics is a skill that develops with time. At times even the most skilful agenda setter will have difficulty separating the wheat from the chaff. The main thing to remember is that generally each party has an interest in each issue that emerges. It is not necessary to put each side's version of the same event on the list as a separate issue. The technique of mutualising (see below, p 52) avoids this.

Issue identification is, of course, much easier where the co-mediation model is used (see Chapter 9 — "Co-mediation"). In co-mediation the mediators have usually divided their procedural roles so that the "agenda setter" can sit back and more easily note the emerging issues while the other mediator is reading back the summaries.

Solo mediators can adopt the technique of underlining or highlighting apparent issues as they are summarising each party's statement and then co-ordinate the highlighted material when the summarising is completed. Another way to identify the issues is to consult one party's summary when both summaries have been read back and then, in the interests of mutualisation, cross-check with the other summary for the same issue, possibly expressed in a different way. Mediators may, if they wish, mention that they are taking time out to review both summaries in order to isolate the discussion topics. Identification by cross-checking is not as difficult as it may seem. The second speaker often feels compelled to comment on the first speaker's summary, even though the mediator may have encouraged that person to proceed as if or he or she was speaking first (see Chapter 3 — "Parties' opening statements and mediator's summaries").

Mutualisation may not be possible for every topic. One party may have an exclusive issue. Techniques for handling any problem on a one-party issue are outlined below (see p 55). When parties see the issues they have referred to in their opening statements listed on the board they feel the mediator is taking them seriously. They feel acknowledged and validated. This creates confidence in the mediator and the process.

Overcoming difficulties

As mentioned, it is much easier to set the agenda when the co-mediation model is being used as it often is in community and family mediation. However, solo mediators, when faced with a complex matter or complicated opening statements, should not feel pressured into having an instant agenda at their finger-tips after summarising the parties' statements. It is not a beat-the-clock exercise. Our preference, if solo mediating in a matter where opening statements have covered a lot of ground, is to tell participants: "Let's have a short break, as I am just going to take a few minutes to consult my notes on your opening statements. It is important I get it clear and I will call on your assistance later."

At this point, a short break might be in order in any case. Following the preliminary paper work, the mediator's opening statement, the parties' statements and mediator's summaries, parties often wish to get a coffee or stretch their legs. It also enables them to digest what they have heard in the other party's opening statement.

Introducing the phase

When ready to record the topics on the board, the mediator might say:

> I mentioned earlier that we will be compiling a list of topics for discussion. The list is really a snapshot summary of things you have already spoken about which you might wish to elaborate on. I have identified some things from what I have heard you say. I will list these on the board and then check them with you. I have identified some things from what I have heard either one or both of you say. Now in your opening statement I note that you both mentioned X ...[1]

---

[1] Charlton, R, *Dispute Resolution Guidebook* (LBC Information Services, 2000), p 25.

What type of heading?

Some mediators simply write as their heading "Agenda" after having explained what it is. Others write "Issues". Some feel more comfortable with "Discussion Topics", "Matters for Discussion" or "Points from Statements". This is a matter of personal preference, although some consider that the word "Issues" carries the connotation of matters to be determined, which is not always the case with agenda items. Some prefer to make no heading at all.

Encouraging co-operative problem solving and mutualising individual issues

In the previous chapter it was stated that summarising the parties' statements was a way of recognising and acknowledging their individual issues and concerns. The agenda advances this individual acknowledgment a step further. We are still acknowledging their issues, but are converting the individual into the mutual as far as possible. This is because we need to set the scene, and provide an avenue, for mutual exploration of the issues and concerns that have been isolated. We are using the terms "issues" and "concerns" interchangeably.

Avoiding the "mediator's agenda"

By extracting the issues and concerns which have emerged from the parties' opening statements and listing these, the mediator avoids the trap of the "mediator's agenda" (see Chapter 22 — "Party- and mediator-driven problems" and Chapter 20 — "How neutral are we?"). Thus, initially, the agenda simply reflects what is important to the parties based on what they have actually said, rather than what the mediator thinks they should be talking about. This strategy is important at this early stage where the mediator is trying to gain the parties' confidence, and avoid perceptions of mediator pre-judgment or bias.

Avoiding a professional focus

Although the traps of the "mediator's agenda" will be discussed in more depth later (see Chapter 22 — "Party- and mediator-driven problems"), it is appropriate to mention here that legally qualified mediators in the early stages of their mediation practice often focus on issues with legal implications which may be more relevant to the courtroom scene than the mediation forum. Whilst legal issues are obviously relevant, legal interests do not necessarily coincide with, or rank higher than, personal needs and interests. Similarly, some mediators from a social welfare background tend to concentrate on the "touchy-feely" components rather than balance these issues with the more practical matters that need to be addressed. We all need to be aware of the tendency to bring our own baggage into the mediation forum.

Including expressed concerns

Mediation issues do not just include dry items such as "cause of the accident" and "amount of compensation". It is tempting to follow such a path, as ultimately these are the matters that may require a decision in order for a settlement to occur. The agenda should also contain discussion topics that may not require a resolution. More personal concerns such as "effects of the accident" should be included if a party, in their opening statement, has mentioned "effects".

Our advice is: Ignore concerns at your peril! It has been proved time and again that parties often cannot focus on settlement until they have been allowed to get off their chest some personal concern and will keep harking back to this until it has been addressed. If these concerns are not addressed in a timely way, it might block a desire to reach a settlement, let alone a particular type of settlement.

Case Note

A personal injury case came to mediation prior to an appeal. The appellant needed time to ventilate against the judge who handed down the initial "paltry" award before he could even begin to contemplate any renewed settlement offers! As he had mentioned his views on the award with some vigour in his opening statement, the mediator wisely noted this as a discussion topic.

Providing an early opportunity to co-operate on an action plan

An agenda is a plan of action — an indication of direction. Just as at a committee or public meeting there are certain issues to be addressed and to not be overlooked, at a mediation, the agenda brings some structure to the meeting which prevents it from meandering along without any particular focus. It also provides a golden opportunity for all participants to co-operate on formulating the action plan, with the mediator consulting the parties and inviting their comments on the list.

Making the dispute manageable

Parties' issues and concerns have been likened to a serving of spaghetti. It sits on one's plate tangled, confused and intertwined. The mediator's job is to stick in the fork and separate the mass into identifiable, individual strands or risk being left with the unenviable job of dealing with a large serving of glug throughout the session.

Setting the scene for discussion, negotiation and problem solving

How can this be done effectively? These guidelines can help the parties steer away from pointless argument and to focus on the main object of the mediation — co-operative problem solving.

Using the whiteboard or butcher's paper

This focuses parties' attention on the "plan of action" to be followed for the next X hours. The skill of the mediator at this point lies in promoting an atmosphere of "We are all working on this plan together". Some mediators are not familiar with, or not comfortable with, whiteboard use. The authors of this book, in fact, practised mediation for several years before being introduced to whiteboard techniques. After the initial unfamiliarity, tension was overcome and we were able to assess that the smoothness and streamlining that resulted made our previous method (using notepaper placed in the middle of the table) seem unduly clumsy by comparison. (See Chapter 18 — "Effective use of information — note-taking and application of visual aids".)

Getting the agenda on the board efficiently

Getting an agenda in place should be done as expeditiously as possible once the scribing has commenced. The mediator should take active control of the agenda formulation by not allowing counter-productive arguments to develop between the parties about what is, or is not, an issue. Agenda setting is a part of the process and the exploration stage that follows should not be pre-empted by the parties being tempted to start arguing or dialoguing on substantive matters before all relevant matters are listed. Excessive consultation and cross-checking with each party about each potential issue can promote these arguments and cause delays. It is far more difficult to find holes in a completed agenda than it is to argue over the relevance of each separate issue. This stage should be used to engender a spirit of co-operation with regard to the issues, not encourage a division.

Our preferred method is to approach the whiteboard, armed with our notes for consultation, either as soon as the parties' statements have been summarised where the statements have been fairly simple or, in a more complex case, after a short break as discussed above. We then "talk to the agenda" by briefly clarifying what we have heard in the statements while at the same time commencing the writing. It is still "their" agenda, because it has been extracted from their opening statements and the mediator is doing no more than setting out what has been spoken of by them. If arguments do break out, it is useful to remind the parties that they are going to have ample time to discuss things in more depth shortly and that at this stage we are all trying to get our "action plan" in place.

Consultation or checking back can occur once the list is on the board. The mediator might say:

> This is the basis of our action plan for the next few hours. Does this cover all the things you both wish to talk about? Is there anything else you need to talk about? Is there anything on this list that neither of you sees as an issue? Remember, this list is not set in concrete and you can add to it at any stage of the mediation.

Mutualising the issues as much as possible

Mutualising involves emphasising commonality of interests. How do we do this? Well, usually the parties have done it for us in their opening statements. They may have used different words or expressions, or given their version, but generally they are talking about the same thing. The mediator should find a trigger word or expression that covers both versions. A suggested mediator script might be:

> I heard you both speak about the bank loan so that seems to be something for our list. You both mentioned the repayments to your parents, so I've made a note of that item. Bob, you were reluctant to tell Mary about client concerns and Mary, you spoke of Bob being too busy to approach, so what if we have a discussion on "past communication" as they both seem linked to that.

Having one list — not two — and focusing on the problem, not on the people

Some mediators draw a line down the middle of the whiteboard and say: "These are your issues A, and B those on this side are yours." There is no need for this. It can create divisiveness at a time when we are trying to generate an atmosphere of co-operation and stress commonalities. In summarising the parties' statements we have already acknowledged their concerns individually. However, the divided listing technique may be useful on paper where a novice agenda setter is merely using it as a tool for visual mutualisation and using it as a springboard to compile a single list.

Order of listing

In some cases it may be possible to first list the issues that appear to relate to past events and then list those that focus on future resolution. This is a useful method of advancing the mediation. It enables the mediator to move smoothly into a future focus at the appropriate time and, where necessary, to prevent backtracking to topics already comprehensively explored. In a farm debt mediation, for example, the past matters might be "effects of drought"; "bank manager's advice"; "original loan conditions"; and "previous negotiations". The future-focused items may contain such topics as "servicing the debt" and "restructure options". Even if the parties have not referred to future-related issues, it is still useful to add "The future" as the final topic on the agenda. The mediator could say "I've added this to the agenda as I am assuming that you will be making decisions about the future. What do you think?"

Using neutral language

This entails reframing potentially inflammatory or judgmental language into something both parties can accept without losing the meaning of what was conveyed. This is sometimes referred to as "removing the toxicity". Although the parties do, and are entitled to, express things as they wish in their opening statements and should hear back a reasonably accurate summary of their own words, this phase places a greater emphasis on co-operative problem solving. Neutralising allows them to talk about their differences more readily. It also serves to reinforce the mediator's impartiality.

Case Note

A trainee's agenda was observed to list certain issues in the following manner:

▌ Breach of contract

▌ Late delivery

▌ Defective work

"Anything wrong with that?" asked the coach.

"Well," responded the trainee (who happened to be a lawyer), "that's what it says in the Statement of Claim."

"Oh, I see, but whose Statement of Claim is it?"

"The plaintiff's", responded the trainee.

"And is the defendant agreeing that the plaintiff's claims are valid?"

"Er . . . No . . . I see what you mean . . . point taken."

What happened in the above case was a combination of the "mediator's agenda", that is, what the mediator had decided were the issues, and a tendency to fall into using familiar legal terminology to classify an issue. If, in this particular simulation, the other party was denying that there was a contract in the first place, this other party may have been outraged to see an alleged breach on the list. Assuming that all those issues were mentioned during the opening statements, a neutral agenda would read:

▐ Contract

▐ Delivery times

▐ Quality of work

In terms of "mutualising 'n' neutralising", the above agenda assumes that both sides have an interest in the existence of a contract, that a delivery time may have been stipulated, and that both parties have some views on the quality of work, even though one is denying, and the other alleging, quality.

Occasionally there can be confusion and possible resentment when an expression in a party's opening statement is reframed for agenda purposes. To avoid this the mediator might consider explaining that "part of my role" is to write up the discussion topics using non-judgmental language, as the following case note illustrates.

Case Note

In a nervous shock claim a deceased person's daughter asserted in her opening statement that the hospital "killed my mother". When compiling the agenda the mediator wrote "Cause of Death", a description that mutualised a subject raised in each party's opening statement. The daughter challenged this reframe by again speaking of "the killing" and asking: "Are you trying to take the emotion out of this?" The mediator's response was: "I do acknowledge the emotion. However, you will remember that I emphasised my neutral role at the beginning. I should also have explained that this role includes using non-judgmental written language." The daughter then acknowledged that the neutral role had been stressed and accepted the explanation. However, this exchange reinforces the necessity, in some very emotionally loaded cases, for a mediator to explain at the outset that the neutral role includes scribing the written word in those terms.

Using simple succinct wording

Succinct, explicit terms such as those used in the reframed agenda in the above contractual matter are more useful and appropriate than long drawn-out sentences. Agenda items expressed in terms of "Was there a contract?" or "What was the quality of the work?" not only take up board space, which is better utilised to list options, but promote an investigatory approach. In a family law matter, rather than write "Value of property as at time of purchase", it may simply suffice to list "Purchase price" under a heading, "Property". (There are times during the exploration of a particular agenda item, such as "work practices", where it can be useful to expand the wording by writing up a future-focused problem solving question on a separate sheet of butcher's paper. Thus "work practices" can be converted into "How can work practices be restructured to give Bob and Mary equal time at the office?")

Dealing with a one-party issue

What about an issue that one party mentioned, but not the other, or an issue one party wants to discuss but the other does not? An apparently one-party issue should be dealt with during the recording stage. It is simple to say:

> Bob, you mentioned the impact on clients. Mary, I think we both heard Bob talk about this during his statement, didn't we, so I will include it at this point.

This method includes some consultation and assumes the other party's co-operation regarding a one-party issue. It effectively nips in the bud any potential argument about whether an issue should be included. If, despite your fancy footwork, an argument does arise you can simply say:

> Well, Bob does seem to want to say a few words about the clients, so we can add it to our list so it's not forgotten.

This will ensure that Bob's issue is acknowledged but at the same time it reassures Mary that she is not committing herself to negotiating on that issue in detail, but merely to listen to what Bob has to say about it. Some mediators put the disputed issue in brackets or isolate it from the other issues. A skilful mediator will avoid this. Some parties feel put down and hostile towards a mediator who trivialises their issue in this way, especially when they highlighted it in their statement.

Having dealt with the one-party issue(s), ideally half way through the compilation, the mediator can then go on to mutualise any remaining issues.

Dealing with the unmentioned (or unmentionable) issue

We have made the point that the issues are initially isolated from the parties' opening statements. What about an issue that emerged, say, at a preliminary conference or appears to be evident in intake data, correspondence or in pleadings, but has not been brought out by the parties in their opening statements? This is a play-by-ear situation to some extent. It may form part of a hidden agenda or it may simply no longer be an issue. Generally, the chances are good that it will emerge during the dialogue. If in doubt, the mediator should leave it to the private session. However, if it appears to have been inadvertently overlooked because of an intense party focus on other things, the mediator may safely say:

> I know neither of you has mentioned this, but do the different valuations need to be discussed if we are going to be agreeing on the best time to sell the property?

Case Note

A traineee mediator recorded "Injunction" on the agenda on the grounds that "this is what this mediation is all about". Neither party had mentioned an injunction in the opening statements and had deliberately refrained from doing so in order to emphasise a co-operative approach. This is another example of the "mediator's agenda" (see Chapter 22 — "Party- and mediator-driven problems") and highlights the possible danger of inflaming matters by injecting the unmentioned issue into the equation without a careful prior analysis.

Avoiding the one-issue agenda

Although some ADR (Alternative Dispute Resolution) writers maintain that there is no such thing, it can often seem that there is only one issue to deal with. For example, in personal injury matters, where liability is acknowledged and the only issue appears to be the amount of compensation due. The purpose of agenda expansion is to create some understanding of where each party is coming from, instead of plunging straight into the horse-trading. Instant bargaining is likely to occur with a single monetary issue and can cause hardening of positions. In such a case, it can be useful to expand the agenda if there is scope to do so. In a personal injury claim, where liability is not an issue, there can still be discussion on:

1. cause of accident
2. effect of injuries on lifestyle
3. basis of offers and claims
4. past loss
    (a) economic
    (b) general
    (c) out of pocket expenses
5. future loss.

The first item, "cause of accident", gives each party the opportunity to clarify perceptions; the second item gives the claimant the opportunity to inform the insurer of how he or she has been affected by the injuries (thus introducing the human element); the third item, "basis of offers and claims", gives the insurer the opportunity to acknowledge the claimant's concerns and at the same time explain the range of compensation usually awarded in similar cases, and how it could realistically be seen to apply in this particular case.

Not making the list too long

No matter how many issues are apparent, an agenda with about 10 items may overwhelm the parties. A long list of issues usually emerges when the parties and the mediator are trying to cover every contingency. This is not necessary. Some items can be usefully condensed and discussed under one heading. Some mediators adopt the ABC method, that is, listing a main heading in the interests of mutualising and then placing the individual facets into subheadings. The subheadings under an agenda item such as "Property" might be (a) Purchase price; (b) Present valuations; (c) Sale prospects. In a parenting matter, the single issue of "Contact Arrangements" can be expanded to include facets such as (a) Weekend contact; (b) Weekday arrangements; (c) Telephone and email contact.

Describing each item in specific terms

The descriptions should not be so general and broad that each party has a different understanding of what falls under that item or all parties forget what scenario the item is supposed to identify. It has been noted in training courses that, in some cases, the care taken to scribe neutrally and mutually can result in over-simplification. Thus, when a particular agenda item is reached everybody has forgotten what led to the item being included. "Communication" is a favourite agenda item and is often included without defining what falls under that heading. If several alleged miscommunications or misunderstandings have occurred, in, say, a medical matter, it might be more useful to list these separately, such as First consultation; Consent information; Discharge notes. Alternatively, they can be listed as subheadings under the "Communication" banner as discussed above. (See also "Specific focus — preventing meandering", below.)

Avoiding whiteboard prioritising

Once the list of issues is written up, or even while writing them up, the mediator should make it clear that they may be discussed in any order of priority. This is better than numbering the items, and getting stuck with a particular order, or being seen to be putting one's own priority on them.

AGENDA IMPLICATIONS FOR THE JOINT SESSION

Where to begin

The mediator should ask the parties where they want to begin. Often they do not know. Alternatively, the mediator can encourage them to discuss an item that promises to be an easy winner, and ask:

> Would it be easier for you to talk about this first?

In personal injury mediations, for example, it is usually easy to get agreement on out-of-pocket expenses. In child parenting arrangements, parties usually co-operate on the joint guardianship issue or on proposals for Mother's Day and Father's Day. Where parties have already shown a tendency to argue or point-score, the mediator can use the mutualising technique and say:

> You both felt this was important, so you are probably looking forward to discussing this.

Even while steering the parties towards the "easy winner" or avoiding arguments about where to start, the mediator should always use "You" language ("You might prefer . . ."). It then appears to be the parties' decision where to start, not the mediator's.

Specific focus — preventing meandering

Where parties are tending to slide unproductively all over the place, the mediator should use the agenda to promote focus. This has the effect of helping parties to concentrate on one thing at a time. The mediator can take them back to the issue under discussion by saying:

> I'm a little confused here. I thought you were talking to each other about the delivery times.

Flexibility — prevention of impasses

Some mediators may feel the need to reach some common ground on each agenda item before moving to the next. This is not necessary and can lead to unproductive and unnecessary dissent at a very early stage of the mediation. The agenda may be used merely to generate discussion and allow further information to be relayed about points in the opening statements. The agenda should be used flexibly when the parties are becoming unproductively enmeshed. If the discussion on one item appears to be creating a roadblock, the mediator should suggest moving on to another item (see Chapter 17 — "Practical strategies").

Highlighting progress

Positive agenda use throughout the session includes highlighting progress. The mediator could say:

> Just to summarise your progress, let's have a look at the agenda to see what you have achieved so far.

This is called a "focused summary" because it is a wonderful way of getting the parties to focus on the whiteboard. It operates as a diversion where the heat is rising. A "Let's look at our progress" comment reinforces the collaborative approach the mediator was trying to achieve at the beginning. Some mediators will tick agenda items where agreements or agreements in principle have been reached on a particular item. The "tick" method can also be used to reinforce progress as parties exhaust discussion. This takes the agreement pressure off the parties once an issue has been discussed, leaving them with a feeling of achievement at an early stage. Progress is then seen in terms of discussion, not just agreement. It is also a technique that discourages unproductive revisiting of old ground, and moves the session forward.

Where the technique of dividing issues into the past and future is employed, the point of transition to the future is a good reference point to indicate progress.

Keeping the agenda on the board

The agenda can be kept in view if space permits, or transferred to a separate sheet if the board space is required later, which it usually is (see

Chapter 18 — "Effective use of information — note-taking and application of visual aids"). If transferring from the board the mediator could say:

> Sometimes it is a useful reminder of things you asked each other to take into account in coming to a settlement today.

Occasionally though, some people are not keen to be reminded of positions they came in with, so it is always a good idea to check with both parties whether they wish the list to remain on display, or at least retained.

THE USE OF PRE-MEDIATION ISSUES STATEMENTS IN AGENDA SETTING

The advantages and drawbacks of pre-mediation issues statements are discussed in Chapter 14 — "Pre-mediation issues". Some mediators request parties to provide an issues statement prior to the mediation conference and may use this as a springboard to formulate an agenda. One of the drawbacks of this practice is that a mediator may be tempted to substitute such a statement for the parties' opening statements or to predetermine the agenda. In court-based mediations, such statements tend to focus on legal issues only or are often a re-statement of the legal pleadings.

WHAT ARE OTHER WAYS OF DOING IT?

Some practitioners have been trained to compile an agenda in the form of problem solving questions, which are mainly future-focused, although they can contain some elements relating to the past, depending on the mediator's philosophy. Below is an illustration of these open-ended questions containing both past and future focus. In a defamation claim the agenda may be compiled in the following way:

Past Focus

How did the publication occur?
What was the personal impact?
What was the business impact?

Future Focus

How do we restore reputations?
How can future publicity be avoided?

Advocates of this method find it works well for them, particularly in interpersonal matters, and it is certainly a model worth considering. The questions that come to mind are:

1. do the past-focused questions tend to promote an investigatory approach; and
2. does the employment of problem solving questions at an early stage focus on solutions too early?

Undoubtedly a list of problem solving questions is an extremely useful tool. The question for mediators is whether the list may be used more productively at the problem solving or brainstorming stage (see Chapter 17 — "Practical strategies").

Table 4.1: Dos and Don'ts for Issue Identification and Agenda Setting

Dos	Don'ts
1. IDENTIFYING AND VALIDATING THE PARTIES' ISSUES	
• Refer to the agenda to acknowledge its ownership by the parties.	• Don't refer back to the agenda needlessly if smooth progress is evident.
• Avoid being driven by your own private agenda on what the issues are.	• Don't record what you think the issues should be.
• Avoid a professional focus, eg, a legal or counselling approach.	• Don't forget to explain that you are drawing on their statements as a basis for the agenda.
Avoid over-consulting with the parties prior to listing an issue.	
• Reassure the parties that you will be asking them to check the agenda.	
2. PRESENTING A MUTUAL ACTION PLAN	
• Present the agenda as a useful action plan.	
• Assure parties that listing of a particular topic does not necessarily require their joint agreement.	
• Introduce a topic for discussion by referring to opening statements.	

Dos	Don'ts
3. ENCOURAGING A CO-OPERATIVE APPROACH	
• Express issues in mutual terms where possible.	• Don't separate each party's issues unless it cannot be avoided.
• Include personal concerns as issues.	• Don't just identify and record substantive issues.
4. BREAKING THE DISPUTE INTO MANAGEABLE PROPORTIONS	
• Convert a confused and intricate opening statement into manageable distinct issues.	• Don't merge too many topics under one heading.
• Use succinct but precise wording.	• Don't use vague or jargonistic terms
5. SETTING THE SCENE FOR EFFECTIVE PROBLEM SOLVING	
• Use the whiteboard or butcher's paper to help parties to focus on a mutual action plan.	• Don't consult excessively with the parties over the agenda.
• Get the agenda up on the board efficiently.	• Don't use judgmental language that might validate only one party's views.
• Refer back to the parties' statements as you record each issue on the board, ie, "talk to the agenda".	• Don't omit from the list an issue referred to by only one party just because the other objects.
• Record a full list of the agenda before seeking the parties' approval.	• Don't confine the agenda to one issue only.
• Incorporate the issues of both parties into the one list.	• Don't make the list of issues too long, eg, 10 items.
• Mutualise the issues by accommodating the parties' differences in the one issue.	• Don't number the listed items, which might imply an order of priority.
• Use simple and neutral language.	• Don't encourage argument about the selection of the first topic.
• Validate a one-party issue.	
• Expand the one-issue agenda into multiple issues.	• Don't divide the board into A's and B's issues.

Dos	Don'ts
• Amalgamate multiple issues where the list of issues becomes too long and unwieldy.	
• Stress that the issues are not listed in order of priority.	
• Assist the parties in selecting the first issue for discussion.	
• Guide the parties to an early winner as a starting point.	
• Group issues into past and future where logical.	
• Ensure parties have exhausted discussion on a topic before moving on.	

6. ENCOURAGING THE PARTIES TO FOCUS ON THE ISSUE UNDER DISCUSSION

• Redirect the parties' focus on the agenda if they "lose the plot".	• Don't encourage indiscriminate unproductive meandering from one topic to another.

7. ENCOURAGING FLEXIBILITY IN THE USE OF THE AGENDA

• Move the parties from one item to another if they become enmeshed.	• Don't promote intense focus on a topic that may encourage entrenchment.

8. USING THE AGENDA TO ASSESS PROGRESS ACHIEVED BY THE PARTIES

• Highlight progress by referring to the agenda, eg, by placing a tick against relevant items.	• Don't allow progress to be unacknowledged.
• Use to effect transition from past to future.	

# Chapter 5

Stage 4 — Clarification and exploration of issues: the first joint session

WHAT PURPOSES DO ISSUE CLARIFICATION AND EXPLORATION SERVE?

Once agreement has been reached on issues, and they have been listed, each issue is now ready for open discussion, clarification and exploration by direct communication between the parties facilitated by the mediator. This occurs in what is generally described as the first joint session. Up to this stage, the parties have been encouraged to communicate with the mediator rather than with each other. Thus, the session heralds an important change of focus. It is also, apart from the negotiation stage, a very challenging one for the mediator who needs to have recourse to an array of skills and strategies, which are outlined under Part 4 — "Mediation skills and strategies", Chapters 15–18. If the mediator handles this first joint session effectively and, providing the parties commit themselves to participating in the mediation in good faith, the prospects of their reaching a satisfactory agreement are greatly enhanced.

Because of its inherent difficulties, the more inexperienced mediator tends to spend as little time as possible on the first joint session and is tempted to go prematurely into private session. Such an approach by the mediator risks turning the mediation into a series of private sessions with the mediator conveying messages, offers and counter-offers from one party to the other; such a process cannot really be described as mediation.[1] We have observed, with trainees in particular, that there may be a loss of confidence in their ability to control the situation and they are thus tempted to go into private session unnecessarily.

The purposes of the first joint session are:

1. To allow parties to identify and explore in detail the major elements of their dispute, including new issues that might emerge.

2. To encourage and facilitate direct communication between the parties and provide them with opportunities to express their feelings.

3. To provide parties with the opportunity to clarify the past, which facilitates their mutual understanding of past events and perspectives and maintains a level of optimism about the future.

4. To facilitate parties' shifting from entrenched positions and demands to identifying needs and interests.

5. To provide opportunities for noting options, emerging common ground, concessions and agreements in principle.

6. To enable the mediator to understand the parties' perspectives on the past and the future in order to set the scene for reality testing in ensuing private or joint sessions.

WHAT DOES THE MEDIATOR DO DURING THE FIRST JOINT SESSION AND HOW?

1. Allowing parties to identify and explore in detail the major elements of their dispute, including new issues that might emerge

The major elements of the dispute

The most important benefit of the clarification and exploration of issues step is that it provides opportunities for the parties to analyse the major elements of their dispute through direct communication. It helps them to articulate, or the mediator to identify, what their needs and interests are and it provides a realistic backdrop to their negotiations.

The mediation probably affords the parties their first opportunity to go into detail about the background to the dispute in a systematic way in the presence of a neutral third party who will not be offering opinions; making value judgments about who is right or wrong; making a decision about the outcome; or giving unsolicited advice. This is one

---

[1] See "Shuttle negotiation" in Chapter 12.

of the features that most clearly distinguishes mediation from any adjudicative process, or even the settlement conference.

Setting the groundwork for future negotiations

The mediator facilitates the parties' direct communication in order to set the groundwork for negotiations. Facilitating direct communication is discussed later in this chapter.

The mediator empowers the parties to take responsibility for the antecedents of their dispute and the part they played in it, rather than relying on the mediator's assessment of it, or whatever approach their colleagues, friends and relatives and perhaps even their lawyers might have advised them to adopt.

New issues

It is not uncommon for new issues to emerge at this stage of mediation, notwithstanding that they may also emerge at a later stage, especially during private sessions.

Information about the past may be imparted for the first time, with parties stating that they had not realised this or that; had they known, they would have viewed things differently. Commercial disputes are no exception, with misinformation having been allowed to build up with little or no opportunity for explanation or clarification of what had actually occurred.

Even though these issues have not emerged from the parties' opening statements, any new issue should be added to the list to be dealt with later in the course of this first joint session.

The mediator's role in relation to the exploration and clarification of issues in general

Up to this point the mediator has played an active part in explaining the process and the role of the mediator, taking notes of the parties' statements, summarising them and setting the agenda. At this stage the mediator's role continues to be an active one but less didactic and more strategic.

It is very important for mediators not to harbour any preconceptions about the way the mediation ought to proceed and how the parties ought to respond to each other. Such private agendas, when acted upon by the mediator, remove opportunities for the parties to play a leading part in defining the nature of their dispute and as a result the parties may be encouraged to rely on the mediator to suggest an appropriate outcome.

The mediator's role in the selection and exploration of the first issue for discussion

(a) **Selecting the first issue.** Once the agenda has been set, not necessarily in any order of priority, or numbered in any way, the mediator's first task is to assist the parties to choose the first issue for discussion. There are a number of ways to tackle this task. Four options are:

(i) The mediator selects the first issue, preferably one that both parties raised in their statement. This avoids a perception of mediator bias in the selection.

(ii) The mediator asks the parties for more information on an issue.

(iii) The parties select the first issue.

(iv) The issues may have been listed in a chronological fashion corresponding to the unfolding of events. In such a case it is natural to work through them in the same chronological order.

(i) The mediator selects the first issue. This option has the advantage of steering the parties towards an item that does not bog them down. The issue selected should be a non-contentious one or one which promises to be an easy winner. The mediator may have gleaned from the parties' opening statements, which of the issues has the best potential of generating common ground and goodwill.

The mediator's selection of the first issue prevents the parties from selecting an item focused on settlement such as "compensation", which might encourage them to maintain entrenched positions rather than to understand each other's perspectives. It is important at this early stage not to allow the parties to get involved in premature settlement discussions without having first reaped the benefits of clarifying what happened in the past and expressing their feelings about it. This process may well lead to a softening of their positions and should be communicated to the parties.

The mediator might say to the parties:

'Well, where do you think we should start? In your opening statements you both spoke quite strongly about office management. Perhaps we could start with that issue. Would that suit you both? Just before we start exploring the past, remember that it might be premature to talk about settlement at this stage, unless you both come up with early ideas on how an issue might be resolved.

(ii) The mediator asks for more information on an issue. This is a more subtle form of steering and can also work effectively. The mediator might say:

> You remember how you both spoke quite strongly about office management in your opening statements. There's something I'm not quite clear about and I wonder if you could give me more information about it.

The drawback is that the parties are once again communicating with the mediator rather than with one another. The mediator must be cautious about asking a series of questions for the purpose of getting "the big picture".

An alternative approach would be for the mediator to say:

> I wonder if it would help you, Bob, to hear from Mary about other aspects of the office management issue, for example, what difficulties she was experiencing with the staffing structure?

(iii) The parties select the first issue. Parties are, of course, capable of ordering the issues and some mediators prefer to ask them to do this. The danger in allowing the parties rather than the mediator to select the first issue has been identified in (i) above. There are also other dangers. It might provide an opening for unnecessary argument. One of the parties may wish to start with the issue that they alone raised in their opening statement and the other party might not be prepared to discuss it at all and certainly not at that time, resulting in:

> That's not an issue for me. I do not wish to discuss it at all.

If the mediator has chosen the third option and it has resulted in unproductive arguing, it is important to revert to either of the former options in order to restore a positive tone to the mediation.

(iv) Where the topics have been listed in the order of unfolding events, there should be no controversy about beginning at the top of the list.

(b) Exploring the first issue. Once the choice of the first issue for discussion has been made, we have found it useful to say:

> This is an opportunity for each of you to go into more detail than you were able to when you gave your opening statements and we asked you to be brief.

If the parties are finding it difficult to get started, the mediator needs to facilitate direct communication between them on the selected first issue. For example, the mediator could say to one of the parties:

> Mary, I remember you said in your opening statement that you were having difficulties meeting deadlines and that you had accepted the responsibility of the office management side of the partnership. Can you provide Bob with a little more detail?

When Mary has done that and Bob does not respond immediately, the mediator could say:

Bob, it might help Mary to know how you see it. Could you tell her?

2. Facilitating direct communication

The above procedure is far preferable to reminding the parties that at this stage of the mediation they need to speak to each other rather than to the mediator. However, although it is important for the mediator to assist the parties to communicate directly with each other, initially they may feel more comfortable addressing their remarks to the mediator. In rare cases, parties have been known to resist talking directly to each other until after the private sessions.

The mediator can steer them gradually towards direct communication if they don't fall into it naturally, as they often do. Not infrequently when this approach is adopted, the parties find themselves continuing to communicate directly with each other. If they persist in directing their comments through the mediator, the mediator can point out that they really need to inform and convince the other party, rather than the mediator. Statements such as "Tell me about ..." or "What I need to know is ..." should be avoided by the mediator and replaced with:

It might help Mary to hear what your future plans are.

or

Bob, would it help if Mary told you about what she hopes to do as far as practising law is concerned once she gets married?

How does the mediator elicit information from a reticent party? And how does a mediator make sure that equal attention is given to each party?

Parties sometimes find it difficult to express themselves or may be too focused on their positions and demands to articulate what their concerns are. The mediator can assist by asking open questions such as:

What other financial concerns do you have? Please tell Mary.

or

What other concerns do you have about the children's contact visits with their father? Can you explain them to Joe.

Throughout the mediation, the mediator must be constantly aware of the importance of maintaining neutrality. Neutrality does not just concern the type of statement made by the mediator. It also concerns the amount of time spent focusing on one party rather than the other, which may make the other party feel neglected or sidelined. If the mediator asks one party a question, this should, if possible, be followed by a similar question directed at the other party, for example:

And what concerns do you have, that Sue needs to know about?

followed by:

Sue, what are your thoughts on what John said?

When should the mediator intervene?

Where direct communication is flowing well, the mediator should intervene as little as possible even if he or she is confused or curious and would like to gain a better understanding of the past events. It is the parties who need to understand each other, not the mediator who needs to obtain more facts. The mediator need only know enough to advance the mediation, and need not embark on a factual inquisition. However, if one of the parties appears to be confused or uncomprehending, then the mediator should note that and respond to that party's need for more information by asking the other party to provide it. The mediator should not say: "I need to know more about X. Could you give me more details so that I can get the full picture", but:

I think it would help Mary to know more about X so that she can understand it from your point of view. Can you provide her with more details?

If a party is not being clear, or either party appears to have difficulty in grasping a point the other is making, the mediator might say:

Are you telling Mary that the clients are becoming dissatisfied?

Another way is to summarise, perhaps by reframing, in order to promote some clarity.

The mediator should intervene when one of the parties is tending to monologue or dominate the other or if a party raises so many points regarding the particular issue that the other party is not given the opportunity to respond. An appropriate intervention might be to say:

I noted that you made three points there, Bob. So that we don't lose them (or before you go on), Mary might like the opportunity to comment on each of them. Mary, the first thing Bob said was ...

The mediator should also intervene if a party becomes repetitive. Instead of pointing out to that party that the points have already been made, the mediator could summarise what the parties have said about that issue so far. It is important for the mediator not to cause either party to lose face or feel that they are being reprimanded.

The mediator need not intervene just because the exchange appears to become robust. The mediator must not lose sight of the parties' need to ventilate. The mediator should avoid taking the easy way out and resist the temptation of (i) reminding the parties about the ground rules; or (ii) breaking into private sessions. On the other hand, if a heated exchange continues and the communication becomes too negative and unproductive, the mediator could then suggest that it is time to move on to the next issue:

> Perhaps we've gone as far as we can on that issue. As you know, at this stage we're not seeking agreement. That would be premature. This stage of the mediation allows you to clarify understandings about the past, to clear up any misconceptions and to begin to understand each other's point of view even if you don't agree with it. How about talking about the next item on the list?

By intervening in such a way, the mediator helps the parties not to become despondent about settlement prospects and allows them to continue to discuss past events.

Exploring the other listed issues: moving from one issue to the other

The mediator now helps the parties to move from one issue to the other, making appropriate use of some of the intervention techniques described above, including giving a summary of the parties' exchange on a particular issue. The mediator could say:

> Let me summarise for you what I've heard you say so far on this particular issue.

Avoiding premature private sessions

Some mediators feel uncomfortable in the presence of parties who are arguing with each other and they are therefore tempted to rush into private session. Others have not developed enough confidence in applying a whole range of mediation techniques, and it is certainly easier for them to deal with a one-to-one relationship, with which they may be more familiar in their professional lives.

It is usually only necessary to separate the parties early if they find it impossible to speak to each other, or even the mediator, on any of the issues without verbally abusing each other destructively and impeding any clarification or exploration of issues. However, private sessions should generally be used to benefit the parties and the mediation session as a whole, not to provide refuge for an insecure mediator, who may have interpreted parties' exchanges as "being out of control" or "putting each other down". (In one current training course, trainees are obliged to justify their use of private sessions at a particular time and to consider whether the private session achieved any more than, or hindered, what could have been achieved in joint session.)

As a rule no private sessions are held, or held productively, until all issues have been explored, all information exchanged and, in some cases, where settlement options have been generated. Even then, there may be occasions where a private session is just a formality.

In such a case, the private session is very short and is focused on providing details for the agreement in principle that the parties might have reached already, and making sure that all necessary aspects have been covered.

Some techniques that can be used before resorting to private sessions, such as paraphrasing and reframing (always making sure the content is checked with the parties for accuracy), are discussed later in the book. These techniques are applied to take the heat out of "toxic" exchanges and also to encourage the parties to begin to focus away from the past, particularly towards the end of the first joint session.

3. Clarifying the past and facilitating mutual understanding

The mediator's purpose for asking clarifying questions is to assist the parties' understanding, not the mediator's. The mediator remains in the background to "catch" rather than actively generate early options, common ground or even agreements in principle. The mediator might, however, actively elicit underlying needs and interests from the parties' expressed positions and demands.[2]

The mediator should encourage parties to ask each other clarifying questions by saying: "Would you like to ask Joe about that?" The answers to such questions may pave the way to a better understanding of what happened in the past.

Maintaining a level of optimism about the future

Although the parties may have agreed to come to mediation rather than have the matter litigated, they may at different stages of the mediation become discouraged by the nature and extent of their disagreements. Unless the mediator helps to maintain a level of optimism about their

---

[2] See Chapter 17 — "Practical strategies".

ability to reach a mutually satisfying outcome, they may lose heart, become even more entrenched in their positions and conclude that mediation is a waste of time. It is important for the mediator to set a tone of optimism, without overdoing it, by helping the parties accept that the disagreement between them is to be expected and should be expressed and clarified; if not, it may be difficult to reach a settlement that is both realistic and satisfying for each party. A mediator might say:

> What you are experiencing is quite normal, and does not mean that you cannot reach agreement.

The mediator should resist the temptation to divert the parties' communication away from areas of disagreement. Rather, the mediator could say:

> You're bound to see things differently and disagree on details, otherwise you wouldn't be here. We have found that it's useful for parties to explain to each other what it is they disagree about.

Some mediators are over-zealous in seeking common ground as soon as the parties identify and define areas of disagreement. It is certainly useful to note emerging common ground but not at the expense of providing the parties with opportunities for explaining to each other why they are disagreeing. Otherwise any attempt to delineate any common ground relating to peripheral and minor issues, rather than the central more relevant matters, may be seen by the parties as trivialising the significance of their disagreement.[3]

4. Facilitating parties' shifting from entrenched positions and demands to identifying needs and interests

Demands, needs and interests

When parties are in dispute, they are, initially at least, likely to remain entrenched in their demands, which are based on what they feel they are entitled to in their aggrieved state. This entrenchment also justifies in their own minds why they are in dispute and in mediation. Parties have a need to express their demands; demands which they consider to be so eminently fair that they cannot understand how anyone could question them. However, one of the greatest advantages of this first joint session is that, with the mediator's assistance, they not only clarify, explore and explain each issue in dispute, but are also encouraged to shift their attention to what their needs are for the future and how their interests

---

[3] See Chapter 3 — "Parties' opening statements and mediator's summaries".

can best be served. Interests are needs that a party wants to have satisfied. In the Bob and Mary case, some of Mary's interests were the need to:

▌ have Bob acknowledge her efforts in helping to build up the partnership through her unique contributions in family and criminal law;

▌ continue to practise in the areas of family and criminal law and to repay the bank loan as well as her parents' loan;

▌ combine a legal career with married life.

Some of Bob's interests were the need to:

▌ retain the family and criminal law clients in order to be able to repay the bank loan;

▌ keep the partnership going, at least in the short term.

One need the parties may have in common is to achieve finality. In some cases parties look forward to having no future contact. However, in the rare case where a party has a "need" to continue with the conflict, there is not much a mediator can do about it, except confront the party privately, if appropriate.[4]

It is important that the mediator is aware of the fact that parties do not just have needs relating to their future, but also what could be described as "process needs", that is, immediate needs in the course of mediation which include the need to be heard by the other party. Sometimes these needs should not be met by the mediator, for example, the need for sympathy or for the mediator to acknowledge that "they have a case".

Identifying needs and interests and their relevance to emerging options

It may be useful for the mediator, once the issues have been explored, to ask the parties to tell each other what needs they are looking to have satisfied by any agreement coming out of the mediation (if they have not already done so in the course of making their statements or during the exploration of the issues). The mediator can help parties by identifying, via their dialogue, some of the underlying reasons for their demands and then mentioning these.[5]

With this identification process it is important for the mediator to avoid parties getting bogged down with details relating to the how, what, who

---

[4] See Chapter 17 — "Practical strategies".

[5] See Chapter 17 — "Practical strategies".

and when of a particular outcome. Once needs and interests are identified, the scene may be set for the framework of an agreement to emerge.

A downside to asking parties about their needs may result in a rehash of wants or demands. If the parties begin to reiterate their demands, the mediator can then explore with each of the parties what their needs are for the future, for example:

> What do you need to see happen to avoid the problems you've experienced in the past, for example, your loss of business opportunities? Could you tell him?

or

> You mentioned that you would not accept anything less than $20,000 by way of compensation. Could you explain the significance of that specific amount? Could you tell him how you arrived at that figure?

or

> You've just told him that you're only prepared to allow him contact with Billy one Saturday a month. Could you tell him in what way it would be in the interests of the whole family?

The identification of each party's needs and interests could lead to the generating of options, which could be developed further during the joint and private sessions and finalised at the negotiations which follow.

If exploration of needs results in a further tabling of positional demands, with the potential for a deadlock, the mediator could say:

> Do you have any other ideas?

These responses could also be treated as options by the mediator who might say:

> Well these are certainly two options to be considered later when we brainstorm a whole range of options. Let me make a note of them on the board.

5. Noting options, common ground, concessions and agreements in principle

At an early stage of the joint session, the mediator needs to note, rather than elicit, any options, common ground or agreements in principle incidentally generated by either party. An option may be extracted from a positional statement, for example, if a party says:

> I refuse to accept anything less than $20,000 to compensate me for the loss you have incurred me.

or

> As far as I'm concerned he can only have the children one Saturday a month.

The mediator might say:

> So an option for you is to accept $20,000 as compensation for your loss.

or

> So an option for you is monthly contact visits.

The mediator might note the options on the board and tell the parties they will be looking at a wider range of options later in the mediation. In those cases, parties may indicate that they are ready to do so now rather than later. The mediator should respond to their request rather than adhere rigidly to the process. *This is where a flexible approach is useful.*

However, premature negotiation should be discouraged if parties are still entrenched in their positions and are not in conciliatory mode. This is where dividing the agenda into past and future, or into "what has happened" and "how do we resolve it?", can be useful. The mediator needs to acknowledge common ground and note any agreements in principle identified during an exchange between the parties. If the common ground is significant and has the potential to lead to an agreement, then it can also be noted.

The mediator can summarise exchanges between the parties and draw out any common ground or agreements in principle on any of the issues. In relation to the latter, the mediator could add:

> You don't have to go into any detail at this stage. I'll make a note of your agreement on the board to refer to later when finalising it.

The mediator's acknowledgment of common ground should not be confined to factual information in relation to the past. It should focus on opinions or value judgments the parties might have on any aspect of the matter: past, present or future.

6. Setting the scene for effective negotiations

In the course of the joint session, the mediator will have been privy to a wealth of information about the parties' perspectives on their dispute, both while listening to their opening statements and summarising them as well as while facilitating their exploration and discussion of issues.

The mediator is interested in absorbing all this information not only for the purpose of gaining a thorough understanding of the elements and dynamics of the dispute, but also to facilitate the parties' better understanding of each other's perspectives. All of this knowledge and understanding can be put to useful purpose in the future facilitation of the parties' effective negotiations. Entrenched positional statements and unrealistic demands should not be allowed to mar the final negotiations. However, at this early stage of the mediation, it may be counter-productive to stop the parties from telling each other what they feel they really want, however unacceptable it may be to the other side.

The mediator should remember these statements and demands (which at this stage could be converted into options), and refer to them later for reality testing purposes, for example, to encourage the parties to assess how realistic their demands are in the light of the other party's response and the need for mutual satisfaction with the outcome. Depending on the parties' sensitivities, reality testing may need to occur during private sessions to avoid a loss of face.

By then, the mediator will have had the opportunity to observe, in the course of their exchanges, the effect the parties have or are having on each other. In private session, the mediator might comment on what has been observed and encourage parties to talk about whether these attitudes might get in the way of them negotiating on practical matters.

WHAT ELSE CAN THE MEDIATOR DO TO MAKE THE MOST EFFECTIVE USE OF THE FIRST JOINT SESSION?

1. Assist the parties to gain a sense of progress.
2. Give the parties undivided attention.
3. Foster a sense of realism in the parties' expectations.
4. Help parties identify what worked well in the past for them.
5. Perform a consistent facilitating role.

1. Assisting the parties to gain a sense of progress

From time to time the mediator needs to report on the progress made by the parties. Summarising their exchanges in the course of the joint session and at the end of it constitutes one way of helping the parties gain a sense of progress and encourages them to persevere in their efforts to reach settlement. Parties can feel emotionally drained and so the mediator needs to encourage them to renew their energy and to help them to be ready to move on.

For example, one way of summarising could be:

> I'd like to summarise what I've just heard you say. You both agree that you want to avoid going to court, and that, although you have different ideas about the outcome, you would like to explore ways of settling your differences out of court. You've suggested at least two ways of doing that. I'd like to make a note of these suggestions and we'll get back to them later.

Another example could be:

> We have clarified your understanding of ... We can now move on to explore the next item on the agenda.

It is important for mediators to avoid sounding condescending and exaggerating any minor agreement between the parties, such as an agreement relating to the process, for example, when to have coffee breaks or which of the listed issues to begin exploring:

> Oh good! We're making real progress here. You've managed to agree on something.

On the other hand, if the parties seem to be on a constant collision course, the mediator could point out that it is not unusual for this to occur and to make use of progressive summaries, making notes on the board, reframing and moving from one stage to another. Such summarising should be pertinent and relevant. Useful techniques and strategies are discussed in more detail later in Chapters 15-18.

2. Giving the parties undivided attention

It may seem obvious, but it is necessary to stress that the parties need to feel that they have the undivided attention of the mediator throughout the whole of the mediation, particularly in the early stages where dissension and emotive exchanges are to be expected, tolerated and even encouraged. If parties feel that they have the mediator's undivided attention, they feel their point of view has been appreciated and that the mediator is listening to them attentively. Communication skills, such as active listening, will be discussed later in the book (see Chapter 15).

It is sometimes difficult for mediators to sit back and listen patiently to the parties discussing each issue in turn, seemingly getting nowhere fast. Mediators who earn their living from certain professional practices often have a low tolerance for joint sessions because they seldom need to spend more than about an hour with their clients and often their role is an advice-giving one. However, some mediations require several hours of talking about the past before decisions about the future can be made. For example, in farm debt mediations, mediators may listen to the parties for three hours while they talk out the past including the fire in the hayshed and even World War II service: "I didn't save Australia in the war so that my own countrymen could kick me off my land." Some parties may need this sort of catharsis.

Mediators need to divide their attention as fairly as possible between the parties so as to avoid any suggestion of bias. If they ask one party to provide more information to the other party, wherever possible they ought to make the same request to the other party. They should invite that other party to give their thoughts on what they have just heard.

One word of warning: when the mediator listens attentively they often nod occasionally and may not be aware that they are doing so. The parties need to be reassured that the nodding does not denote agreement with what is being said but that he or she has heard what the party/ies have said.

What about note-taking?[6] Whilst it is important for the mediator to take notes of the parties' statements in order to accurately summarise back what they have said, it is not so crucial during joint or private sessions. Note-taking should not distract the mediator from being attentive. On the other hand, the parties might well feel that the note-taking is an indication that the mediator is taking them seriously, particularly if later they are quoted back.

Mediators in training often continue unnecessarily with their note-taking during joint and private sessions instead of concentrating on the parties' communication and observing the effect they are having on each other. Whilst it is useful to note any options generated by either party or common ground or emerging agreements in principle, this should be done with the knowledge of the parties and eventually recorded on the board during an appropriate pause in the parties' communication. The content of the board or flip chart represents what is sometimes described as "The group memory".[7]

The mediator might say:

> While you've been talking I've noted some of the points you've made which will be useful a little later in the mediation when you're ready to negotiate and seek agreement about future arrangements. I'll just jot them on the board and I need your help in getting it right. Let me know if I've heard you correctly.

....

[6] See also Chapter 18 — "Effective use of information — note-taking and application of visual aids".

[7] For extended discussion, see Chapter 18 — "Effective use of information — note-taking and application of visual aids".

Noting points on the board is also useful when the parties have reached an impasse. It also distracts them from a potentially unproductive exchange and focuses them on the problem rather than on each other.

3. Fostering a sense of realism in the parties' expectations

It is not uncommon for parties to develop doubts about whether mediation is the right forum for their dispute and whether a better outcome could be achieved by going to court. They may have had doubts even prior to the mediation. Mediators need to remember the principle of voluntariness. Even if mediation is conducted under a mandatory programme, the parties still have the right to decide that their interests might best be served by resorting to an alternative dispute resolution process, including the courts.

Without being too discouraging, the mediator could say:

> You may decide that mediation is not for you and you are free to leave at any stage if you feel it's a waste of time. Why don't you go on for a while before you finally make up your mind?

or

> Certainly mediation usually can't give parties 100% of what they want, but you might get much closer than if you left it up to an independent person to make decisions affecting your future.

4. Encouraging parties to identify what worked well in the past

When parties are making decisions for the future, it is important to remember that not everything in the past was catastrophic. In certain types of mediations it is not unusual for parties, or at least one of them, to make comments such as "We used to get on really well". It can be encouraging and constructive in the course of such exchanges for the mediator to focus the parties' attention on the more positive aspects of their past relationship whether in a commercial, domestic or neighbourhood matter. The mediator could say "What do you think worked in the past for you? Is it something you would like to maintain in the future?".

5. Performing a consistent facilitating role

A mediator's most important contribution is to facilitate communication and negotiation between the parties. Sometimes this can be achieved simply by keeping quiet and allowing parties free rein to discuss matters. In such cases the mediator need only intervene to summarise or move the discussion on to the next item when discussion fades. Where a more interventionist approach is needed, as a facilitator, the mediator needs to tread carefully to avoid arguing with the parties, cross-examining them, advising them or making judgmental statements about their conduct or the merits of their individual cases. Such approaches are more legitimate for investigating officers, barristers, teachers, specialist consultants or counsellors.

Therefore, a mediator should be mindful to avoid the following:

▌ Arguing with or cross-examining the parties.

▌ Making judgmental statements and advising parties.

▌ Deterring the parties from a rushed and superficial handling of the exploration of issues.

Arguing with or cross-examining parties

There will be enough arguments between the parties without the mediator adding to them. Parties will contradict themselves in the course of the session. Rather than highlight the contradictory statement, the mediator should just ignore it. It would be preferable for the other party to pick it up rather than for the mediator to do so. If necessary, it can be clarified in private session. Highlighting it in joint session can promote a loss of face. This is particularly important with parties who come from different ethnic or cultural backgrounds where loss of face should be avoided at all costs.

Where clarification is needed the mediator could ask questions in a way that facilitates communication between the parties while at the same time allowing parties to clarify or expand on facts relating to the past. For example:

> Bob, would it help if Mary gave you more details on how she thinks things started to go wrong and why?

A mediator with an inquisitorial approach delays the parties' direct communication and negotiation and often creates an imbalance in the level of attention directed at each party. The party who is being questioned may feel ambushed while the other party may feel neglected or sidelined. On the other hand the party not being questioned may feel favoured if the mediator adopts an accusatory style of questioning. As already noted, the mediator should encourage the parties to ask each other questions, but not to robustly cross-examine each other. If parties do cross-examine each other, the mediator needs to summarise and make use of reframing.

Making judgmental statements and advising parties

When mediators give their opinion or make judgmental statements about one of the parties, they risk compromising their neutrality and may encourage the parties to seek further advice from them, including perhaps what the outcome should be. For example, the mediator might say:

> As I see it the problem has been caused by poor management and lack of long-term planning.

and

> What I suggest you do is to seek specialist advice from management consultants. I'm sure that the consultants would agree with me.

What the mediator could say instead is:

> What do you think has caused the difficulties you've been experiencing with the business?

and

> Have you thought of seeking expert advice?

or

> How useful would it be for you to seek expert advice.

Judgmental statements about the conduct of parties, what they say or how they say it should be avoided unless communication between the parties becomes uncontrollable. A comment from the mediator, which needs to relate to the conduct of both parties, could be helpful, for example:

> It seems to me from what you are saying to each other that there is a lack of trust between you. Am I on the right track?

During a mediation simulation, a trainee mediator objected when one of the parties told the other: "You've just ripped me off!" The trainee mediator intervened by saying: "Now, now let's not use emotive terms." What he could have said instead, using reframing, was: "Could you tell him in what way you feel that you were dealt with?"

Deterring the parties from a rushed and superficial handling of the exploration of issues

The mediator should actively deter the parties from a rushed and superficial handling of the exploration of issues. Instead, the mediator should facilitate a genuine exploration and discourage the parties from each simply stating their position on a particular issue then moving too quickly to the next issue.

The mediator could reassure the parties that they do have plenty of time to discuss each issue:

Is there anything else you would like to tell each other about issue X or Y. [Pause] If not, are you ready to move on to issue Z?

There should be no time constraints on the first joint session, as it is probably the longest and most vital segment of the mediation. Experienced mediators learn to relax at this stage of the mediation. They learn to be "alert but not alarmed" at emotionally charged exchanges or toxic challenges which are not focused on settlement. If the parties talk themselves out they are more likely to be better prepared for the later generation of settlement options and associated reality testing components by the time they get to their first private session.

A summary is always useful at the end of the first joint session.

CONCLUDING THE FIRST JOINT SESSION

Before concluding the first joint session and moving on to the private session, it may in some cases be useful, if parties are receptive, to launch into a brainstorming session. This may include an early consideration of offers. If, on the other hand, the parties find it difficult to shift from talking about the past or need a break to digest what they have heard, the mediator should not persevere with brainstorming.

At the end of the session, when all issues have been explored, and perhaps options and/or offers tabled, the mediator should remember to summarise the progress made by the parties as this provides a springboard for discussion in private session:

I'll just summarise what you've both said. It seems that you have a common interest in preventing a recurrence of the difficulties that gave rise to the delays that occurred. You would also like to look at ways in which you could continue in partnership at least in the short term and at the same time introduce changes to accommodate your lifestyles away from work.

The mediator then informs the parties that they are about to break into private and confidential sessions. It is useful for the parties to be told about the purpose of these sessions, that is, they provide an opportunity to allow each party to critically explore the issues and options in more detail and to consider the extent to which they are prepared to make concessions and to prepare for negotiations. Some mediators like to focus on the advantage of parties feeling free to talk about matters they may have felt reluctant to air in the presence of the other party. This may raise unnecessary suspicion and anxiety about what the other party might raise in private session. We have found that a more productive approach is to concentrate on looking for realistic and mutually satisfying outcomes and being able to discuss them in more detail in private session prior to final negotiations in the following joint session.

Mediators need to find their own way of introducing the private sessions. The following suggestion is not intended to be taken as a script to be adhered to rigidly, but should assist novice mediators.

> You remember I spoke about us breaking into private sessions. We find them to be very useful. It provides you with the opportunity to consider options in more detail without having to talk to each other about it. It's also a good time to begin to think about options that might suit you both. I'll be playing devil's advocate with each of you, encouraging each of you to think of how a particular option would suit you both. It can also be a time to talk about things you didn't have the opportunity to raise during the joint session.
>
> Mary, as you were the one to make the first opening statement, I'd like to meet with Bob first. Is that okay by you both? Fine. Mary, you know where the tea and coffee facilities are. Please help yourself to a cup. You might like to think of further options while you're out there. We should take no longer than about 10 or 15 minutes. If we do take longer, I'll come out and let you know. You will of course get equal time as far as possible.

In some cases, depending on how the session has gone, it may be more useful to have the first private session with a particular party, not necessarily the one who made the first opening statement. In such a case the mediator might say: "It doesn't really matter who goes first, but I might start with Bob." Where legal representatives are present, parties and advisers usually want some time out without the mediator being present. In such a case the mediator might advise they will be popping in to see one or the other in about 10 or 20 minutes respectively.

Some dos and don'ts for the exploration and clarification of issues during the first joint session are set out below.

Table 5.1: Dos and Don'ts for Clarification and Exploration of Issues: The First Joint Session

Dos	Don'ts
1. IDENTIFYING AND EXPLORING THE MAIN ELEMENTS OF THE DISPUTE	
• Help the parties play an active role.	• Don't inform the parties what you think about the dispute.
• Help parties select the first issue by suggesting a non-contentious one.	• Don't encourage argument over the selection of the first issue.
• Assist exploration and clarification of issues for the parties' mutual understanding.	• Don't seek clarification of issues for the sole purpose of helping you understand, don't say: "Tell me ..."
• Proceed to next issue when exchange is bogged down or exhausted.	
• Note emerging new issues.	
2. DIRECT COMMUNICATION BETWEEN THE PARTIES	
• Direct the parties' communication towards each other rather than you.	• Don't force direct communication if the parties are clearly not ready for it.
• Facilitate free expression of feelings and emotions.	• Don't break into private sessions at the first sign of disagreement.
• Ask open-ended questions rather than make statements about the matter.	• Don't refer to the ground rules as a way of controlling the parties just because they are ventilating feelings.
• Avoid focusing on one party more than on the other.	• Don't imagine you have lost control of the mediation by giving the parties free rein to express their feelings.
3. FACILITATING MUTUAL UNDERSTANDING OF PARTIES' PERSPECTIVES	
• Help the parties to tolerate the differences in their perspectives.	• Don't minimise the differences between the parties or exaggerate minor common ground.
• Be aware that parties' needs are not confined to the future but that they have needs relating to the mediation session itself.	

Dos	Don'ts
• Maintain a tone of optimism when parties become discouraged and argue with each other.	

4. IDENTIFYING UNDERLYING NEEDS AND INTERESTS

Dos	Don'ts
• Allow parties to articulate demands in the early stages of the joint session.	• Don't insist on parties identifying their needs and interests immediately.
• Elicit needs and interests from positional demands.	• Don't allow demands to become entrenched.
• Reframe demands into options or ask questions to elicit underlying needs and interests.	• Don't seek early evaluation of options.
• Recognise that parties' needs differ in relation to how they can reach finality, including the possibility of no future contact.	

5. NOTING OPTIONS, COMMON GROUND AND AGREEMENTS IN PRINCIPLE

Dos	Don'ts
• Acknowledge and note emerging options, common ground, concessions or agreements in principle on any issue.	• Don't prematurely ask for options, common ground, concessions or agreements in principle on any issue.
	• Don't adhere rigidly to a particular process if the parties' needs can be otherwise met.
	• Don't focus unnecessarily on common ground.

6. SETTING THE SCENE FOR EFFECTIVE NEGOTIATION

Dos	Don'ts
• Listen carefully to gain an understanding of the parties' perspectives to prepare for later reality testing.	• Don't encourage the parties to help you understand but to help each other understand.
• Observe carefully the parties' reactions to each other.	

7. CREATING A SENSE OF PROGRESS AND ACHIEVEMENT

Dos	Don'ts
• Report regularly on the parties' achievements by progressive summaries.	• Don't draw the parties' attention to the lack of progress.

Dos	Don'ts
8. GIVING PARTIES UNDIVIDED ATTENTION	
• Maintain attention on the parties.	• Don't get distracted or look uninterested.
• Give equal attention to each party.	• Don't take notes continually and thus stop observing the parties or actively listening.
• Observe the parties' reactions to each other.	• Don't distract the parties' communications by writing on the board and interrupting their flow.
• Explain your notes on the board during a natural pause.	
• Explain that your nodding denotes that you have heard what is being said, not that you agree with it.	
9. FOSTERING REALISTIC EXPECTATIONS	
• Expect and accept the parties' expression of doubts about the mediation outcome.	• Don't exaggerate the advantages of mediation.
• Assist the parties to lower any unrealistic expectations in order to enhance concession-making.	• Don't over-sell mediation on the basis of a "win–win" outcome
10. IDENTIFYING WHAT WORKED WELL IN THE PAST	
• Encourage parties to identify what worked well in the past.	• Don't let parties focus only on what did not work in the past.
• Help parties decide what they wish to retain from the past.	
11. PERFORMING A CONSISTENT FACILITATING ROLE	
• Ignore contradictory statements.	• Don't argue with a party.
• Encourage an in-depth exploration of issues.	• Don't adopt an inquisitorial role.
• Avoid making comments which might lead to loss of face to either or both parties.	• Don't ask too many questions.
	• Don't give your opinion or advice.
	• Don't make judgmental statements about the parties' conduct or their issues.

Dos	Don'ts

12. CONCLUDING THE FIRST JOINT SESSION
- Summarise progress achieved so far.

- Explain the purpose of ensuing private
  sessions focusing on the exploration
  of settlement options.

Stage 5 — Private sessions

What is meant by private sessions in mediation? What purposes do they serve and how can mediators make use of them to the parties' best advantage? What are some important dos and don'ts?

WHAT ARE PRIVATE SESSIONS?

Private sessions (often referred to as "caucus") are held in confidence with each party in the absence of the other. While one party is in private session with the mediator, the other party takes a break. Private sessions are always confidential. Whatever might be revealed in ensuing sessions relating to the private session will be up to the parties, not the mediator. Not all models of mediation include private sessions as an integral or necessary part. Some mediation models, family mediation in particular, only make use of private sessions as a strategy to be applied in exceptional circumstances rather than as a distinct stage of mediation, with a preference towards dispensing with it altogether. The rationale for the limited use of private sessions is that for mediation to work, the disputing parties need to be frank and open and not withhold information from each other.

In other models of mediation private sessions constitute a distinct stage in the mediation process; in very rare instances the parties and the mediator may agree to dispense with it.

We have a preference for including it as a stage in the process to ensure that the parties are really satisfied with the way the mediation is progressing and that the proposed settlement is regarded by them as being in their interests and preferable to any alternative to the mediated outcome that might be available to them, including adjudication.

However, private sessions can be deferred when parties have made good progress and, after the exploration and discussion of all issues on the agenda, have begun to generate options, negotiate and table offers. The purpose of the private sessions in such a case is more limited and will focus on making sure that there are no new issues or options and that the parties believe that it is in their interests to continue in joint session for their final negotiations.

A private session usually lasts anything between 5 and 20 minutes and sometimes longer. It is important to give both parties equal opportunities in terms of time spent during the session.

There is a decided change of atmosphere and tempo during a private session. You can almost feel the tension lift. Both the mediator and the party are no longer faced with having to relate to at least two others in the room or having to deal with interruptions and a high level of emotion. This change of atmosphere can be fraught with danger and the mediator needs to be wary of at least three perils:

1. The party in private session could, without the other party there, mislead the mediator by making false allegations about the absent party or give misleading information about herself or himself.

2. The party in private session could succeed in getting the mediator to take sides, or at least give an appearance of taking sides, by buying into negative comments about the other party, for example, "I know that you understand me and will agree with me" or "Yes, he is being difficult, isn't he" or "Yes, he does appear to have an attitude problem".

CASE NOTE

A mediator gave into the temptation to make a comment about the other party in the course of a private session. When the joint session reconvened, the first party told the other party that even the mediator thought he was a "pain in the butt".

If the party tries to draw in a mediator in this way, the mediator should simply respond by reinforcing her or his neutrality.

3. A party may make monumental disclosures that affect any agreement in principle previously made during the joint session.

WHAT PURPOSES DO PRIVATE SESSIONS SERVE?

Private sessions serve many useful purposes including the following:

1. To ascertain what a party thinks of the mediation so far.
2. To expand on, raise new issues or complete unfinished business.
3. To allow parties to unwind and express their views in private.
4. To uncover the parties' "bottom line", that is, what their negotiation limits are.
5. To review the agenda, explore issues in more depth and explore new issues.
6. To reality test parties' entrenched positions and identify underlying needs and interests.
7. To test options listed in joint session and to generate new ones and to respond to offers.
8. To act as an impasse breaker.
9. To foster a joint problem solving approach and re-affirm the parties' ability to resolve their dispute.
10. To set the scene for final negotiations: exploring settlement options and rehearsing negotiations.
11. To proceed, as a last resort, with the mediation as a series of private sessions.

HOW CAN MEDIATORS MAKE BEST USE OF PRIVATE SESSIONS?

Preliminary steps

Timing of private sessions

Although private sessions can be initiated by the mediator at any stage of the mediation, they are generally held after all the issues have been explored at the first joint session. Private sessions can be used by the mediator as a strategy to deal with an impasse between the parties. The mediator should remind the parties of the confidential nature of the private sessions and that information offered by either party will not be revealed by the mediator to the other party unless the party offering the information has expressly requested the mediator to do so. We prefer to encourage the parties not to invite the mediator to act as their agent of negotiation for reasons that will be outlined later.

Which party goes first?

This is not usually a contentious decision to make. The mediator could ask the parties who would like to start or who would like a coffee break. If the parties do not object, the mediator could suggest a rule-of-thumb that whoever was the last to make their statement would be the first to have the private session. In some cases the mediator might consider it to be more useful to hold a private session first with a particular party, in which case the mediator can tactfully steer the parties towards that decision. For example:

> Perhaps we could start with you, Bob, if that's okay by you, Mary?

The duration of the private session

It is important to make sure that the party who is not in private session knows approximately how long the first private session will take; that he or she will be notified if the session takes longer than anticipated; and that parties will be given equal time if they want it. It should be remembered that breaking into private sessions can create a feeling of suspicion and loneliness on the part of the absent party. This is particularly so if the session is held too early in the process. It is useful, therefore, to give the absent party something constructive to think about during their break, for example:

> While you're out there, you could think of other options to add to the list.

or

> If there are any other issues which haven't been addressed you might like to make a note of them to raise them when we all get back together.

Acting as agent for a party

It is important for the mediator to state that it really makes no difference who starts first because parties will be treated equally during the private sessions in terms of what will be discussed. This is one reason the mediator should resist agreeing to take offers from the first party in private session and conveying them to the second party in their private session without exploring issues and options with that second party. Acting as the negotiating agent of the first party in private session may also give the message to the second party during their private session that the offer made has the mediator's approval or even that the mediator recommended it. Furthermore, the second party does not benefit from having an equal opportunity to use the mediator to convey offers unless another series of private sessions is held, which in some ways defeats one of the primary aims of mediation, that of empowering parties to conduct their own negotiations.

Another danger in adopting the role of a party's agent of negotiation is that the mediator may make mistakes in conveying the messages; a situation which one of us actually experienced. On the other hand a party may feel too intimidated and lack the confidence to negotiate directly with the other party. The mediator may then agree to act on the party's behalf. It would be prudent, however, in such circumstances to have the offers written down and at least initialled or bearing the party's signature to minimise the possibility of error.

Beginning the private session

What the mediator does first in a private session depends on what has occurred in the course of, and towards the end of, the first joint session. The mediator's approach depends also on whether the private session was conducted as one of the stages in mediation or whether it was resorted to as a strategy, in order to, for example, deal with an impasse, consider an offer or to enable the mediation to continue as a series of private sessions if the parties are unable to persevere with the mediation through joint sessions and would otherwise abandon it.

Note-taking

The mediator should take care not to add to or delete what has already been noted on the whiteboard or, any other recording aid, as the session is confidential. Newly trained mediators have a tendency to take too many notes during private sessions rather than concentrating on the parties' needs. If what is being noted is relevant and important enough to raise in the ensuing joint session, then it is the party who should be taking the notes. Certainly if the mediator takes notes, it indicates that the matter is important or significant enough to do so and it may be very satisfying for the party to think that the mediator is taking it seriously. However, that message may be conveyed in other ways that are just as effective. The mediator can ask the party how important the matter is to them and if it is important, would they like to make a note of it so that they remember to raise it during the following joint session.

One of the pitfalls of the mediator taking copious notes is that when the second party comes into the private session, there may be a temptation for the second party to glance in the direction of the mediator's note pad, which could raise their level of suspicion and perhaps cause them to be privy to a piece of confidential information.

HOW CAN THE MEDIATOR BEST ACHIEVE THE PURPOSES OF THE PRIVATE SESSIONS?

The following section deals with ways the mediator could best achieve the purposes of private sessions as identified above. The mediator needs to maintain a balance between giving undivided attention to the party present while at the same time making use of the opportunity to encourage the party to consider not just the party's own interests but those of the absent party. In this way the mediator conveys that her or his neutrality is maintained.

1. Ascertaining what the party thinks of the mediation so far

A useful and neutral way of launching into a private session is to give the party an opportunity to ventilate about the first joint session. It allows the mediator to test out her or his views about the parties' reactions to each other. It also allows the parties, in private, to talk about what they regard to be important. This may not necessarily relate to the agenda items discussed during the first joint session. The mediator could ask the party: "How do you think the mediation is going so far?"

2. Expanding on, raising new issues or completing unfinished business

There may be insufficient time or opportunity for the mediator to achieve all the purposes of the first joint session. Private sessions provide a useful forum to expand on or to complete unfinished business, including dealing with all the listed issues, expanding on some of them or exploring new issues.

The new issues raised may be ones that the party did not feel comfortable raising in the presence of the other party or may be ones that emerged spontaneously.

3. Unwinding and expressing views in private

The first private session provides an opportunity for the parties to unwind for the first time since the commencement of the mediation. Providing the mediator has succeeded in winning their trust and confidence, parties can express their views more freely than in the presence of the other party. Unlike the situation in joint sessions, they do not have to worry about the effect they are having on the other party. The mediator should resist any premature analysis of the absent party's perspective and should instead focus on meeting the need of the party in the course of the private session to ventilate in the absence of the other party. Resisting premature analysis is particularly important when conducting a private session with the second party who should be treated as though they were the first party to get into private session. Prior to the first private session, some parties, in spite of the mediator's efforts, may have felt under stress, especially if the dispute has been prolonged and acrimonious.

The party may have wanted to express views about the mediation or about the conduct of the other party that they did not feel comfortable mentioning in the presence of that party. The mediator could start the session in a number of ways, for example:

> Is there anything you'd like to talk about before we go back into joint session?

or

> Do you think you've covered all the issues on the agenda? Shall we just check?

or

> Now that we're alone, is there anything you'd like to talk about? As you know this is a confidential session, so please feel free.

4. Uncovering the bottom line

Parties feel far more at ease talking in private about the limits to which they are prepared to go in their negotiations. The mediator can assess whether the party is positional and create doubt in that position by helping them to identify their underlying interests. The way to deal with positional parties is discussed under Item 6 below.

5. Reviewing the agenda, exploring issues in more depth and exploring new issues

There may have been insufficient opportunity to explore all issues in depth. Private sessions provide the parties with the opportunity to do so without interruption. The mediator's role is to encourage the party in the private session to explore the issues from both parties' perspectives. It is not always possible for the parties in the course of the first joint session to explore and discuss all the issues listed on the agenda.

The list of issues may be too long to cover during the joint session without the need for a break from direct communications, which can be stressful especially if the dispute has been long-standing. This applies to commercial as well as interpersonal disputes. If the list of issues was too long to cover in the joint session; the parties cannot continue to communicate productively; or there is an escalation in the level of conflict, the private session provides the opportunity for relief and for the parties to begin to review the agenda and explore the issues in more depth. It may also have been unnecessary for all issues to be explored because parties quickly moved to settlement options and the tabling of offers.

If the issues were not explored in-depth during the joint session, the mediator could take the party through them and encourage commentary at two different levels — the personal level and from the other party's perspectives asking appropriate open-ended questions such as:

> You didn't have much opportunity to discuss this particular issue. What are your views about what happened?
>
> How did it affect you?
>
> What do you think he or she thinks about it?
>
> How do you think he or she has been affected by it?
>
> How effective do you think it might be if you were to say what you've just told me when we get back into joint session?

Open-ended questions allow a rich array of information and views to be expressed by the parties unlike the style of questioning some television journalists are prone to adopt which reveals what the interviewer wants the interviewee to agree with, for example: "Don't you think that ...?" or "Wouldn't you say that ...?"

Not infrequently, a party might not feel comfortable raising a particular issue and may therefore exclude it from the opening statement. Thus, a new issue may emerge in the course of the private session. The mediator should be careful not to add it to the list of issues on the whiteboard because of the confidential nature of the private session. However, the mediator needs to obtain the party's views as to whether that issue should be explored in the subsequent joint session and how it should feature in the future negotiations. The party should be encouraged by the mediator to discuss the new issue from the perspectives of both parties, as well as how it might be raised when the joint session is reconvened.

6. Reality testing parties' entrenched positions and identifying underlying needs and interests

During the prior joint session, although the mediator would have attempted to identify the parties' underlying needs and interests in the course of their exploration and discussion of issues, there may not have been enough time or opportunity to do so in relation to each of the issues. For example, the mediator might ask a party:

> When you insisted on him only seeing the children once a month, in what way would that help you?

or

> What effect do you think this arrangement will have on the children?

or

> You said that you wanted at least $60,000 compensation. How did you get that figure? How important is it to you to get that money now?

The mediator should emphasise that "part of my role is to play devil's advocate".

It is most important to complete that task before any serious generation and selection of options is undertaken, otherwise the option generating and final negotiation will proceed on the basis of entrenched positions rather than mutual interests. A private session is also useful for encouraging the parties to examine the needs and interests of the absent party.

7. Testing options listed during joint session, generating new options and responding to offers

Sometimes parties in joint session are reluctant to generate options in case they might be conceding too much. Because the mediator might have asked them not to evaluate the options just yet, the party may be uncertain about the possible reaction of the other party. A private session provides the opportunity for evaluating the options already generated as well as generating and evaluating new options from both parties' perspectives, and assessing the merits of offers made.

8. Using private sessions as an impasse breaker

At any stage of the mediation, breaking into private session can be a useful way of breaking an impasse between the parties. It may be necessary to make use of private sessions when the parties find it difficult to continue in joint session. Perhaps one or both parties have reached the point when they simply regress and resort to making unrealistic demands on each other? Perhaps one or other feels that they would be losing face if they continued to negotiate?

A private session can be a useful time for helping parties reassess the reality of a position they may have taken, including the likelihood of the other party's acceptance of that position. It is also useful to discuss with the parties the benefits and drawbacks of adhering to that position.

The mediator may conclude that strategies need to be re-assessed and that focusing on the future may, for some reason, be difficult for either or both parties without the help of a private session. If only one of the parties would benefit from having a private session, it is always wise to have a private session with the other party also.

9. Fostering a joint problem solving approach and re-affirming the parties' ability to resolve their dispute

The mediator should foster a joint problem solving approach to the issues, which by now should have been fully explored either during the first joint session or private session. The mediator can achieve this by asking questions which are framed in such an open-ended way that the party is directed towards a solution which aims at the parties' mutual satisfaction, for example:

> How do you think the difficulties you both had in your partnership such as X, Y or Z can be avoided in the future?

or

> What worked well for you in the past? Is there anything about the past arrangements that you want to retain in the future?

or

> What sort of arrangements for contact with the children would satisfy your needs to have time out and for him to have the opportunity to continue to be a parent?

or

> How can you avoid the constant bickering with your neighbours and maintain your privacy while at the same time allow your neighbours to feel that their concerns are being taken seriously?

The mediator could direct the party towards reviewing the options already generated during the joint session in terms of how they would meet the other party's needs and interests. New options and offers could also be explored in the same way. For example:

> What do you think would assist the other party to accept your offer?

10. Setting the scene for final negotiations: exploring settlement options and rehearsing negotiations

The mediator should assist in setting the scene for final negotiations. One of the main objectives of this important purpose of private sessions is to encourage the party to develop a strategic approach to the final negotiations. The options of mutual benefit discussed and assessed may well crumble if proposed in a way that would attract animosity and resentment on the part of the other party. Thus, the mediator's role is to enhance positive, and minimise counter-productive, communication during the final negotiation session.

Another important strategy that the mediator could apply is that of encouraging the party to adopt an analytical approach to the progress or lack of progress achieved so far in the mediation. The mediator could ask the party questions such as:

What do you think of the progress achieved so far?

Why do you think it's not going well?

Can you think of ways to move it along a bit?

The mediator can assist in the analysis of one party's impact on the other party, for example:

Do you remember when you said X, Y or Z? How did he or

she react? Why do you think he or she reacted that way?

How do you think you can avoid that reaction when you get together again?

Practise on me. What exactly could you say to avoid that negative reaction?

If the party is tending to remain entrenched and positional, the mediator could reality test by asking:

What sort of settlement would really satisfy you today? What do you really want to get out of the mediation?

followed by:

What do you think would really satisfy her? What do you think she really wants out of mediation?

followed by:

How can you help her give you what you want?

Such questioning paves the way for a more conciliatory frame of mind and the need for a give and take approach that is conducive to a fruitful final negotiation session.

Rehearsing final negotiations

The mediator could also assist by rehearsing final negotiations with the party in private session, for example:

> Practise on me. Let's say I'm her. How would you approach that new issue in a positive and constructive way?

One of the dilemmas faced by parties in Western-style negotiation is the fear of losing face or a potential advantage by being the first to make an offer. This is particularly so in mediations where sums of money are being negotiated. One way of dealing with this dilemma is to explore ways in which neither party is put at a disadvantage. For example, an offer could be incorporated into a number of options so that it does not represent a definite offer. The options could then be evaluated by both parties in terms of mutual satisfaction during the final negotiations. Another strategy at the mediator's disposal is the "simultaneous offer strategy", which will be discussed in Chapter 7 — "Negotiations and problem solving". (See also Chapter 17 — "Practical strategies".)

Options may have been generated in the course of the joint session and the list of options may be either very lengthy or very brief. A private session could be used for discussing the merits of expanding a very short list or condensing a very long one for the purpose of final negotiations. As the private session is a confidential one, the mediator should encourage the party to record options to raise later in joint session.

If the party has run out of ideas, then the mediator could generate options as long as more than one is suggested for the party's consideration so that the party does not associate the mediator with any preferred option, which could be seen as compromising the mediator's neutrality. For example:

> I know you think that the way out for you is to leave the partnership. This, of course is one option open for you. Have you thought of any other options? What if you asked him if he would consider employing a full-time office manager to relieve you of that burden? Or what if you asked him to help you with the office management? Or how do you think he would react if you agreed to work part-time in the partnership, concentrating your efforts on the family and criminal law clients?

At this stage of the mediation it is important not only to focus on the exploration of specific, mutually satisfying settlement options, but to explore the implications of other avenues for resolving the dispute. The mediator could explore with the parties in a private session what the best or worst alternatives to a negotiated agreement would be for them. For example, the mediator could ask the party:

> If you don't settle today, have you thought of what you would need to do? If you went to court, has your lawyer told you how much time and money you would have to spend? How certain can you be about the outcome if you left it to the judge to decide?

And again:

> What's the worst that could happen if you didn't settle today? Would that be better than settling at mediation? In what way would it be better than settling today?

The same series of questions could be asked about the worst alternatives to a mediated settlement.

11. Proceeding with the mediation as a series of private sessions as a last resort

The use of private sessions to replace joint sessions for direct negotiation should be a strategy of last resort when the mediator fails to maintain communication between the parties and there is a very real possibility of the mediation being abandoned by the parties. We have rarely had to resort to doing this and mediators should not do so without applying other strategies that will be dealt with in detail later in the book.

It should be remembered that the rationale for breaking into private sessions should not be based on the comfort level of the mediator but that of the parties. Only as a last resort should mediators continue the mediation as a series of private sessions. However, in those cases where parties are horse-trading over a sum of money, and it would not be efficient to keep re-assembling them to merely exchange small monetary concessions, those exchanges might be better done through shuttle negotiation. (See Chapter 12 — "Shuttle negotiation and shuttle mediation".)

Some dos and don'ts for private sessions are set out below.

Table 6.1: Dos and Don'ts for Private Sessions

Dos	Don'ts
A. PRELIMINARY STEPS	
• Agree on who starts first.	• Don't allow the decision about who should start first lead to unnecessary argument.
• Remind parties about confidentiality, equal time and equal treatment.	• Don't focus only on the use of private sessions for confidential information.
• Give absent party constructive tasks, eg, to think of other settlement options or new issues.	
B. PRIVATE SESSIONS **1. General Hints**	
• Give party your undivided attention.	• Don't follow your own agenda.
• Encourage party to take notes of what is important to them for negotiation.	• Don't take copious notes (preferably don't take notes at all).
• Ask open-ended questions.	• Don't offer your opinions rather ask for the party's opinions.
• Avoid making statements.	• Don't be discouraging about lack of progress made.
• Ask parties to assess progress made, and encourage them about progress achieved so far.	• Don't, in the private session with the second party, act as agent for the first party.
• Treat parties equally in both private sessions as far as possible.	
2. Specific Hints (a) Expanding or completing unfinished business	
• Expand list of issues.	
• Complete unfinished business from joint session.	
(b) Expressing views in private	
• Allow for free expression of ideas and feelings.	• Don't focus prematurely on how the absent party would feel.

Dos	Don'ts
(c) Reviewing agenda and exploring issues in more depth	
• Review agenda and expand or contract List of issues.	• Don't focus on what you need to know but what they need to find out from each other.
(d) Exploring new issues	
• Probe for any new issues for exploration from both parties' perspectives	• Don't discourage party from raising new issues not listed on the agenda.
(e) Identifying needs and interests	
• Continue to identify needs and interests prior to option generating.	• Don't focus only on present party's needs and interests.
(f) Fostering joint problem solving approach	
• Ask open-ended, mutual problem solving questions.	• Don't recommend solutions.
• Encourage review of options generated to satisfy both parties.	• Don't encourage focus on options that only satisfy the party present.
• Generate new options for mutual satisfaction after parties have run out of ideas.	• Don't generate just one option in case the party thinks that this is your favoured option.
• Focus on the past only to explore what needs to be avoided or retained in the future.	• Don't encourage the party to dwell on the past.
(g) Setting the scene for final negotiations	
• Assist party to develop strategies for final negotiations.	• Don't focus on strategies for final negotiation that might only suit that party.
• Rehearse final negotiations and help party to enhance productive future communication and avoid negative communication.	• Don't assume that mediation is necessarily in the party's best interests.
• Explore best and worst alternatives to a negotiated agreement.	• Don't have a private session with only one of the parties.

Dos	Don'ts
(h) Breaking an impasse	
• Use private sessions to break an impasse.	• Don't resort to a series of private sessions to replace joint negotiation sessions without trying other strategies first.
(i) Conducting a series of private sessions	
• If parties are ready to give up the mediation, resort to a series of private sessions.	

Stage 6 — Negotiations and problem solving

PREAMBLE

There are no hard and fast rules that apply to these final stages of mediation. What happens at the negotiation stage, which precedes the outcome, depends on what progress has been made thus far. It may also depend on the type of mediation being conducted (ie, interpersonal or commercial etc).

Many mediations resolve quickly after a reasonable exploratory time in the first joint session followed by the first private sessions. In such an event, Stage 6 may just be a wind-up session making sure that there are no misunderstandings pending the final agreement.

Similarly with some ADR programs, particularly those that are time constrained, the joint session stages of exploration and negotiation are completed before the first private sessions. The scene is normally set for resolution in the post-private joint session. That joint session will essentially be a wind-up session focused on fine tuning the terms of the agreement or on terminating the session if the parties have failed to agree.

It may also be the time to transmit offers based on options that have been fine tuned or firmed up during the private sessions. So, for those mediations, Stages 6 and 7 become the final joint session.

However, for many other mediations, separate stages of negotiation and of agreement-making are necessary and usually follow the first private sessions. It is at this stage that a mediator is called upon to determine what is the most appropriate process to follow and what are the most appropriate skills and strategies to apply at any point in time. In complex mediations, it is normally only in Stage 6 that the scene is set for resolution and often the mediator needs to be creative in process design.

Transition from exploration to problem solving

The negotiation stage, following the first private sessions, is the point of transition from discussing the past to solving the present problems and dealing with the future. The parties may also have generated a number of options.

As a result of holding a private session with each of the parties, the mediator should now be aware of the areas of potential agreement and those where further clarification or detailed negotiations are needed. The mediator will have prepared each party for this next joint session. The mediator will also have formulated a tactical plan as to how best to progress the matter. Permutations that may be identified from the private sessions include:

▮ if issues still need clarification, then further exploration is necessary before proceeding to offers and negotiations;

▮ if one or other party has options that have not been raised, or if the parties are devoid of ideas or reluctant to make suggestions, then the negotiation stage might commence with a brainstorming session; or

▮ if the mediation has reached the stage where the parties are expecting offers to be made, these can be tabled and negotiations commenced.

At whatever point this second joint session starts, it will normally progress to one of the above step(s) unless the parties agree that they are unable to resolve their dispute. At the stage where offers are exchanged, there can then be a succession of joint and private sessions (or a shuttle exchange of offers) as the recipient of an offer privately considers and discusses the offer with advisers and the mediator.

A challenging stage

The final negotiating stage is possibly the most challenging for both the parties and the mediator. Until now, a mediator can generally rely on the Process to progress the matter to the offer and negotiation stage. In Stage 6, it is the mediator's use of flexible process, skills and strategies that will be needed to bring about a resolution.

The future focus of Stage 6 brings many stresses for the parties all at a time when they are probably tired and on edge. There may be the frustration of slow progress, the need to deal with a party that has not heard of principled negotiation, the pain of compromising beyond "a bottom line", or simply the need to save face. For the mediator, there is the need to be alert to parties' stresses, to choose the appropriate tool to keep negotiations progressing,[1] close "the last gap",[2] and to avoid "mediator's settlement hunger",[3] among other things.

PURPOSES OF THE NEGOTIATION AND PROBLEM SOLVING STAGE

After the first private sessions following exploration of all issues, the parties are generally ready to table offers and ideas for settlement, or if better progress has been made, their proposals for those items that have not yet been agreed. Where parties have not reached the stage of formulation of offers or options, or if ideas that have been tabled have yet to be accepted, then the mediator can assist in either encouraging the parties to generate options or to expand on or vary existing ones.

So the negotiation and problem solving stage has the following purposes:

1. To facilitate the tabling and clarification of offers and negotiation of an outcome.

2. If necessary, to generate settlement options through brainstorming or other means, and to generate offers based on those options.

1. Tabling and clarification of offers

Process

Whilst it is possible for Stage 6 to be conducted entirely in joint session, it may, in certain types of disputes, become a succession of private sessions with the party whose turn it is to consider and respond to an offer, followed by a joint session where the response and counter-offer is given. If the only outstanding issue is the amount of monetary settlement, there is often little point in getting together in joint session. In fact, if parties react negatively to each other, remaining in joint

---

[1] See Chapter 17 — "Practical strategies".

[2] See Chapter 17 — "Practical strategies".

[3] See Chapter 20 — "How neutral are we?"

session may well jeopardise settlement prospects. The mediation at that stage is best handled as a shuttle[4] until agreement is reached.

With private sessions at this stage of the mediation, the focus is on resolution. The mediator's role is to assist the parties:

▉ to formulate the offer or to consider the other party's offer;

▉ to reality test the offer or response to an offer;

▉ to rehearse what is to be said to the other party in the next joint session.[5]

Where parties have legal representation, their lawyers often wish to discuss matters with their client in the absence of the mediator. While this should be respected, the mediator should insist on a session with the party prior to reconvening in joint session in order:

▉ to understand what that party's approach will be in the next joint session (if only to be forewarned); and

▉ to reality test that approach in terms of the mediator's assessment of the position reached in the mediation.

Offers for all issues together?

It may simply be that a global offer, usually of money, is the only element of a settlement. However, the settlement of most disputes has rarely such a simple structure.

In such cases, some mediators prefer to facilitate the generation and evaluation of offers for one issue at a time and then work out specific agreement terms for that particular issue before moving to the next issue. This method is conducted on the basis that "nothing is agreed until agreement is reached on all issues". This basis frequently overcomes a party's concern that a concession given early may not be reciprocated. It allows a party to change an earlier concession as the situation develops with agreement being reached on later topics. This approach is particularly appropriate for family mediation of property settlements and parenting arrangements.

Other mediators prefer to encourage parties to make all-encompassing offers covering all issues ("a global proposal"). The advantage of this approach is that the issues are not always self-contained and tend to overlap. There may be greater opportunities for

---

[4] See Chapter 12 — "Shuttle negotiation and shuttle mediation".

[5] See generally Chapter 17 — "Practical strategies".

trading on some aspects of the offer when the totality of the offer is considered at the same time.

Experienced mediators make use of either approach depending on the nature of the dispute and the parties' reactions. Frequently, the approach to settlement is determined by the first offeror and her or his adviser.

Who goes first?

Sometimes, it is appropriate for the parties to exchange offers at the same time. On resumption of the joint session, the mediator may adopt an appropriate process that will enable both parties to table their offers in this manner, for example, a simultaneous exchange of written offers.

However, the majority of matters require someone to open. Unless it has been previously agreed as to whose responsibility it is to make the first offer, the mediator can say on resumption of the joint session:

> From the private sessions I have held with each of you, I am aware that there are offers to be tabled that have the potential to resolve matters between you. However, I remind each of you that these opening offers may only be the starting point and we may have some more work to do before you both reach an outcome that is satisfactory to you. Now, who would like to go first?

This statement conveys a positive, although realistic, message. It also emphasises the mediator's neutrality in not favouring either party or their offer in terms of who starts the offer process.

A common difficulty, which mediators then face in the tabling of offers, is the reluctance of parties to make the first move. The mediator could acknowledge this as a situation that occurs frequently and then use mediator silence to force someone to fill the void. Alternatively, stress that there is no disadvantage as to who starts first.

Delivery of offers

Offers are best delivered by the parties or their advisers, rather than the mediator. Where advisers are present, there are advantages in the adviser communicating the offer. They may be more articulate than their client and certainly less emotionally involved. An offer communicated by an adviser is also seen as third-hand and so can be regarded by the other party as less personal or "insulting" than had it been communicated by the offering party. This can take the heat out of initial offers, particularly those in the "insult zone".

Where parties are not represented, the mediator needs to manage the delivery of the offers within the limits of the abilities of the parties. If one of the parties has difficulties in communicating, especially when making an offer, the mediator can provide the necessary support by clarifying what is being offered. For example:

> Are you saying that you would like to offer Peter the opportunity to keep the children for a longer period on Saturdays, or are you offering him the opportunity to have the children stay overnight with him?

Clarification of, or summarising, the offer has the additional advantage of slowing the process down and allowing the other party to digest and understand what is being placed before them, rather than immediately rejecting the offer.

Offers transmitted by mediator

Mediators are sometimes asked by a party to convey that party's offer to the other party. This might be asked in all innocence because a party is not comfortable with making offers and negotiating. For experienced mediators, there is a great temptation to do this having witnessed how poorly offers are often communicated by parties, as well as by advisers.

Where the mediation has reached the stage of simply closing a monetary gap, it can be appropriate for the mediator to convey final offers without re-convening in joint session. But the mediator needs first to obtain the agreement of both parties to this process and to establish clearly that in doing so, the mediator will merely be conveying offers and not advocating or agreeing with the particular offer being conveyed.[6]

In other cases, the authors advocate that a mediator should rarely agree to convey an offer from one party to another. There are a number of reasons for this:

1. the mediator may create a perception of endorsing the offer or being the advocate of the offeror;
2. the mediator will be unable to clarify an offer or respond to a counter-offer without referring back to the other party: spontaneity is lost;
3. the other party will be unable to "read" the body language of the offeror to understand whether it is a soft offer or really a "final offer"; and
4. the offeror might simply be using the mediator as a blind for insulting offers that the offeror could not and would not make

---

[6] See Chapter 12 — "Shuttle negotiation and shuttle mediation".

face-to-face. Be particularly suspicious of manipulation when the request for the mediator to convey an offer is made by a party's adviser.

Rather than convey a party's offer, the mediator should encourage parties to present their own offers and if need be, spend time in private session to coach a party in the presentation of that party's offer.

> ## Case Note
>
> One of the authors conveyed an offer orally to the other party who was in a separate room. When the parties came together to agree on the final settlement terms, the offeror turned to the mediator and said:
>
> > That's not what I offered at all!

If a reluctant party still feels uncomfortable in making the offer face-to-face, with that party's approval, the mediator could do so in her or his presence when the parties come back together again in the following way:

> Susan, when we were talking a few moments ago, you said that you would be prepared to do X. Am I right? Is that what you are prepared to do?

Non-conveyed offers arising in private session

There will be times where a party does not bring out their private session proposals. If the joint discussions or the mediator's gentle prompting does not flush the idea out, the mediator will need to wait till the next private session with that party to see if the idea is still a possibility. It may simply be that the party had second thoughts as to whether it was a good idea or it may be that the offer tabled by the other party has made it obsolete or less attractive.

Keeping parties focused on the future

If parties believe an offer made to them, or a non-acceptance of their own offer, is unreasonable, they tend to regress by reiterating past incidents that led to the dispute because they feel the other party has not taken into account their statements or perspectives conveyed during the exploration stage. The tendency to go back to the past may also indicate that insufficient time has been spent on discussing some aspect of the past and that that party may still have a need to express feelings or revisit arguments that they feel have not been taken into account. This is why it is so important not to go into private sessions prematurely or to force parties into generating options. Unexpressed feelings have a way of coming back to haunt both the parties and the mediator.

A mediator cannot ignore a party's desire to revisit past events. However, the mediator needs to be firm to keep the focus on the future. The party should be encouraged to link the past with the offers being considered or to bring forward new ideas that will address past events, for example:

> I wonder if you could at this stage link those past events with what you would prefer for the future. Knowing what you believe went wrong in the past, can you think of what you would like to be done differently from now on?

Emphasising progress

As the negotiations progress, it is important for the mediator to take detailed notes as the parties reach broad consensus on a developing settlement proposal. In addition to these notes being needed when the final agreement is being drafted, summarising from the notes of what the parties have decided so far often helps the parties to come to an agreement more readily on outstanding issues. They are reminded of the prospect for resolution and can create a renewed focus on solving the remaining unresolved issues.

Will they never agree?

A difficulty faced by mediators at this offer stage is when parties are close to agreement and yet are unable to finally settle, a situation described by Professor John Wade as the "last gap".[7] Strategies to overcome this "last gap" need to be brought into play.[8]

In doing so, the mediator should not bring too much pressure to bear on the parties to come to an agreement as it may be counter-productive. Persistence, optimism and patience are all personal qualities that prove to be invaluable at this time.

---

[7] Wade, J H, "The Last Gap in Negotiations. Why is it Important? How can it be Crossed?" (1995) 6 ADRJ 93.

[8] See Chapter 17 — "Practical strategies".

2. Option generating

Options often emerge in the course of the first joint session and set the scene for the making of offers in Stage 6. Where those options are limited and the mediator becomes aware through the first private sessions that the parties are not yet ready to exchange offers or that there are options yet to emerge, the mediator will need to assist the parties to generate and evaluate options in the next joint session.

Ways and means of doing so follow.

Options prompted by problem solving questions

When facilitating option generating, the mediator can assist the parties by posing questions in a problem solving framework to elicit possible options without critically evaluating them. Examples include:

> How can the client's best interests be served if the business were to close on Thursdays?
>
> What are your ideas on how these tasks might be shared?
>
> What do you suggest you both might do when XYZ happens in the future?

This helps the parties move away from:

(a) entrenched positions and demands;

(b) making offers and counter-offers and prematurely reaching an impasse;

(c) the temptation to be critical of options or details associated with any option generated by the other party.

For example, one party might comment on the other party's options:

> That option would not suit me at all. I don't know how many times ... (I have to tell you that unless I get X from mediation, this whole session has been a complete waste of time).

The mediator might quickly intervene (before the words above in brackets are uttered) by saying:

> I wonder if we could just defer any comments on the options for a little later. At this stage, let's just add options to the list without looking at the merits of any particular option.

Brainstorming

Brainstorming, although a staple of training courses, is only usually effective in certain limited circumstances and is not often used in practice. Those circumstances are where there exists the possibility of multiple outcomes, in inter-personal matters or where there is an ongoing relationship. There is a need to obtain the parties' agreement to proceed in this fashion otherwise there will be less than full participation in the process.

A "brainstorming" exercise involves primarily the parties but also includes their advisers. It involves the mediator standing at the board, marker pen in hand, seeking ideas from each party in turn as to ways in which the several components of the dispute might be resolved. Before commencing, the mediator needs to explain how the exercise will be conducted:[9]

> We need to list as many ideas or options to resolve this matter before we begin evaluating and selecting what works best for both of you. I will be asking each party in turn to provide an idea until we exhaust all possibilities. If you are stuck for an idea, I will ask the other party to make a suggestion and that may prompt other ideas. There are a couple of simple rules that apply until we have everything on the board:
>
> 1. there can be no comment or judgment passed at this time; and
>
> 2. you may offer as many ideas as you think of, no matter how bizarre or possibly unworkable they may at first appear.

The mediator may need to set a time limit to the brainstorming session. Naturally, if the parties were experiencing no difficulty in continuing to generate the options, it would be fruitless to adhere rigidly to a time limit.

Invite options in turn

Whether or not the mediator conducts the exercise as formally as a brainstorming session, it is important that the mediator provides the parties with equal opportunity to offer options. This avoids being seen as favouring one party's ideas. For example, a mediator might say:

> John, you've just suggested the option of giving Mary more time for her personal life by appointing a part-time secretary to do some of the work Mary is doing now. Mary, can you think of any other options to add to the list?

Apart from issues of neutrality,[10] this approach can prevent the impasse that can occur when an early formal offer is made by one party, and is then rejected by the other party, who then either makes a counter-offer

---

[9] See also Chapter 17 — "Practical strategies".

[10] See Chapter 20 — "How neutral are we?"

or no offer at all. This often leads to a stalemate in the mediation at a critical stage.

If a demand or a formal offer is made during the generating of options, the mediator should convert it into an option. For example:

Party A: "What I'm only prepared to do is to give B another two weeks to deliver the goods."

Mediator: "Delivery in two weeks' is an option which I will list on the board and we can consider it when we're discussing the other options."

Leave details till later

At the option-generating stage it is not necessary and may indeed be counter-productive to insist on details. The mediator should stress the usefulness of developing options in broad terms without critical evaluation.

Later, there will be a need to provide sufficient detail to see if an option is workable or attractive. However, if the mediator or a party insists on too much detail, the parties may well get embroiled in a secondary conflict that could jeopardise any final settlement prospects. Instead, the mediator should elicit broad agreement in principle prior to fine tuning the option for the final agreement.

Mediator suggested options

When the parties can think of no further options, brainstorming or otherwise, the mediator could add to the list. This should be done with caution, and only if the mediator can suggest several options, rather than a single option to avoid the perception of a preference. The mediator can preface the suggested options by saying:

> There are other options which you haven't mentioned. You can if you wish add them to the list. For example: What if each of you did X, Y or Z in order to avoid A, B or C which created a problem in the past? Are these possibilities?

or

> Have you thought of D, E or F so that you can both benefit from the arrangement?

or

> Others in similar disputes have decided on G, H and I. Is that a possibility?

Depending on how the mediator assesses the situation, it may be safer to save any suggestions until the next private sessions.

Limited options

Certain types of disputes do not have the potential of giving rise to many options. For example, some commercial disputes where the parties may not continue to have a business relationship; a partnership dissolution; or a personal injury matter where sums of money loom large as a major or sole issue. On the other hand, some other commercial disputes may involve a continuing relationship and therefore give rise to a wide range of options.

In disputes that generate a narrow range of options relating to one apparent issue, such as a claim for monetary compensation, the mediator needs to think of ways of expanding the possible options, rather than encouraging a global offer. At the agenda setting stage, the mediator will have broken the one issue up into a number of sub-categories. This will assist the parties to think of options for each of these sub-categories rather than focusing on the one global amount of monetary compensation.[11] However, despite the best efforts of the mediator, some negotiators (mainly positional) or advisers resist a split-up of a global sum as they fear it will attract too many lines of argument on the composition of the offer. It is then a matter for the other party to insist on a break-up, rather than the mediator.

Option evaluation, clarification and selection

However options are generated, the mediator then needs to help the parties evaluate the relative merits of the options that have been generated in order to bring a sense of reality to the final proposals for settlement. By its nature, the process of mutual evaluation, clarification and selection of options can only be effectively done face-to-face. If the mediation has become a shuttle, then this process is undertaken with each party individually as part of the consideration of formal offers.

The mediator can assist the parties to examine the options by highlighting one of the options, or a combination of options, which appear to meet their respective needs and interests. For example:

> Bob, you suggested a moment ago the option of appointing a part-time secretary to do some of the clerical and administrative work which Mary is no longer happy doing. Mary, does that option allow you to do what you said you needed to do, more legal work? If so, would you both like to include that as part of your agreement?

---

[11] See Chapter 4 — "Issue identification and agenda setting".

If the positive momentum is maintained and the parties are encouraged by the mediator to feel that they are making progress, an exchange of offers can often occur without the need to continue to consider the other options listed. On the other hand, the mediator may need to do more work with the parties on other options that appear to satisfy only one of the parties. The mediator could help the parties to re-examine the one-sided options by focusing on ways in which the needs and interests of both could best be met. For example:

> What changes do you need to make to option X so that it's acceptable to you both?

or

> What do you need to inject into M's proposal to make it work for you?

Transition to formal offers

The selection of options can simply progress into defining the terms of the final agreement. However, in many cases, the process of formal offers needs to be undertaken.

It is at this point that each party and their adviser(s) adjourn to consider what they have heard and to formulate the offer they are to exchange with the other side. Alternatively, it may have been agreed that one party would make the first offer on the basis of an agreed structure of the final settlement. If no advisers are present, the mediator may need to speak privately to each party to assist with the formulation of offers.

Table 7.1: Dos and Don'ts for Negotiations and Problem Solving

Dos	Don'ts
1. TABLING AND CLARIFICATION OF OFFERS	
• Use private sessions if the only outstanding issue is the amount of monetary settlement.	• Don't "shuttle" unless there is only one outstanding issue.
• In private sessions help parties focus on resolution.	
• If legal representatives wish to discuss matters in private with their clients, insist on holding a private session prior to the joint session in order to understand and reality test the approach they plan to adopt.	

Dos	Don'ts
• Be flexible re the management of offers eg, evaluate one issue at a time or all offers.	• Don't favour one party over the other in who goes first in making offers.
• Be flexible about who goes first in making offers.	
• Allow parties or their advisers to deliver offers.	• Don't let unrepresented parties struggle with delivering offers if they have communication problems.
• Convey final offers in private session only if parties request it.	
	Don't put pressure on a party to bring out in joint session an offer or proposal raised in private session.
• Encourage parties to focus on the future.	• Don't assume you can convey an offer in private session without checking with the offeror that you have correctly interpreted the offer.
• Emphasise progress made towards reaching consensus on settlement proposals.	• Don't block a party's desire to revisit the past.
• Be persistent, optimistic and patient even when parties are close to agreement yet seem unable to finally settle.	• Don't put too much pressure on parties to come to an agreement.

2. OPTION GENERATING

• Facilitate option generating by posing questions in a problem solving framework.	• Don't allow parties to critically evaluate options at this stage.
• Encourage parties to defer critical evaluation of options generated.	• Don't impose brainstorming without the parties' agreement.
• Limit brainstorming to situations giving rise to multiple outcomes.	• Don't appear to favour one party's ideas by focusing on her or his options.
• Provide parties with equal opportunity to offer options.	• Don't encourage parties to be too specific when generating options in order to minimise premature undue criticism.

Dos	Don'ts
• Convert a demand or final offer into an option.	• If you do suggest an option, don't suggest only one option to avoid a perception of preference for that option.
• Encourage parties to develop options in broad rather than specific terms.	
• Only suggest additions to options already generated when parties have run out of ideas.	
• Assist parties to re-examine one-sided options by focusing on mutualising parties' needs and interests.	

Stage 7 — Range of mediation outcomes

Mediation sessions conclude with a range of possible outcomes:

■ adjournment;

■ partial or interim agreement;

■ total resolution; or

■ no resolution.

If the parties have reached a settlement, the role of the mediator is a very pleasant one. The parties are congratulated for their efforts and there is a pervading air of optimism. If no settlement is reached, the mediator needs to conclude the session in a way that does not result in any of the parties losing face.

ADJOURNMENT

A mediation may be adjourned for any number of reasons:

■ There may be a need to obtain more information or take action prior to the next session, for example, to obtain a property valuation.

■ It may simply be that discussions are not concluded and it is often better to adjourn to another day when everyone is fresher rather than carry on late into the evening with everyone becoming tetchy and closed in mind (including the weary mediator).

▌ The parties may have agreed to trial an arrangement for a period of time and contemplate another session at the end of the trial period to iron out any hiccups that may have emerged.

Whatever the reason, the mediator needs to conclude the mediation session with:

1. a summary of the progress made;

2. parties' agreement on what, if any, action is to be taken prior to the next session, by whom and by when;

3. agreement on the time, date and venue of the next mediation session; and

4. noting matters written on the whiteboard, including agenda items covered and not covered, common ground, options and any areas of agreement.

Subsequent to the mediation session, if time permits, the mediator should in writing (marked "Confidential for the purposes of mediation") confirm items 1 to 4 above to the parties or their advisers. Where the adjournment is more than a week, the mediator (or the agency, if one is involved) should contact the parties several days before the resumption date to ensure they have done all that they agreed to do and/or are ready for the next session.

PARTIAL OR INTERIM AGREEMENT

Some matters come to mediation with a number of separate issues that are capable of separate agreement. Where agreement is reached on some but not all matters, the parties may be happy to resolve such matters, leaving the remaining issues to be determined later.

The mediator should then proceed to document what was agreed. The mediator should also identify, and perhaps draft a statement of, issues yet to be resolved. The advantage of this is that after the mediation, it may still be possible for the parties to settle these remaining issues. Even if they do not settle out of court, the issues will have been clarified or narrowed in the course of the mediation and the statement of unresolved issues serves as a useful agenda for future action.

COMPLETE RESOLUTION

Structure or component parts of proposed agreement

As the mediation is in the final stages, the mediator and the parties need an understanding of the broad shape of any settlement agreement in order to understand on what matters agreement is needed.

The matters to be addressed and included in any settlement agreement will often be evident from either the nature of the dispute or from the issues in dispute. For example:

▐ A parenting agreement will need to cover at least a child's residence, contact with other parent, long- and short-term welfare.

▐ Damages to property will usually simply involve a payment in return for a release and indemnity.

However, with complex disputes, whether involving an ongoing or terminating relationship, the settlement structure can be unique to that particular dispute. Further, institutions often require boilerplate clauses or recitals in any settlement agreement. Whilst these should have been identified at the preliminary conference stage, and the clauses provided prior to the mediation, the other party needs to be aware of the totality of what it will be asked to accept before putting forward settlement options.

So before commencing the recording of an agreement reached, the mediator should check with the parties as to what is their understanding of all the matters that need to be addressed. This exercise may take a very brief time or it may generate considerable further discussion. Whatever the case, it is a necessary step to reduce the chances of a settlement being derailed at the eleventh hour by one party introducing new elements to a settlement agreement (for example, warranties or guarantees).

Reality testing

The parties should be informed that experience has shown that it is useful for the mediator to reality test the agreement by fine tuning its terms to ensure that both parties can live with it, not only in the short term but also in the long term. This involves the mediator exploring with the parties what they realistically expect of the agreed solution.

Although there are dangers in the mediator playing devil's advocate once the parties appear to have agreed on a final settlement, it is nevertheless important to do so. Parties often begin to have doubts after the mediation about the compromises they made to reach agreement and this can lead to a breach of that agreement. If this is a possibility, it is better that these reservations be addressed prior to the final agreement being executed.

The following types of questions could be asked:

So you both agree that you will consult on the reserve sale price. What is your understanding of "consult", and what will happen if you don't agree?

Are there any difficulties you can think of which might get in the way of making it work at the present time?

How do you envisage this working for you a year from now?

If you found that these arrangements were not working well, how would you deal with that?

You have agreed to get a new property valuation. Who will obtain/pay for it?

Writing up the agreement

This final stage of the mediation calls for the drafting of the agreement reached by the parties. If lawyers are present, they usually draft the agreement with little involvement from the mediator. If lawyers are not present, the mediator has the responsibility of drafting the agreement with full participation of the parties. The mediator should ask the parties "to give me the words", or should make it clear that what is being written is a draft only and they are free to suggest changes and additions. Where the mediator prepares the agreement with the assistance of the parties, the agreement might be expressed as being subject to the parties seeking legal advice depending on the circumstances. In some cases, in neighbourhood disputes for example, parties are not required to seek legal advice regarding their agreement.

Unless stated otherwise, most agreements reached at mediation are legally enforceable. Sometimes further action is required, such as the filing of consent orders in court or expansion of the settlement terms into more formal documentation. In such an event, heads of agreement may be entered into expressed to be either binding until replaced by orders or other documentation or not binding until such further action is taken.

Where the mediator has the role of drafting the final agreement, some of the guiding principles include:

(a) The agreement commences with:

▌ Description of document: Agreement; Heads of Agreement;

▌ Terms of Settlement;

▌ The date of agreement;

▌ A statement that it has been reached as a result of mediation (to seek to preserve confidentiality of the prior negotiations during the mediation);

▌ Names of parties; and

▌ A description of what issues the agreement is addressing.

(b) The content of the agreement should be written in a positive tone.

(c) The agreement clauses should be sufficiently detailed to avoid future interpretation conflicts, but not so convoluted as to create confusion. The clauses requiring action need to address "What", "Who", "When" and "How".

(d) The agreement should not appear to be one-sided, that is, the respective responsibilities and commitments should, as far as possible, be written to reflect a balance between the parties. For example:

> A will pay $X to B by bank cheque within 14 days of today. Within 7 days of the receipt of the cheque, B will commence the repairs. A will provide ...

(e) If further action is required after the mediation, this should be clearly stated, along with by whom and by when.

(f) The agreement should be signed (or at least initialled if not binding) in sufficient copies to allow one copy for each party.

FAILURE TO RESOLVE

Mediators should not expect all mediations to settle. Moreover, since in most cases mediation is a voluntary process, it is also important for the mediator to respect the parties' decision not to persevere with mediation and to accept the possibility that their interests may in fact be better served by resorting to another form of dispute resolution, including litigation.

Mediators should not be tempted, at this stage in particular, to refer to the high success rate of mediation and risk the parties experiencing a sense of failure if they fail to resolve.

Where it appears to the mediator that the parties will be unable to agree, or if one or other party indicates a desire to withdraw, a final series of private sessions should be conducted with each of the parties ensuring the mediator that this is their wish. It may be that the mediator's perception is wrong and it has simply been that each party has not wished to lose face by making the next concession.[1] In other cases, the parties could, in private session, be encouraged to analyse why it was not possible to reach agreement and the mediator could act as an agent of reality testing the consequences of not settling in mediation.

If all efforts to keep the mediation going fail, the mediator should nevertheless maintain a positive approach, by, for example:

▌ seeing if the last offer can be kept open for a few days;

▌ proposing that the parties enter into a partial agreement for those matters on which they could agree, or that they reach an interim agreement on what is to happen pending final adjudication;

▌ encouraging the parties to agree to have a cooling off period, and perhaps a teleconference to review the status, before they seek to embark on, or continue with, litigation;

▌ highlighting the benefits achieved by the parties, through the clarification of issues and, if relevant, agreement on the fewer issues to be resolved if the dispute did proceed to litigation; or

▌ inviting the parties to come back to mediation at a later stage if they feel it would be of some assistance then.

The mediator should terminate the session by summarising what has been achieved, and should take care not to make the parties experience a sense of failure by their inability to reach agreement. The situation can be normalised by saying:

> Over the last few hours we have given the tree a good shaking but unfortunately the fruit that has fallen has not been sufficiently ripe as to be attractive to both parties. Not all disputes can be resolved through mediation, and this seems to be one of them. As you progress down the litigation route, a time will arise when you will wish to revisit settlement discussions. If you then wish, I will be available to assist you again to see if the fruit is then ripe for all parties to reach a satisfactory outcome. In the meantime, I wish you each well.

Just as it is important for the parties not to experience a sense of failure when agreement has not been reached, mediators, too, should not feel that they have failed.[2]

---

[1] See Chapter 17 — "Practical strategies".

[2] See Chapter 20 — "How neutral are we?"

Some dos and don'ts for the mediation outcomes are set out below.

Table 8.1: Dos and Don'ts for Mediation Outcomes

Dos	Don'ts
1. ADJOURNMENT OF THE MEDIATION • Identify the reason for the adjournment and record requirements for the adjourned session. • Ensure parties are well prepared for the adjourned session.	• Don't let the parties leave until all issues relating to the adjourned session are understood and agreed to.
2. PARTIAL OR INTERIM AGREEMENT • Document what agreement parties have reached. • Draft a Statement of Unresolved Issues (SUI) where relevant. • Refer to clarification of issues and SUI matters for future action.	• Don't make parties feel that they have failed just because they have not reached total agreement.
3. COMPLETE RESOLUTION • Check the parties' understanding of all matters which need to be addressed re the agreement	• Don't risk last minute derailment of the settlement by a party's introducing new elements re the settlement agreement.
4. REALITY TESTING • Stress the value of reality testing by fine-tuning agreement terms to ensure short-term and long-term liveability. • Explore with the parties what are their realistic expectations of the agreed solutions.	• Don't forget to address parties' reservations relating to compromises made and normalise possible future doubts that may emerge.
5. WRITING UP THE AGREEMENT • If lawyers are present, let them draft the agreement with minimal involvement from you. • If lawyers are not present, then assume responsibility for drafting the agreement. • Ensure the parties understand that you are only preparing a draft of the	• Don't make the parties feel left out of the working of the agreement.

Dos	Don'ts
agreement with their assistance, and that it is subject to the parties' seeking legal advice.	
• Where further action is required (eg, filing consent orders or need for additional formal documentation) enter into binding or non-binding heads of agreement.	
• Formulate the agreement clauses succinctly and positively.	• Don't formulate the agreement clauses in a convoluted way.
• Focus on the necessary details for implementation to avoid future unnecessary problems.	
• Ensure that agreement clauses include details re "what", "who", "when" and "how" in relation to future action.	• Don't omit relevant details for the parties' future guidance.
• Provide each party with a copy of the agreement.	

6. FAILURE TO RESOLVE

Dos	Don'ts
• Respect the parties' decision not to persevere with mediation.	• Don't refer to the high success rate of mediation.
• Accept the possibility that the parties may be better served by another form of dispute resolution, including litigation.	• Don't take it for granted that a party's reluctance to make the next concession indicates a desire to abandon mediation.
• Resort to private sessions to assess whether your view that parties might wish to abandon mediation is correct.	• Don't make the parties feel that they have failed because of the inability to reach agreement.
• Highlight in summary what has been achieved in the mediation so far.	
• Suggest a cooling off period and offer your availability for another mediation session.	• Don't let the parties leave with a sense of failure.

Part 2

Procedural Variations to the Mediation Process

Co-mediation

What is meant by co-mediation and what are its features? What are its advantages and limitations, what is its impact on settlement rates and how can it be applied effectively?

WHAT IS MEANT BY CO-MEDIATION?

Co-mediation is mediation conducted by two or more impartial and neutral third parties working together to assist participants in the negotiation of a mutually acceptable settlement of the issues in dispute.

THE FEATURES OF CO-MEDIATION

Co-mediation has a number of features unique to it, some of which, such as teamwork and the opportunity for debriefing, are in direct contrast with those of solo mediation.

Equality of standing

Co-mediators should have equal standing. If mediators have someone to assist them, and one of the mediators is introduced as the mediator and the other as the assistant mediator, then it would be inaccurate to describe the process as co-mediation. The parties should not perceive the relationship between the mediators as a hierarchical one, even if one of the mediators is far more experienced than the other or one possesses professional qualifications in, for example, law, commerce, social work, psychology or counselling and the other is a lay person.

Teamwork

The key to successful co-mediation is effective teamwork. Unlike solo mediation, the ability to work as a member of the team is a prerequisite for co-mediation. This feature, as we shall see, has both advantages and disadvantages. There are several elements associated with teamwork which become evident at specific stages of the mediation, for example, the division of tasks between the mediators is important at the preliminary stages, while sharing of tasks is assumed throughout the mediation.

Debriefing

Co-mediators are provided with the opportunity to debrief at the end of a mediation session. Mediation agencies make debriefing an essential ingredient of co-mediation, thereby affording mediators the opportunity to give each other "open and honest feedback". Co-mediators are required to complete debriefing schedules at the end of the mediation session.

Mediators are also required to attend workshops on how to give each other positive and constructive feedback. These form part of the quality control which the agencies need to demonstrate to maintain professional standards and to fulfil their obligations when applying for the continuation of government grants.

The content of debriefing schedules includes an assessment of teamwork and an analysis of the dynamics of the dispute. The debriefing schedules encourage constructive comments on the mediators' performances.

THE ADVANTAGES OF CO-MEDIATION

Advantages for mediators

Co-mediation offers significant advantages for mediators. Most mediators find co-mediation very rewarding. We have found after mediating with about 60 different mediators that there would be only two or three we would prefer not to work with again.

The advantages of co-mediation can be general, in relation to issues such as the need for newly-trained mediators to gain knowledge and experience in an effective and expeditious way and the need to maintain quality control and professional standards. The advantages are also specific in relation to the mediation session itself. Advantages of co-mediation which become evident in the course of the mediation include the following:

▌ It combines the skills, insights and talents of two or more mediators: two heads are always better than one in sensitive, complex and contentious situations.

▌ It provides mediators with back-up and support when they might need it most, for example, impasse situations.

▌ It helps to prevent physical and emotional fatigue.

▌ It avoids a sense of isolation.

▌ When a mediator's personality traits or background professional training might encourage a bias towards a particular communication style or strategic approach with one or other of the parties, the other mediator can provide the necessary balance to enhance mediator neutrality and absence of bias.

Advantages which are of a more general nature

▌ Co-mediation serves as a form of apprenticeship for newly-trained mediators.

▌ Mediators are afforded the opportunity of working with a specialist mediator, that is, someone who specialises in particular types of disputes, for example, building disputes, environmental disputes, medical negligence or other personal injury matters. Such an arrangement enhances the prospects of widening the range of options that can be generated when parties run out of ideas.

▌ It allows for quality control through peer-group review and constructive self-criticism.

▌ It provides opportunities to observe a variety of mediation skills and strategies.

Advantages for the parties

▌ It allows a party who is ill-at-ease with one mediator to relate to the other mediator.

▌ It may assist the matching of mediators to parties in terms of age, gender or ethnic background. However, even if one of the mediators comes from the same country as one or both of the parties, it may not necessarily mean that rapport can be readily established, for example, they may come from different regions with a history of hostile relationships.

▌ It is the rule rather than the exception for mediation agencies to have a male/female team in family disputes.

▌ It provides opportunities for the mediators to demonstrate different communication and negotiation styles to the parties.

It should be stated that more research is needed on parties' perspectives on co-mediation in terms of their level of satisfaction; their views on the pros and cons of solo and co-mediation (somewhat difficult to assess as very few parties would have been a party to both solo and co-mediation); the effects of matching efforts; and the use of a combination of different professional backgrounds and experience.

THE LIMITATIONS OF CO-MEDIATION

There are, of course, limitations to co-mediation. Not all mediators feel comfortable with co-mediation and may feel more at ease working alone. Moreover, personality and style clashes can cause stress and conflict between the co-mediators. One mediator may have a need to play the dominant role in the mediation, thus depriving the co-mediator of valuable opportunities to gain more experience. There may also be a continuing lack of agreement on the choice of strategies to apply in the course of the mediation. Parties should not be subjected to conflict between the mediators.

It is preferable for mediators to recognise that they feel more comfortable with solo rather than co-mediation. It does not mean that they will perform effectively when mediating alone. However, it is generally accepted that the more comfortable mediators feel with co-mediation, the more likely it is that they will become effective solo mediators.

It should be kept in mind that there is a dearth of empirical evidence to show that co-mediation necessarily results in higher settlement rates than would be the case with solo mediation.

HOW CAN CO-MEDIATION BE APPLIED EFFECTIVELY?

The need to devote ample time to preparation and planning

This requirement applies to both solo and co-mediation in terms of physical arrangements including an adequate supply of note paper and pens for the mediators as well as the parties, seating arrangements, for example, ensuring that one party is not sitting too close to one of the mediators, the availability of whiteboard and markers and so on.

The division of labour between the co-mediators

Before the mediation, the co-mediators should reach:

█ Agreement on a division of tasks in the initial procedural stage of the mediation process and a sharing of tasks for the remainder of the mediation.

█ Agreement on the method of communication between the co-mediators, especially on how a lack of consensus on strategies will be handled in the presence of the parties, including how to handle interruptions between them and when to hold private sessions.

Open communication between the mediators is very important and can serve as a useful model for the parties, especially of how to handle differences.

Examples of open communication can include requesting the other mediator to come in:

> I seem to be running out of steam here, John, perhaps you could take over.

or

> I don't know where we should go from here. Does anyone have any ideas?

> David, do you have anything to add at this point?

Different ideas on procedure are also handled openly. If one mediator thinks it is time for a private session, he or she can communicate this openly. The other mediator might respond by saying something like:

> Yes, I think that would be a good idea in a few minutes, but I'd just like to explore this idea a little further if you don't mind before we break into private session (or I think Mary was just about to elaborate on why she is fed up with the present working arrangements. Can we just hear her out?).

In general, however, both mediators will come to the "private session" decision at the same time.

A suggested way to co-mediate during the first three stages of mediation is outlined on p 140.

Mediator's opening statements

Each mediator will introduce herself or himself, rather than one doing it on behalf of both. With the mediator's opening statement, one mediator could describe the role of the mediators and the features of mediation (neutrality, voluntariness, flexibility, confidentiality, courtesy rules and the status of the mediated agreement), and the other could describe the process to be followed for the remaining period.

Parties' statements

The parties' opening statements will be taken down, and summarised back, by one mediator, while the other mediator maintains eye contact. At the end of each statement either mediator can ask clarifying questions if necessary. While the "scribe" mediator is summarising back, the other will pick out the issues which emerge from the summaries and will compile the interim agenda. The agenda setter is generally the one who will list the issues on the whiteboard in consultation with all participants and will consult on which item to begin with.

Joint sessions

Both mediators can be active in facilitating dialogue between the parties in the first joint session which follows. However, if one mediator is pursuing a particular line or strategy to good effect, it is perfectly in order for the other to sit back if there is nothing constructive to add to what the active mediator is doing. The less active mediator is then in a better position to actively listen, absorb what is occurring, take notes, pick up points that may be emerging or subtleties the other may have missed, for example, a hint that there is scope for an ongoing relationship. The second mediator will then have the opportunity to reinforce the other's line of action if necessary, or to intervene with a line or idea that may have occurred to him or her while the other mediator was being more actively interventionist. This does not mean that one mediator has to sit back. In the context of the dispute it may be in order for both to be equally active throughout at certain times.

Another advantage of co-mediation in the joint session is that the passive mediator can observe the effects on one party of the dialogue between the active mediator and the other party as well as the parties' reactions to each other, and intervene appropriately.

Private sessions

Both mediators are present at each party's individual private session. If one has been more active in joint session, the other may take a more active role in the private session, particularly if handling the private session is one of their fortes. But this is a play-by-ear situation. It is not unknown for one mediator to play the "heavy" reality agent in a private session, leaving the other to be "sweetness and light". With a male/female co-mediation team, it may be less threatening to a party for the same sex mediator to take the major reality testing role.

MEDIATORS' PRIVATE SESSIONS

Although this is not a general feature of co-mediation, the mediators can adjourn briefly for a private session if it is appropriate. In such a case, one mediator will inform all participants that:

> I'd like to have a few minutes alone with Sue before we proceed.

The private session can be constructive in that it allows one mediator to check with the other a perception of bad faith participation and how to handle it, or allows both mediators to consult on a proposed strategy to break an impasse.

SETTLEMENT

At the end of the session, if one mediator is summarising or drafting the settlement terms, the other will provide input if necessary or will check details with the parties and/or the legal representatives.

DEBRIEFING

Mediators can use debriefing as an opportunity to hold a frank discussion on their strengths and weaknesses and the difficulties they might have encountered, but they need to avoid too much self-indulgent introspection and self-analysis and should keep the debriefing practical to maximise mutual learning.

Positive and constructive feedback can also be useful and encouraging, for example:

> I was glad when you came in there as I was really stuck.

> I felt a bit lost when you did so and so, and thought we went off at a tangent at that point.

or

> Thanks for taking the reins in the first private session, I was finding it difficult to remain neutral.

The mediators could ask each other: "Do you think there's anything I could or should have done differently?"

Table 9.1 Division of Tasks During Mediation Stages 1–3

Mediation Stages	Mediator A's Tasks	Mediator B's Tasks

Stage 1:
Mediators' Opening
Statements
	• Introductions
	  Mediation Process
	• Features of Mediation
	  and Role of Mediators
		• Outline of the

Stage 2:
Parties' Statements
	• Keeps eye contact with
	  the parties
		• Takes notes of Parties'
		  Statements

Stage 3: Mediator's Summaries of Parties' Statements and Agenda Setting	• Sets the Agenda Statements	• Summarises Parties'

Table 9.2: Dos and Don'ts of Co-mediation

Dos	Don'ts
1. PREPARATION and PLANNING • Dedicate sufficient time to prepare and plan for the session.	
• Ensure appropriate seating.	• Don't seat parties where they may have difficulties talking to each other.

• Ensure availability of equipment eg,
  whiteboard, markers etc.
	• Don't allow one party to sit closer
	  to the mediators than the other
	  party/ies.

2. DIVISION OF TASKS DURING INITIAL PROCEDURAL STAGE
• Allow each mediator to introduce
  herself or himself.
	• Don't imply one mediator has higher
	  status than the other.

• Agree on who does what.	• Don't let one mediator undertake all tasks in the initial procedural stage.

• Agree on general guidelines for the
  sharing of tasks for the remainder
  of mediation session.
	• Don't be inflexible in the sharing
	  of tasks for the remainder of
	  mediation session.

Dos	Don'ts

3. METHOD OF COMMUNICATION BETWEEN CO-MEDIATORS

Dos	Don'ts
• Communicate openly over different ideas on how to proceed.	• Don't go into a mediators' "private session" too readily.

4. CO-MEDIATING FROM FIRST JOINT SESSION TO DEBRIEFING

Dos	Don'ts
• Share mediation tasks flexibly according to the relative levels of skill and comfort of each mediator.	• Don't intervene unnecessarily if your co-mediator is working effectively.
• Be open and frank about progress achieved and normalise periods of difficulty that the parties might experience.	• Don't oversell mediation by referring to high rates of settlement.

Doing the job by phone

TELEPHONE MEDIATIONS

There has been an increasing trend to conduct mediations and concili-ations by teleconference. This is often for economic and efficiency reasons, particularly with those mediation agencies that have a maximum time set aside for the meeting. In a non-agency situation, a teleconference may be the priority choice in the particular circum-stances, or even a necessity in other contexts.

Geographic separation, age, disability, time factors and economics may prevent parties from participating face-to-face. Teleconferencing enables these difficulties to be overcome so that the benefits of mediation or conciliation can be delivered regardless. Preliminary conferences are often conducted by teleconference where it is not efficient to gather everyone together for a meeting that may last less than an hour. Similar principles apply for a telephone preliminary conference as for the mediation itself.

A DIFFERENT LANDSCAPE

With a teleconference there is a departure from many of the traditional aspects of mediation. One of the main lynch pins is omitted — that of the parties having the opportunity to sit down and discuss matters with each other face-to-face. Other factors enter the forum. Certain dynamics are reduced or minimised; others are more pronounced. Different skills are required. Other skills may need different emphasis and timing. It may not be possible to apply the range of skills and strategies normally relied on. There may be noticeable differences with voice only connection in the way parties behave with traditional face-to-face communication.[1]

COMMUNICATION DYNAMICS

"Some people may feel more inhibited by telephone contact, while others are less so than in a face to face meeting".[2] It has been observed that men and women tend to communicate differently by phone. Men often favour the "No frills, let's get down to it" style, while women can be more responsive than in a face-to-face meeting.

The mediator/conciliator has to establish telephone rapport and confidence. This includes drawing out a poor or "no frills" telephone communicator and, in doing so, there may be a need, at some stage, to request a speaking moratorium from a participant who has a tendency to babble on or become strident.

The two edged sword

Obviously, a party and mediator cannot observe, react to or pick up on a non-verbal message. Impressions conveyed by clothing, physique, body movements, facial expressions and eye motions which can produce both positive and negative messages, such as goodwill or hostility, are all eliminated. Face-to-face encounters can, however, result in interpretations that are encouraging and reassuring in one situation, but may be threatening or intimidating in another. This is the two edged sword.

With teleconferences, non-linguistic characteristics such as tone of voice, pitch, volume, intake of breath, accent and sighs are accentuated by the telephone and become some of the tools the mediator must work with and interpret, perhaps providing clues on how to proceed. More than ever, listening skills come to the fore to compensate for the absence of the non-verbal nuances. A mediator's own telephone manner may come under scrutiny. Mediator impatience or frustration may be more easily discernible by the parties. On the other hand, impatience or frustration conveyed by body language alone would provide an outlet for the mediator that is not discernible by the parties.

There are additional positive and negative effects in parties not being in the same room.

---

[1] Charlton, R, *Dispute Resolution Guidebook* (LBC Information Services, 2000), p 239.

[2] Charlton, n 1, p 329.

Positives for the parties:

▌ It may be less inhibiting where one party is not faced with the other's physical presence, particularly where there is a history of violence or in other cases where one party may feel nervous or disempowered by the presence of the other. As well, there may be more comfort in not being physically confronted with the other party's lawyer or other professional adviser.

▌ It allows each party to take control of their own involvement on their own territory or that of their lawyer. Confidence may be enhanced.

▌ A person who has more comfort with the telephone, has good "telephone relationships" and productive telephone networks, can feel more at home and thus more empowered than they might face-to-face.

▌ Responses may be more thoughtful where participants have more time to think things through. "Sometimes the telephone contact, with its pauses in the flow, may allow for more reflection on what has been heard."[3]

▌ The increased necessity to make notes may enhance recall and assist a "visual" person to reflect and thus promote creativity.

▌ A party who cannot visibly focus on the opposition may be better able to focus on the merits and demerits of a proposal. There may, as a result, be more focus on issues than on personalities.

▌ The physical absence of the mediator may also be a relaxing factor. The parties may feel there is less need to make a good impression, although this may be a negative factor for the mediator in some instances.

Positives for the mediator:

▌ There is a certain relaxation in not being obliged to maintain eye contact and in not being the focus of the visual attention of all participants.

▌ Note-taking can proceed unimpeded by the need to write unobtrusively or minimally as occurs in face-to-face.

▌ For some mediators it may be easier to convey neutrality when purely relying on the spoken word.

---

[3] Charlton, n 1, p 330.

▊ Additional relaxation may come from not having to respond to a number of visual stimulants.

▊ It has been observed that mediators who feel ill-at-ease working with the whiteboard (as some mediation agency models require), see this impossibility as a bonus.

Negatives for the parties:

▊ A person who is more familiar with business-like telephone communication may feel disadvantaged when emotionally-linked topics arise or require exploration. Some may have been shielded from telephone tyranny by support staff.

▊ There is not the same scope for parties to exchange friendly reassurances and courteous introductions — "How was your journey?"; "Where did you park?". These exchanges involve the personal touch, which can warm, give confidence and soften a potentially tense situation.

▊ There may be more leeway to get locked in to positions when distance provides more time to reflect. Separation may also provide more scope for parties to change their minds. Freedom from the direct encounter may enhance a tendency to be aggressive. Truncated or blunt communication may be more likely to occur without the eye contact or physical atmosphere.

▊ Phone talk may inhibit opportunities to unlock the emotional content, the release of which can sometimes lead to a focus on practical arrangements. Physical distance may not enhance the achievement of emotional understanding.

Negatives for mediators:

▊ Diminished is the mediator's ability to create the "atmosphere in the room" which can be promoted by the personal exchanges such as a simple handshake or the "putting of a face to a name" which occurs when parties and lawyers have previously only communicated by phone or through correspondence.

▊ There are no visual aids to enable the mediator to separate people from the problems, to list and compare options, to workshop proposals or solutions or to validate parties' suggestions and amendments to data already visually recorded.

▊ Poor telephone equipment can contribute to delays and communication interference.

▌ With some parties the telephone may inhibit spontaneity. This can deprive the mediator of the ability to tap into the spontaneous, unguarded response.

▌ The mediator cannot maintain complete control of the process. Confidentiality can be jeopardised when the mediator is unable to observe what parties are doing. As an example, one of the authors observed a party tape-recording the proceedings and had to request that it cease. The mediator has less control over the activities of advisers, support persons and interpreters.

▌ Private meetings lose their important features of immediacy and personal touch.[4]

▌ When private sessions commence, the mediator may have inadvertently failed to disconnect one of the parties or speaker link ups may be disrupted. As Boulle reminds us, "Technology often follows Murphy's law and goes wrong when it is not needed."[5]

▌ It has been observed that there is a more frequent tendency for parties to challenge a speaker's opening statement or demand a right of reply.

How does the lack of visual aids affect the meeting?

There are no visual aids such as whiteboards to provide an objective focus of the problem. The agenda is verbal and is more easily disregarded. Unless the mediator is keeping scrupulous track of the conversation, there is the potential for it to skip from one topic to another without necessarily making progress in regard to any one topic. A mediator with good whiteboard skills may experience the loss of a "good friend", although some report that even in their isolation, they continue to use the whiteboard as a reference point and to maintain their comfort and relaxation level.

Following the process

In order to facilitate a common focus at the mediation, the parties could be furnished with an outline of the process prior to the call so that they have reference to this road map when the mediator is outlining the process.

---

[4] Boulle, L, *Mediation Skills and Strategies* (Butterworths, 2001), p 209.

[5] Boulle, n 4.

As the process is not so easily followed, initiated or controlled, there may be a need for ongoing reminders of the stage "that we are at" than in the usual forum. The prior furnishing of a process diagram can be useful not only as an aid to understanding initially, but later when, for example, the mediator is clarifying the stage reached during the conference.

Some people are more visual than others and not so tuned in to the spoken word. Helpful whiteboard diagrams have to be substituted with verbal descriptions. Articulation skills are emphasised. With the increased tendency to skip around or drift from the original topic, the mediator may find themselves saying:

> We need to go back a couple of steps. This conversation began on topic X and what you both said was ... We are now discussing Y. Have we exhausted topic X or do we now need to revisit it?

In this regard, once the parties have approved the agenda, the mediator might ask them whether it would be helpful to have it faxed to them, particularly if the agenda is fairly comprehensive. Alternatively, the mediator might just dictate the agenda and ask the parties or their professional advisers to record it to enable all participants to be on the some wavelength.

Documentation

Parties are usually required to sign an Agreement to Mediate, which may include a separate confidentiality document to be signed by support persons and advisers. These signed documents should be with the mediator prior to the commencement of the session.

Documentation issues have their positives and negatives. File notes or other records in support of a position or explanation may sound less convincing and credible when read out over the phone, and are more easily dismissed by the other party. Explanatory plans and photographs cannot be tabled. On the positive side this may eliminate the generally unproductive "I have proof" aspect which features in some mediations as the supporting "evidence" is not readily available. Thus, the absence of documentation may be a plus for one party but a minus for another.

Who is participating?

At the outset the mediator needs to confirm who is present at the mediation and what is their status. If an uninvited guest or an unexpected "tagalong" is revealed this person's presence needs to be conveyed to the other party whose permission should be sought. The status of this person should be clarified. Are they present as an adviser, a support person, a scriptwriter or merely an interested observer? Pauses may indicate that someone is ghost writing for one of the parties or feeding them a script. If an undisclosed presence is suspected once the conference is underway, it is quite in order to ask "What was that noise?" or "Did someone enter the room?"

COUNTERBALANCING THE ABSENCE OF PERSONAL CONTACT

Introductions

In order to establish rapport with, and gain the confidence of, both parties it will generally assist if the mediator has a private word with each party before the general link up. First to make or renew introductions. Then to check, or reassure, that the Agreement to Mediate has been signed and faxed in by all participants. That particular party's participants can be confirmed at that time and information provided on the other party's "team", if not already known. This initial conversation may provide some clue as to a party's telephone communication style or comfort level, but not always.

The parties may have met or spoken previously. They may not have done so where someone is representing an organisation such as an insurance company, and there has been no preliminary conference. The mediator should make this inquiry and if necessary introduce the parties to each other when the joint link up commences. Legal representatives should also be introduced. The lawyers may have had some previous dealings with each other, but if they have not the mediator might say:

> Mr X is advising Mrs Black, and Ms Y is advising Mr Green. I understand that you have not spoken before so I would like to introduce you to each other.

A mediator pause will usually produce a "hello", to which the other will respond. In this regard, it has been observed that telephone inhibitions need not be just the exclusive province of the parties.

During these preliminaries, the mediator might mention that one or other of the lawyers will be required to prepare the settlement terms and ask, "Is anybody 'offering'?" If so, what will be the process for the others to review any draft, to comment upon and then sign? The responsibility for filing terms with the court or vacating a return date can be mentioned then or, if more appropriate, later.

The parties should be requested (and will often need to be frequently reminded), to state who is talking. Equally, the mediator needs to follow this rule.

Mediator's opening statement

It is doubly important in this forum to take a minimalist approach to the mediator's opening statement. As in a face-to-face mediation, parties are anxious to get on with it. In this forum, however, there is far more scope for parties to switch off when there are no other props to keep them alert, for example, where eye contact is being maintained; the mediator's body language is being observed; or where the parties are at least going politely through the motions of paying attention. Listening is exhausting and the mediator should prioritise the parties' needs for concise bite size information and subjugate their own impulses to make a verbal splash. At the best of times, it is easy to switch off during what is perceived as a boring ongoing monologue. Varying the delivery style by changing pace, tone and emphasis can hold the listener's attention and thus assist in establishing the telephone rapport.

Is anybody listening?

The mediator/conciliator can discuss the listening aspects with the parties by saying:

> This will be a listening exercise for all of us.

or

> This will really test our listening skills, won't it?

It is important for the mediator, when mentioning the ground rules, to emphasise that:

> I can only listen to one person at a time, and will have to call time out
> if two people are talking at once.

Where the mediator suspects that one or other of the parties is not really listening, or there are ongoing interruptions, it may be appropriate to keep checking that they have heard what the other has said, or to ask a party if they could summarise what they thought they heard the other party say.

It has been noted that telephone participants, even more than in face-to-face conferences, simply do not take in all that is being said. Parties' dialogue is the main tool the mediator has to work with. Every word may be a gem and this is where the mediator must remain sharp-eared even if the parties have, or one of them has, temporarily switched off.

Nuances in speech can be revealing and hidden agendas can sometimes be more easily detected through the exaggerated telephone tones. The mediator also needs to practice what they preach in terms of listening and not interrupting.

Interpreters

The involvement of interpreters can create a double jeopardy for mediators. Ongoing checks that the conversation is being interpreted are required if this is not clearly apparent over the telephone line. As in face-to-face mediations, the mediator needs to ensure that the interpretation is comprehensive and some of the dialogue is not being left out. The mediator's suspicion may be aroused if the interpretation seems too brief. It is difficult to check whether the interpreter is offering an opinion, as sometimes happens, but if the interpretation is overly verbose it may be that the interpreter is engaging in a conversation with the client, which falls outside the strict interpretation role.

Note-taking[6]

Note-taking needs to be ongoing with the notes set out in an ordered way. To avoid being faced with interpreting scrambled notes it can be helpful to have separate sheets or separate columns to note down the Agenda; the outcomes sought; and the proposals and options, similar to whiteboard use. Additionally and importantly, reasons for proposals and options should be noted. This assists in summarising and reminding. Thus, the mediator may say:

> According to my notes, Barbara is now agreeing to do X, but told us that the reason for sticking to her Y option is because ...

or

> I am just checking my notes and what J said was ...

or

> I am taking down what you just said. Could you please repeat it slowly?

Parties and their advisers should also be requested to keep on top of the game by taking notes. Where lawyers are present, the mediator needs to remind them that preparation of the agreement terms will be a task for one or both of them and that they may need to consult their notes.

---

[6] See also Chapter 18 — "Effective use of information – note-taking and application of visual aids".

Mediator input

The mediator has, and needs to have, more verbal input than in a face-to-face meeting. Mediator silence can be used effectively at times. Generally, however, the mediator needs to be more verbally active to keep up the communication and procedural flow. The "smiling face", non-interventionist style mediator, no matter how effective face-to-face, may need to change their favoured modus operandi in this forum. The opportunity to facilitate direct communication does not so easily arise. Nor is it so easily achieved and can be hard work. The mediator cannot indicate that the parties should talk to each other by a simple hand gesture or head movement. If a party feels inhibited by the phone forum there may be more reluctance to talk directly to the other party than in a face-to-face scenario. A contributing factor is the tendency to avoid the use of personal names, despite participants' confirmation that first names are preferred. Third party or formal titles seem to be more prevalent than in face-to-face sessions.

The importance of summarising and reframing

As mentioned, parties simply do not take in everything that is said. Frequent summarising is required because of the lack of opportunity to observe whether the parties are really listening to each other or indicating some other type of acknowledgment. This is where meticulous note-taking is important. It can be far too easy for a party to later assert they didn't state, or hear, a particular point.

Participants in a telephone mediation seem more prone to selective listening than usual. Sometimes line interference or poor equipment can contribute to this, as can a soft or indistinct speaking manner. Wrap-up summaries prior to private session are particularly important in the phone forum together with the announcement that this is the information to be considered during the break and discussed in the private sessions.

More reflecting and clarifying is needed where the communication of one or both of the parties tends to be of the "no frills" variety. Thus:

> Let me just clarify this. Are you telling Bridget that the reason you cannot pay for all the renovations is because ... ?

Private sessions

Where legal advisers are present, it is useful for them to have some time out with their client, without the mediator, to discuss any options or how to overcome any deadlocks that may have arisen. The advisers might be asked how much time, approximately, they will require with their client before the mediator rings in for the private session. Whether lawyers are present or not, it is useful for all to have a break at this point. The mediator can state that:

> I am going to take about a 10 minute break to gather my notes together and get a coffee.

This hiatus has the double benefit of ensuring that all lines are disconnected before the mediator rings one or other of the parties for the private session.

Review of positions, assessment of proposals

The mediator may have to persist in asking the parties to review and assess the practical details of any arrangement. Persistence is required because parties are often keen to cut short the conversation when substantial agreement has been achieved — this is "breathe-a-sigh-of-relief" time. However, prior to the faxing of any draft settlement terms (see "Agreement stage" below), it can be important to ensure that the understanding of what is apparently substantial agreement is not superficial, bare bones or broad brush. Because of the intense concentration on the spoken word, parties seem to get weary earlier in a teleconference than in a face-to-face mediation or conciliation. A tendency to avoid fine tuning both by parties and advisers has been noted. Mediators need to be resolute in resisting this avoidance, recognising that a teleconference will also have wearied them (perhaps more so than a face-to-face mediation).

Agreement stage

All participants need to be very clear about the proposed settlement terms. Lack of clarity provides more scope for the agreement to be sabotaged later. There is no on-the-spot, "before your very eyes", document. Nevertheless, in most cases there is scope for the draft agreement or orders to be faxed or emailed immediately for review, comment and, if confirmed, for signature. If approved, the signed agreement can then be secured by return fax.

Where one of the legal representatives is responsible for drafting, this person will be asked to read out the terms as they understand them, with input from the mediator if something has been overlooked by both legal representatives. The faxing or emailing will then be the draftsperson's responsibility. The draftsperson can also be asked to fax or email a copy to the mediator.

In complaint conciliation (in contrast to a mediation), private session offers can be transmitted by the conciliator and, if accepted, the parties may see no point in resuming a joint session and are reluctant to do so. Nevertheless, where the agreement terms are comprehensive or complicated, the conciliator should bring the parties together to review these terms so that there can be no misunderstandings or denial when the terms are faxed or emailed to them. It is only with a one-clause agreement such as "All brokerage fees paid between 1 May 2003 and 1 August 2004 will be refunded within two weeks from today's date" that resumption of the joint session may not be necessary.

Resolution rates

There is some anecdotal information from agencies that telephone mediations and conciliations have a slightly higher settlement rate than with the face-to-face process. Conciliations in particular tend to be more directive and solution based compared to mediations. Whether this perception is confirmed by non-agency mediations is not known. However, there are consistent reports of a more speedy closure than in the face-to-face forum. "The reason has not been analysed, but it is possible that telephone communication, with its more clinical atmosphere, encourages the participants to 'get on with it'."[7]

Time changes

It would seem quite unnecessary to remind mediators and session coordinators to pay attention to time zone differences. Surprisingly, this factor has commonly been overlooked, as have time changes resulting from daylight saving.

Neutrality aspects

The mediator/conciliator cannot be in the same room with a party where that party is participating from the same venue as the mediator. The normal separation should be maintained, even for the private sessions. The other party who is at another venue should receive the assurance that despite Party X and the mediator being in the same building no face-to-face liaison will occur.

---

[7] Charlton, n 1, p 330.

OTHER MEDIUMS

Teleconferencing is, of course, only one of the alternatives to face-to-face mediation. Others emerging include videoconferencing and mediation through the Internet. Review Tribunals are increasingly using video conferencing, and it has been noted that parties seem far less stressed in video-conferencing than in face-to-face hearings.

Chapter

11

Multi-party mediations

Multi-party mediations are more complex and challenging than two-party mediations.

With three-party mediations it is still possible to apply the standard process adopted for two-party mediations although the process will almost certainly take longer.

It would still be possible to ask each of the three parties to make an opening statement, which is then summarised by the mediator once all statements have been delivered. The rest of the process need not vary — including the holding of private sessions. However, when the number of parties exceeds three, the process may need to be varied in a flexible way.

A three-party mediation can occur in a dispute over a will, for example. In one such case, while the mediator was conducting a private session with Party A, Parties B and C got together and formed a coalition that resulted in what amounted to a "ganging up" against Party A. Depending on the circumstances, it may be in order for the mediator to request that those parties left to their own devices during the private sessions remain separated from each other. On the other hand, in some circumstances it may be useful for the others to confer to see whether some common ground can be achieved on what has transpired so far, as opposed to forming a bloc for unfair purposes. Whatever the situation, it is wise for the procedural rules to be agreed upon when the mediator is outlining the process.

Perhaps a mediator could mention the coalition aspect when describing the private session stage. Realistically, a mediator may not be able to enforce a request that unattended parties remain separate. However, the above example does indicate that private sessions should be as short as possible and illustrates the drawbacks of leaving several parties on their own for long periods of time in a multi-party context.

Matters which lend themselves to multi-party mediation are:

▌ Large construction projects.

▌ Environmental disputes.

▌ Local Government proposals which may involve other statutory bodies with potential impact on residents.

▌ Public policy matters.

▌ Proposed government legislation requiring community consultation.

WHAT ARE THE FEATURES OF MULTI-PARTY MEDIATIONS?

The following features characterise multi-party mediations:

▌ The matters tend to be more complex, involving a multiplicity of issues.

▌ A number of different groups tend to be involved.

▌ Not all the issues affect each of the groups.

▌ There can be no standard procedure for conducting multi-party mediations and a flexible approach is essential. Suggestions about a proposed procedure need to be canvassed in consultation with the representative groups.

▌ Co-mediation is particularly useful in multi-party mediations.

INTAKE PROCEDURE FOR MULTI-PARTY MEDIATIONS

The complexity of multi-party matters requires more in-depth consideration to be given to a number of issues.

These may include:

1. Assessing suitability of the matter for mediation.
2. Identifying the parties representing the interest groups and who the main spokesperson/negotiator for each group will be.
3. Contacting the parties.
4. Establishing the role of the participants and the procedure for the mediation.

5. The Agreement to Mediate:
   (a) confidentiality
   (b) authority to settle
   (c) special agreement clauses if relevant
6. Pre-mediation issues statements and chronology of events.
7. Consensus building and customised intake.

1. Assessing suitability of the matter for mediation

Assessment of mediation suitability may involve taking a history of the matter, including whether any action has been taken to resolve it to date. A suitability assessment may include whether the matter has compromise potential or whether there appear to be options for settlement. Settlement may involve a set of recommendations agreed upon by all parties to the mediation, rather than a final settlement of a dispute. Generally, the more options that are available, the greater the promise of success.

With certain types of complaints there may need to be consideration of whether a public interest issue is involved. Multi-party matters sometimes have a long history that may have involved other agencies. Mediation is often a last resort. Where a matter has a long, complex history, which may or may not involve someone's perception of a public interest issue, the parties may have become very polarised.

Public interest type disputes sometimes require more than one mediation session and the parties at the intake stage need to be informed accordingly.

Note: There is a view that matters involving public interest issues should not be mediated, but require a public airing. An assessment of what is in the "public interest" can be very subjective or the term can be difficult to define. Our view is that ultimately the decision to mediate must rest with the parties after they have been given the opportunity to make an informed decision. A party to a so-called public interest debate may not wish to be a whistle blower and may prefer to air any concerns in the privacy of the mediation forum.

2. Identifying the parties representing the interest groups and who the main spokesperson/negotiator for each group will be

Determining who the parties are involves an assessment or an investigation of who should be there and in what capacity. This is particularly so in multi-party matters. The inquiry should include who has been involved so far; whose presence might assist a resolution and whose absence might either prevent a decision or might jeopardise an agreement being carried out. These inquiries might involve initial discussions with the presenting main players. For example, who else might have been affected by a planning decision? It is therefore essential to establish who the final decision-makers are.

The main spokesperson or negotiator should be selected at the pre-mediation stage. Some reference has been made to this in Chapter 3 — "Parties' opening statements and mediator's summaries". Where there is a large number of people at a mediation they cannot all make opening statements. Whilst they often have something useful to contribute to the ongoing dialogue, where there is a "cast of thousands", its members should generally be encouraged to act as support persons or to fill in gaps. There is no scope for them all to give their own particular version of events.

At the end of a particular segment of the mediation the mediator could ask: "Is there anything anyone would like to add very briefly at this stage?"

3. Contacting the parties

Having established who the parties are, the mediator needs to contact each of them.

An approach in writing, accompanied by a mediation information sheet, followed by a phone call is often the most productive and non-threatening method.

Contact with each party should be carried out on a private and confidential basis. At the end of the contacting stage, it will be necessary to confirm in writing who the parties are.

4. Establishing the role of the participants and the procedure for the mediation

Establishing the role of participants

Particularly in a multi-party dispute, a party will agree or even ask to come along but will deny being a party. This can sometimes be based on a concern that they may be seen to be at fault in some way. It can occur, for example, where a local government council involved in a planning decision which is under challenge has relied on advice from a separate authority, such as a government department. The latter may be willing to attend but not be designated as a party to the dispute.

Establishing the procedure for the mediation

In a multi-party mediation there may be a handful of people involved, or dozens, or over 100 (especially when matters involve public interest issues). Obviously the standard mediation process cannot accommodate a large number of participants. In such cases, it may be possible to hold a preliminary meeting to confirm the reasons for the mediation, to outline the standard mediation procedure and necessary variations to it, and to determine the issues that will be brought to the mediation.

The mediator will have already established the identity of the various interest groups during the contact stage. The mediator could then suggest that there should be a selection of parties — each one to represent a particular interest group — to take part in the mediation session. This may have already been agreed upon at the contact stage.

Procedural variations to be determined may include:

▌ the need for the parties to forego making an opening statement and instead to bring with them to the mediation a list of issues they need to discuss at the mediation session;

▌ the need to forego private and confidential sessions if the number of participants is too large;

▌ the need to be prepared to sign a customised Agreement to Mediate before the mediation session begins;

▌ the need to contemplate the possibility that more than one mediation session may be required;

▌ the possibility that the participants to the mediation session may only be authorised to agree to a list of recommendations to be forwarded back to each interest group for their endorsement. The list of recommendations could be considered as an agreement in principle to be finalised.

▌ the need to vary the procedure when facilitation rather than mediation becomes appropriate.

If the number of participants is too large for each party to make an opening statement, the mediator could ask for two or three issues from each party. These issues could then be recorded on the board. The mediator could then seek the assistance of all present to help identify any repeated issue, which could then be deleted. The remaining items would then form the list of issues for exploration and discussion. It is useful for all the issues to be recorded in the first instance as it acknowledges the contribution of each participant.

Very occasionally, when a matter involving a statutory organisation and employees of that organisation, as well as a representative from the community (ie, a three-party mediation) has been referred to mediation, the mediator may discover at the mediation session that the parties had not really agreed to come. They, or at least some of them, may feel that they have not made an informed decision to participate. At one such mediation, the mediator did not adhere to the standard procedure but gave the parties ample opportunity at least to discuss the issues and make recommendations about a possible action plan rather than how to resolve the matter. In that matter, the mediator did not make use of her notes relating to the statements, as one of the parties had been taking ample notes. As that party had a senior executive role in the organisation, the other parties respected him and listened carefully when he was speaking. All parties agreed that they did not want the action plan to be reduced to writing by the mediator. They were all very satisfied with the outcome and wanted to treat the session as a meeting facilitated by the mediator rather than as a mediation.

5. The Agreement to Mediate

As there is far more likelihood of procedural variations in multi-party mediations depending on the nature and the number of participants in the mediation session, it is important for the mediator to tailor the contents of the Agreement to Mediate accordingly.

(a) Confidentiality

The issue of confidentiality is particularly important in multi-party mediations, especially in public interest matters. In such matters, it is not always easy to insist on inserting a confidentiality clause in the Agreement to Mediate. Until mediation was envisaged, the issues could have been very much in the public eye and may have already attracted much media attention. However, the interest groups might want to agree to maintain the confidentiality of what occurs in the course of mediation. It is often the case that an agreement is reached that there will be no communication with the media prior to the mediation and in the course of a multi-session mediation. Misinterpretations by the media could very well jeopardise agreement being reached. On the other hand, the parties may agree on a press statement to be issued, the wording of which may form part of the final agreement.

(b) Authority to settle

Establishing the authority to settle

This is discussed in Chapter 14 — "Pre-mediation issues". There is nothing worse than the situation where agreement has been reached and someone then says, "I'll have to go back and check with so and so". This is the potential graveyard for an agreement.

Where an interest group is represented by only a few people, the authority to settle question is paramount, as they need the authority to bind the others. Some environmental groups, for example, may have branches and satellites throughout a State. Even though they have a common overall goal, they can be factionalised and have separate agendas on some issues. In such a case it is probably more important than ever to establish, not so much which issues will be discussed, but on what issues the representatives can bind the others. This is where a pre-mediation issues statement can be helpful as it is linked to the authority to settle question. (The advantages and drawbacks of pre-mediation issues statements are discussed in Chapter 14 — "Pre-mediation issues"

One possibility, which has already been mentioned in establishing the procedure for mediation, is that there could be an agreement on principle or a set of recommendations to be forwarded to the various interest groups for their endorsement.

(c) Special agreement clauses if relevant

There may be a need to add to the Agreement to Mediate a requirement to report back to an organisation, statutory or otherwise.

Sometimes a statutory authority represented in mediation cannot, under its statute, ratify any agreement until it has been rubber-stamped by a board, council or other hierarchical body. The representatives of an authority, who nevertheless claim to have full settlement authority, can be reluctant to commit themselves in case they have to answer criticism of their decision. They can use the rubber stamp stipulation as an excuse to stall on making an agreement. The absent audience is perceived as having the potential to affect their career.

6. Pre-mediation issues statements and chronology of events

The advantages and drawbacks of pre-mediation issues statements are discussed Chapter 14 — "Pre-mediation issues".

A chronology is discussed in Chapter 14 — "Pre-mediation issues". Its usefulness to the mediator is accentuated in a multi-party matter.

Each side should be invited to contribute. Any variations or omissions can then be co-ordinated into one list by the mediator. It may not be a good idea to ask one to supply the list and then have it checked by the others. This practice has the potential to produce the polarising effect discussed with regard to the drawbacks to pre-mediation issues statements, particularly where one side has omitted an event which the other sees as significant or included one which the other sees as insignificant.

7. Consensus building and customised intake

Consensus building is a form of dispute resolution, most commonly used in multi-party disputes or workplace restructures. In a workplace dispute, for example, at the intake stage there may be a need to visit the organisation in question and to conduct personal interviews in order to get the background to the dispute and to ascertain who should attend. The intake task may be too complex to conduct by telephone or correspondence. This form of customised intake is discussed below.

Case Note

A mediation was requested by a senior manager of a large organisation. The presenting dispute was said to be between two separate sections of the organisation and the mediators were requested to proceed on that basis. The visit of the intake officer opened a "can of worms". There was no possibility of one section mediating with the other unless certain in-section issues were resolved first.

In-section and factionalised disputing held out no possibility of each section presenting a reasonably united front when mediating with the other section. In addition, individuals from one section had extraneous conflicting issues with individuals in the other section.

At the intake stage a series of "mini-mediations" were set up starting with the one-to-one matters. The number of participants in each mini-mediation progressively grew as matters were sorted out in a way that first drew the "lone rangers" into the fold and then members of the wider group. Each mediation had its own agreement terms. Finally, a reasonably workable consensus was reached among members of each section and the mediation, as originally requested, was held.

Customised intake methods, such as that described in the above case study, need to be devised to accommodate particular multi-party situations. These often take the form of a series of personal interviews. How these are achieved needs to be given careful consideration depending on the particular situation.

Case Note

Residents of a huge housing estate were in dispute. The police, social workers and a public housing authority were involved as well as some neighbouring non-residents. Parties were divided along lines that included ethnicity, generation, family and non-family. It was originally decided that the intake should take the form of personal visits. Because the dispute had generated a genuine fear of retribution among many of the residents, some key complainants were reluctant to be seen talking to, or being visited by, intake workers. The alternative proposal of a letter box drop to all residents, inviting them to either telephone or visit the intake workers at a neutral, non-threatening venue proved ultimately to be the most appropriate intake method. As certain residents of another housing estate were involved, the resident group with whom these non-residents were aligned undertook the responsibility of including them in an intake session devised for that particular group.

Shuttle negotiation and shuttle mediation

SHUTTLE NEGOTIATION

In shuttle negotiation the mediator meets separately with each party, moving backwards and forwards between them, conveying their respective ideas and responses. It may occur because the parties cannot communicate with each other face-to-face and can only do so through the mediator. It may, perhaps of necessity, occur later in the mediation session during a heavy bargaining stage, normally because parties want to discuss matters with their own advisers and generally when it is not efficient for a joint session to reconvene simply to exchange some minor concession or to clarify a point in a proposal.

The "instant" private session occurs where no exploration phase is undertaken, and the mediator conducts the rest of the mediation by the shuttle method.

Continuous shuttle negotiation should only be used in special circumstances. A mediator who proceeds this way as a matter of general practice and preference may be displaying insecurity in joint session and people skills, or may simply not have grasped part of the mediation philosophy. There have been increasingly frequent complaints about this practice both with regard to the mediator isolating the parties from each other (and the mediator) for long periods of time and the cost involved in drawing out the mediation longer than it need be. Mediators who are uneasy about dealing with parties together and are only comfortable with parties on a one-to-one basis may need to reassess their joint session skills or consider their own anxiety threshold level for conflict or debate.

Apart from the bargaining stage referred to, shuttle negotiation is appropriate in those cases where it becomes apparent that the parties simply cannot be in the same room together — usually for strong emotional reasons. Even where a separation is considered appropriate, or has been requested, parties may be able to reconvene in the same room once the mediation has progressed. The mediator should, from time to time, canvass with the parties the option of resuming on a face-to-face basis.

Shuttle negotiation may also be useful when parties make a huge effort to be in each other's presence but would appreciate a break from that effort. It is not just a question of negative feelings towards each other but lack of comfort and the inability to be natural. This can become evident at the beginning of the first private session when the mediator asks, "How do you think things are going?" The party might express feelings of relief at being able to speak freely and even hint that they would feel more comfortable to continue on that basis. In such circumstances, the mediator needs to be satisfied that continued negotiations might be jeopardised and that a final settlement is more likely to be achieved by shuttle negotiation. It is still desirable for a final joint session to be held in the presence of all parties to confirm any agreements.

Shuttle negotiation is not appropriate simply because it contributes to the comfort level of a mediator, who in her or his normal professional capacity (whether it be as a banker, lawyer, engineer or social worker), usually deals with clients on a one-to-one basis. Nor is it appropriate simply because mediators who are also lawyers, in their usual legal role, conduct negotiations in pre-trial or settlement conferences in this manner. Such negotiations are quite different in character from mediation.

Case Note

In a commercial matter, the parties, who had daily dealings with each other, flew to the city on the same plane to attend the mediation. By agreement their legal advisers were not in attendance. The parties were separated by the "mediator" after the initial procedural part of the process was completed. At the end of a day-long session, one of the parties complained bitterly to his legal representative (who was a trained mediator) about being face-to-face with the other side for a period of only 20 minutes. According to the lawyer, it was a simple commercial matter that could have been settled by lunch-time. The parties made the most significant progress when they shared a cab on the way to the airport to catch their plane home. As one party put it, "Why bring us to Sydney for this exercise? The mediator could have done what he did over the phone". This party was resentful about the cost of the airfare, the room hire and the mediator's general inability to facilitate, or unwillingness to allow, a face-to-face communication.

Sometimes a legal adviser will request a mediator to separate the parties because they are concerned about their client's strong emotional feelings. Before acceding to this request the mediator might check with that client whether that is her or his wish. If so, a further check is needed with the other party and adviser before proceeding to separate the parties.

The pitfalls that can occur in private sessions[1] are accentuated where continuous shuttle negotiation is used. Particularly accentuated is the danger of the mediator appearing as an advocate or agent for either party or being manipulated in the absence of the other party. Where parties are continually separated, what one party is saying is never directly tested or challenged by the other party. Indeed the mediator may need to be alert to a party who requests separation to avoid being tested.

Mediators need to avoid what may be perceived as discriminatory behaviour or statements. With shuttle negotiation there is a particular temptation for mediators to put their own interpretation on things, to give personal opinions or make promises about their powers of persuasion with the other side. The shuttle method is undoubtedly tempting because it emphasises a mediator's importance and certainly demonstrates how active they are and how worthy of their fee.

There are some common features between shuttle negotiation and shuttle mediation (which is discussed below), but there are also differences.

---

[1] See Chapter 6 — "Private sessions".

SHUTTLE MEDIATION

Shuttle mediation is different from shuttle negotiation in the sense that it has been previously agreed that this is the way the session will be conducted. Such a session has not slipped into shuttle negotiation by accident or design. It is also different in the sense that at no time will the parties meet face-to-face, either for the opening statements or for the agreement writing phase.

Shuttle mediation may be appropriate where previous domestic violence has caused a fear of intimidation despite the mediator's presence. It is also used in those cases where there is no possibility of constructive discussion because the continuing animosity will result in the mediation being used as another forum to continue the fight. Children or adolescents involved in a negotiation can sometimes only talk openly or feel comfortable without the presence of parents or adult carers. Shuttle mediation is also useful where there is a perceived power or status discrepancy between parties (such as between a professional and a lay person or a manager and an employee in a workplace matter). In such cases, it may be more empowering to one of the parties to remain separated.

The shuttle method is usually raised at the intake stage or at the preliminary conference. An intake worker may raise it. Parties or their representatives may request it.

With shuttle mediation the mediator will explain the shuttle process to the parties including the fact that it may be time consuming and that they and their advisers may be left alone for periods of time. The mediator will explain her or his "messenger" role, particularly emphasising that the message being conveyed is not the mediator's viewpoint, nor is the other party's view being endorsed by the mediator. It is often necessary to reiterate this with each visit as the following case note demonstrates.

Case Note

In one case where the mediator had transmitted the message from Party A to Party B, Party B began to "argue" with the mediator, by challenging the content of the message that had been conveyed. The legal representative came to the mediator's aid by saying to his client: "Hey, Dave, don't shoot the messenger."

The flip-side to this type of challenge is the increased tendency for parties in shuttle mediation to try and persuade the mediator about the rightfulness of their argument and attempt to get the mediator on side.

Procedure

There are various options on how to proceed in a shuttle mediation. One of these is to follow the normal process as far as possible in the early stages:

1. Party A makes their opening statement.

2. Party B makes theirs, without knowing the content of A's. The mediator then summarises both statements to Party B, then revisits Party A and undertakes the same procedure.

3. The agenda topics (drawn from both statements by the mediator) are clarified with A, and a similar procedure is conducted with B. It is only where there is any real dissension about the content of the agenda (which is not usually the case), that the mediator will need to sort this out. However, the agenda items should be written up on each party's whiteboard.

4. The first topic is then explored. The mediator can begin the exploration with either party, but it is usually convenient to begin with the party in whose room the mediator is situated once the agenda is settled.

5. More often than not the focus is on the substantive issues because of the limitations of the forum. Communication is often reduced to the bare bones, because there is not the possibility of it really being fleshed out. The main focus is on outcomes rather than the past. In the role of communication agent the mediator needs to be quite clear on what is permitted to be conveyed and what is not, because the session becomes a mix of non-confidential information that would normally be shared in joint session and the usual private session confidential disclosures.

The mediator should note the positions advanced and the rationale behind them. These should be written down and double-checked with the speaker each time. When conveying the message from Party A to Party B, the mediator usually needs to reiterate, "This is what I am authorised to say". When about to deliver the message, the mediator needs to assure Party B that he or she is merely conveying the message and is not negotiating on A's behalf. When relaying the message "he" and "she" language should be used:

Mr Jones said **he** was seeking X and that in **his** opinion this was appropriate because of Y ...

He also said that in **his** case time was running out ...

It is usually safer to keep injecting the "he" or "she" references every couple of sentences. When leaving that party, carrying their response or additional thoughts on the matter, there is the further reminder that in delivering the message the mediator will not be endorsing the comments nor acting as that party's negotiation agent.

A variation on the process, which avoids the mediator being the messenger, is possible where each party is represented. The adviser of one party can be invited to join the meeting with the other party and adviser in order to be the advocate and listener for her or his party. When this joint session is finished the mediator and the two advisers can join the other party for a similar session from which the first party is excluded. This can be a more efficient means of conducting a shuttle mediation, particularly when the exploration phase commences. It has also been noted that the two advisers may wish to confer separately at some stage without their clients.

Part 3

Pre-mediation

Preliminary conferences

WHAT IS A PRELIMINARY CONFERENCE?

A preliminary conference is a pre-mediation meeting that the mediator holds in the presence of the parties and, where they are involved, their legal representatives to ensure that the mediation session is ready to proceed. It usually lasts for between 30 minutes and an hour.

Mediators vary in the way they run a preliminary conference. Some prefer to hold face-to-face conferences so far as possible. This enables them to meet the participants and is seen as the start of building trust between the parties and the mediator.

Others rely on teleconferences that provide a simultaneous link-up between the mediator, parties and representatives in a situation where it is not convenient, usually because of distance or cost, for a combined meeting of less than an hour's duration to occur. Such mediators regard the initial telephone intake and the conference itself as providing sufficient basis for the parties to gain confidence in the mediator and the process.

Occasionally the parties and their lawyers may agree to dispense with a preliminary conference particularly if they are ready to proceed with the mediation and there are no additional documents to prepare or to exchange. There may also be a need to hold the mediation urgently especially if a court case is pending in the very near future. In cases where parties come to the mediation without their legal representatives, the mediator should encourage them to seek legal advice prior to the mediation and to arrange for their lawyers to be at the very least available for telephone consultation during the preliminary conference.

Some mediation agencies do not include preliminary conferences in their mediation process. Some of the related tasks are undertaken by an intake officer at the pre-mediation stage or by the mediator as part of the mediation session.

One statutory agency dealing with retail tenancy disputes actually dropped the practice of holding preliminary conferences as little benefit was seen by mediators and regular users to be gained for such disputes. By contrast, the process for farm debt mediations[1] was changed to require the holding of preliminary conferences as a standard process to ensure that certain matters were discussed, and the appropriate information imparted.

Purposes

The purposes of the preliminary conference are generally:

(a) to make introductions among the mediator, the parties and their advisers;

(b) to outline the role of the mediator, the features of mediation and the mediation process to the parties and their legal representatives;

(c) to discuss the Agreement to Mediate and its execution;

(d) to acquaint the mediator with the broad matters at issue;

(e) to agree on the pre-mediation exchange of information between the parties and to set a timetable;

(f) to establish who will be attending the mediation and to discuss the role of advisers and/or support persons;

(g) to encourage the parties and their advisers to undertake pre-mediation preparation including each party's opening statement;

(h) to establish and define the scope of the authority to settle of any representative of a party;

(i) to agree on the date, time and venue for the mediation.

Arranging a preliminary conference

When contact with the parties or their advisers is made by the mediator, one matter that is raised is the purpose of a preliminary conference, as set out above. Also considered at this stage is the manner of the conference and the time it will be held. The participants in the conference should also be established and generally all those who will be attending

---

[1] See *Farm Debt Mediation Act 1994* (NSW).

the mediation should be encouraged to attend the preliminary conference. This is not always possible, particularly where counsel are to be involved.

Nevertheless, it is highly desirable that the same parties and representatives who attend the mediation also attend the preliminary conference. One of the disadvantages when this does not occur is that the non-attendees at the preliminary conference have not had the benefit of hearing the mediator explain the mediation process, the mediator's role and the role of the legal representatives in mediation. The role of legal representatives differs significantly from the adversarial approach in litigation. They are therefore less well prepared for the mediation session.

In our experience, lawyers who have not been present at the preliminary conference have tended to adopt a more traditional adversarial role and have not encouraged the parties they represent to speak for themselves, especially if they are lawyers who know very little about mediation (they still exist). They have, in some cases, also attempted to cross-examine the other party and to focus on legal issues rather than on interest-based negotiation.

Some lawyer mediators tend to hold a preliminary conference only with the legal representatives. It is suggested they lose the opportunity to establish the full participation of the decision-makers (namely the parties) in the process at this early juncture and for the parties to learn from the mediator what to expect on the mediation day. Such practice raises the question of "whose dispute is it anyway?"

It is good practice for a mediator to confirm the arrangements, send an agenda for the conference so that everyone is prepared and enclose a copy of the agreement to mediate. A suggested pro forma letter, agenda and Agreement to Mediate for each is included in the Appendix.

How to conduct an effective preliminary conference

(a) Introductions

Introductions are always necessary even where the mediator has previously spoken to all participants as part of the intake. They may, or may not, have spoken to each other and it would be a rare case where they have spoken to the other party's legal adviser. Also, where advisers are involved, the preliminary conference is the first opportunity for the mediator and the parties to speak to each other, as often the initial contacts have been between the mediator and the lawyer.

A preliminary conference is the first step in establishing the parties' trust and confidence in the mediator, so the ritual of personalising the introductions should not be ignored. Early agreement on the use of first names assists and emphasises informality.

(b) Outlining the role of the mediator, the features of mediation and the mediation process

Often the explanation given at the preliminary conference is the first time a party has heard in detail what are the features of mediation, including the role of the mediator and the process that will be followed on the day. Even for the repeat players and experienced advisers, this explanation may provide new information as it defines the manner in which the particular mediator intends to proceed. The way different mediators proceed can depend on whether they adopt a facilitative or directive style. It is often best to state specifically: "The manner in which I conduct mediations, is ..."

The content of the explanation is essentially the same as the mediator's opening statement.[2] The opportunity can be taken to provide a fuller explanation at the preliminary conference so that a shorter explanation, by way of reminder, can be given at the mediation.

(c) Discussing the Agreement to Mediate and its execution

The mediator should make sure that the parties in particular understand the terms of the Agreement to Mediate before they are asked to sign it. They should be encouraged to ask questions about it or to suggest changes.

Some of the content of the Agreement to Mediate reflects the mediator's explanation of the process, so if this has already been explained, little more need be said, particularly if a copy of the proposed agreement has been distributed beforehand. One aspect that the mediator should particularly raise is the level of fees and costs being charged, how they are to be split between the parties (normally 50:50) and, importantly, how and when payment will be made to the mediator. A typical Agreement to Mediate is included in the Appendix.

With face-to-face conferences, the mediation agreement can be signed and exchanged there and then if there are no changes. Where the agreement is to be signed later (often at the commencement of the mediation session), undertakings should be sought from each party to observe the confidentiality and privilege provisions of the agreement as from

---

[2] See Chapter 2 — "The mediator's opening statement: what is it and what purpose does it serve?"

the date of the preliminary conference. The agreement should also be expressed as dated as of that date. These undertakings should be noted in any post-conference letter.

(d) To acquaint the mediator with the broad issues

The purpose is to provide the mediator with a sufficient understanding of the background to the dispute and the issues involved so they are able to facilitate the following discussion on the exchange of information. In a lease matter, for example, a brief background could include such items as withholding of rent, state of repairs and interpretation of the lease. Prior to the mediation, and particularly in complex matters, the mediator may need more detail, including a chronology of events. In court-based mediation, pleadings and other litigation documents may be offered. However, it is the experience of the authors that pleadings often offer no greater clarity of background and issues for the mediation than they do for litigation. It is better to ask the parties or their advisers to exchange statements of issues for the mediation.[3]

(e) Agreeing on an exchange of information and setting a timetable

The purpose of this is to optimise prospects for a successful mediation through adequate preparation and exchange of information so that each party can mediate from a position of knowledge (and not experience ambush).

Parties are generally not obliged to provide information to the other side for the purposes of a mediation. If a party objects to providing information, the mediator will need to facilitate the discussion and maintain neutrality on this issue. If that party intends to use such information at the mediation, or if the other party indicates that it is not prepared to consider a particular option unless they have prior opportunity to consider the information (for example, accounts), the mediator may need to speak to the objecting party separately to reality test the objection. In most cases, the requested information is then agreed to be provided. Where it is not, the mediator has little choice but to accept the situation (unless it is a court referred mediation where the mediator can issue directions).

With some mediations, such as in banking or insurance matters, one party may have a requirement that any settlement agreement should contain certain standard clauses or recitals. In such situations, that party should be asked to furnish to the other party prior to mediation a "shell"

---

[3] See Chapter 14 — "Pre-mediation issues".

agreement, which contains those standard recitals and clauses so that they can be considered and, if necessary, advice obtained.

(f) Pre-mediation preparation

The mediator can only encourage the parties and their advisers to undertake the recommended preparation for negotiations. This includes the party's needs to be met, realistic maximum and minimum outcomes, what the other party is likely to be seeking and likely to accept, alternatives to a mediated settlement, and costs of not reaching agreement. Often, these aspects are only faced by a party during the mediation.

One thing a party must do, with the assistance of advisers, is to prepare their opening statement. The mediator should emphasise the need for it to be delivered by the party and that it be a brief outline of the party's perspective of the dispute.[4]

(g) Establishing who will be present at the mediation

Apart from establishing the number of persons to be accommodated in the venue and for any catering, the mediator should establish who will be attending the mediation and what is their role. Parties do not appreciate turning up at a mediation to find that another party has brought along an adviser (or not brought an adviser) or expert when the contrary was agreed, or a person to whom they object has simply turned up. Sometimes a lawyer will turn up at the mediation session with counsel, a colleague or a junior solicitor, which can create an imbalance in representation as well as being discourteous.

Such problems set a very negative tone at the very start of the mediation. Accordingly the mediator should seek both parties' agreement that if the composition of their team changes, they will advise the mediator and the other party prior to the mediation.

The mediator should also make sure that persons not connected in any way with the dispute who wish to attend the mediation for academic or other purposes do not do so. Their presence may well affect the dynamics of the mediation session, especially if sensitive issues are being discussed and negotiated. This comment does not apply to support persons whose presence has been requested by a party to the dispute.

The roles in the mediation of parties, advisers[5] and support persons should be discussed so that there is no doubt as to the expectations of the mediator.

---

[4] See Chapter 3 — "Parties' opening statements and mediator's summaries".
[5] See Chapter 19 — "Role of legal representatives".

(h) Authority of representatives

This can be one of the more critical aspects to be discussed during a preliminary conference and it alone justifies the holding of the conference. The issue can often generate considerable debate, particularly where one party perceives that they have previously been unable to settle their dispute due to the lack of authority of the other party's representative. This issue is discussed in more detail elsewhere.[6]

(i) Arranging the date, time and venue for the mediation

Finally, the mediator will need to obtain agreement on the date, time and venue for the mediation session. These details are normally readily agreed upon, although identifying a suitable venue can sometimes be problematic. Parties generally prefer to mediate in a neutral venue although increasingly the facilities of one of the legal advisers is offered and accepted. Whatever the case, agreement must be reached regarding who will organise the venue — if not already organised — and how the cost, if any, will be paid. An important consideration for the mediator is whether a whiteboard is available, and if not, whether one can be obtained.

Post-preliminary conference

It is helpful for the mediator to confirm to the parties and their legal representatives the matters that were agreed upon during the preliminary conference. This will assist them in fulfilling their mutual undertakings and act as a reminder of the need to prepare for the mediation. A suggested pro forma letter and Agenda for the mediation session have been included in the Appendix.

---

[6] See Chapter 14 — "Pre-mediation issues".

Chapter

14

Pre-mediation issues

AUTHORITY TO SETTLE

Why is authority crucial?

Whether or not a preliminary conference is held, the authority to settle of any representative of a party should be addressed and settled at the pre-mediation stage. If authority to settle is not finalised and confirmed prior to the mediation session, this can lead to frustrating delays, confrontations and sometimes abandonment of the session.

Even if the authority to settle issue has ostensibly been confirmed or finalised, this may not be the end of the story.

Every experienced mediator has a story, or two, or three, regarding a representative's authority to settle or the lack or limitation thereof. The issue can arise despite the fact that an assurance of the requisite authority has been given previously or that they come with "flexible authority". The issue even arises where the representative has signed the Agreement to Mediate confirming that they have "authority to settle within any range which can reasonably be anticipated".

When is authority needed?

Authority is required in those cases where a person is not mediating in their own right, but when representing an organisation or corporation, such as an insurance company or a bank. An employee of a government department or a local council needs the authority to bind the entity they represent. An executor of a will requires authority to settle from the other executors.

The same situation applies with joint property owners or a married couple, where only one will be participating in the mediation. The latter situation can arise in neighbourhood disputes where only one spouse may attend the mediation. The party attending might say to the mediator, in response to a suggestion from the neighbour:

> I really have to discuss this further with my husband/wife before I can agree to it.

What authority is needed?

In a perfect, theoretical, textbook world, full authority means being able to settle up to 100% of the other party's claim if the mediation process, including any new information which emerges, convinces a party that it is appropriate to do so. However, mediators and representatives do not live in a perfect world and it would be unrealistic to imagine that any representative would come to mediation with limitless authority to settle. The standard compromise is "authority to settle within any range which can reasonably be anticipated".

Probing of the extent of authority to settle

The mediator should probe for any limitations on a party's authority and parties should be requested to disclose any limitation to the mediator and the other party. For example, representatives of a defendant insurer in a personal injury matter should be requested to discuss the extent of their authority and encouraged to state their usual policy on authority to settle within a perceived range. Likewise, a party should be requested to reveal that they have an obligation with some types of settlements to obtain final agreement clarification with some person or an entity such as a superannuation board, which may not be represented at the mediation. Ideally, the representative attending the mediation should be the person with the authority.

A limitation or a reporting duty should be disclosed in order to give the other party the choice of whether or not to proceed on that basis. In one case it transpired that the so-called authority did not go beyond pre-mediation offers which had previously been rejected. An inquiry should always be made regarding earlier offers and negotiations, if only to establish whether authority goes beyond points already reached.

It is not satisfactory for limitations to be conveyed at the mediation session itself. Supposed limitations have been known to be used as a stalling tactic. This is particularly so where new information emerges which throws into confusion the preconceived settlement range or a pre-determined bottom line figure. When probing authority to settle, the mediator or intake worker should make it quite clear that new information often does emerge at mediation which may need to be taken into account when parties or representatives are confirming their authority to settle at the intake stage. The question is simple:

If information emerged at the session which did significantly change your view that an appropriate settlement may be different to what you had in mind, would you have authority to settle on that basis?

If the answer is in the negative or unclear, the mediator should ask:

What needs to be done to obtain that authority?

or

Is it possible for the person with the actual, rather than the delegated, authority to attend?

A common response to a probing of the extent of a representative's authority is that they have authority to settle "on a commercial basis". Whilst settlement on "a commercial basis" is quite valid, this explanation still needs to be fine tuned. What is perceived to be a commercial basis may be very subjective and may not fit with the assurance that a person has the authority "within any range, which can be reasonably anticipated". Furthermore, the other party will have a different (or higher) subjective view of a settlement "on a commercial basis".

The mediator should go on to explain the drawbacks of a mediation proceeding on the basis of "the empty chair". They include the risk that the other party may refuse to mediate "with the monkey, rather than the organ grinder" or may be reluctant to disclose a "bottom line" when the person opposite does not have authority to accept it. Sufficient authority is important because lack of authority is unfair to the other party, particularly an individual who has full authority.

The representative is at the mediation to settle the matter. It is only this person who hears all the arguments and is in a position to assess the merits. How can a person elsewhere, or on the end of a phone make this assessment? If someone with authority can be contacted by a local call, ideally they should be at the mediation.

PRE-MEDIATION ISSUES STATEMENTS

Pre-mediation issues statements are a snapshot synopsis of what the parties and/or advisers see as the issues in contention. They are sometimes exchanged between the parties prior to mediation or may simply be forwarded to the mediator for background briefing.

Role of pre-mediation issues statements

Issues statements are most frequently requested in commercial mediations. They probably have their greatest value in multi-party disputes. However, some mediators request them as part of their preparation practice regardless of the context. In some cases they have proved to be a two-edged sword, and their usefulness is questionable in certain types of mediations. An issues statement should not be a substitute for parties' opening statements, used as a pre-determined concrete agenda or to short-circuit a valuable stage of the process such as the issue exploration phase.

Issues statements promote a natural temptation to preset or prejudge the issues. Legal representatives in particular often attend to an issues statement request by providing a copy of all the pleadings, or a restatement of the pleadings, including such declarations as "Liability is denied"! Mediators conducting a preliminary conference may sometimes use this forum to get agreement on the issues as a substitute for an issues statement.

Parties and/or advisers will sometimes request from the other party a statement of that party's position prior to the mediation. Mediators should discourage "Position Papers" as they tend to cement the parties from the outset in opposing trenches and can create a sense of pessimism before the mediation session has even begun.

Advantages of pre-mediation issues statements

A brief issues statement will assist the parties in their preparation for negotiations by clarifying their position and identifying among themselves their strengths and weaknesses. Issues statements also act to identify any supportive documents parties may wish to exchange prior to mediation, or table during the mediation. An exchange of issues statements can prompt the other party to think about issues that may need to be addressed. In a multi-party context, where a person is representing a big group, an issues statement can be used to establish the issues on which that representative can bind the group.

For the mediator, issues statements can give some awareness of the issues in dispute and provide any mediator with an opportunity to become familiar with the factual background. Statements may also provide a trigger later in either joint or private sessions if parties have omitted something from their opening statement that has not emerged during joint session dialogue. Where a person is representing a large group in a multi-party mediation, an issues statement can be used to establish the issues on which that representative can bind the group

Drawbacks of pre-mediation issues statements

Issues statements are usually prepared by lawyers and so may have a focus on legal issues. They tend to avoid the non-legal interests and needs of the party. They sometimes conclude with a "declaration of war" expressed as:

> If this matter does not settle at mediation, our instructions are to pursue litigation to its conclusion.

So, an exchange of issues statements can sometimes have a polarising effect and can promote more pre-mediation defensiveness and conflict exacerbation than might ordinarily have been the case. An exchange of issues statements has been known to encourage the development of entrenched positions and an adversarial rather than problem solving approach. Sometimes they can promote a flurry of concern and suspicion. In extreme cases, the issues statement can provide an opportunity for reluctant participants to pull out of the conference, or threaten to hijack the agenda:

> I'm not coming if they are going to talk about that!

or

> I want to know what they are going to say about that before I attend.

or

> I'm only prepared to talk about X, Y and Z.

In such cases, it would have been far better for the issues to have been isolated at the mediation session itself. The mediator would then deal with any dispute over an issue at that time in the manner we have suggested in Chapter 4 — "Issue identification and agenda setting". Pre-mediation ignorance can sometimes be bliss.

An issues statement can also be misleading. It can be wise to take it with a grain of salt.

Case Note

At a multi-party mediation, a request for an issues statement received the response: "We have no issues but are merely attending to play an assisting role." Although this may have been their genuine belief at the time, it transpired that this party had more issues than any other participant. Because the issues statements had supposedly isolated the issues to be discussed, the other parties (and possibly the mediator) had been lulled into a false sense of security and were thrown off balance when new controversies were introduced.

This case study also highlights the dangers of using mediation jargon like "issues" and "issues statements" without fully explaining what is required and why this information is requested.

CHRONOLOGY OF EVENTS

The provision of a simple chronology of events in complex commercial or serious personal injury matters or any matter with a long and convoluted history can be very useful to the mediator. It is particularly helpful when a long list of dates and corresponding events is involved. For neutrality reasons, both parties should prepare a list. The mediator can request this list of events as part of the pre-mediation preparation if they perceive a chronology might be helpful to keep track of what is being spoken about.

An example of a chronology in a personal injury matter might be:

▌ Date of accident No 1 and brief details

▌ Date of hospital admission

▌ Date of first operation

▌ Date of discharge

▌ Date of first medical report for plaintiff and result

▌ Date of first medical report for defendant and result

▌ Date of second medical report for plaintiff and result

▌ Date of second medical report for defendant and result

▌ Date of accident No 2 and brief details

▌ Date of police report

▌ Date of hospital admission

▌ Date of second operation

▌ Date of discharge

▌ Date of further medical report for plaintiff and result

▌ Date of further medical report for defendant and result

Similarly, chronologies can depict a relationship with the deceased in a contest over a will or the highlights of a commercial relationship.

Part 4

Mediation Skills and Strategies

15

Communication skills and their application in mediation

Unlike mediation strategies that may accommodate a particular situation, the communication skills used in mediation cannot be so neatly compartmentalised. Many of these are usefully employed throughout the session either in particular contexts or simply to oil the wheels and move the session along. Skills and strategies often overlap and merge. Some individual skills do not operate in isolation. Reflecting forms part of the reframing technique and opportunities for the use of both may depend upon active listening.

Listening skills constitute an essential tool in mediation. They are, however, applied for purposes other than understanding the situation in order to give advice or for the mediator to suggest a solution. Listening skills are applied in order to understand the situation so that appropriate interventions and responses occur which will facilitate progressing the session.

PASSIVE AND ACTIVE LISTENING

Passive listening

Passive listening in mediation occurs when the mediator listens in silence to what parties are saying and responds in a passive way, for example, through eye contact, nodding, leaning forward, generally being relaxed, focused and alert, not appearing uninterested, and making use of non-committal acknowledgments such as: "I see" or "Mm-hmm". There is no need to add, especially in joint session: "I hear you" or "I understand". Such expressions tend to be associated more with situations in which the listener has an advice-giving or counselling role. It is wise, however, for the mediator to inform the parties that a nod does not imply agreement with what has been said. It merely means that the mediator has heard what the parties have said.

The mediator could also use encouragement for parties to begin or continue talking, for example:

Please elaborate on that point you made in your opening statement.

Tell John how you felt at that point.

I'm sure John would be interested in what you have to say about this.

Please go on. Take your time.

Passive listening is applied at all stages of the mediation to encourage a party to go on talking and to convey the mediator's interest in what a party is saying. It is important for mediators to demonstrate not only that they have listened to what the parties have said but also that they have heard accurately. Teenagers often accuse their parents of never listening properly to them even though they might very well have heard every word they have said.

Responses such as: "How awful for you" or "That's very interesting" should be avoided as they may lead the other party who is also listening to feel that the mediator is over-identifying with, or biased in favour of, the speaker.

Objectives of passive listening in mediation

The objectives of passive listening in mediation include:

█ to encourage parties to continue talking;

█ to encourage parties to finish a sentence especially when they are hesitating while talking;

█ to convey to parties by keeping quiet and not looking uninterested, that the mediator is genuinely interested in what is being said;

█ to observe the effects parties have on each other.

Barriers to effective listening

Barriers to effective listening occur if the mediator is:

█ Finishing the sentence for the speaker.

█ Talking at the same time as the parties or allowing parties to talk at the same time. If this happens, it is quite in order for the mediator to say: "Hey, we have two conversations going on here. It really helps when only one of us speaks at a time."

▌ Tuning out the speaker while the mediator's mind moves on.

▌ Suggesting that what is being said is untimely.

▌ Playing with an object or doodling while attempting to demonstrate that the mediator is listening to the parties.

▌ Faking attention or looking bored.

▌ Taking excessive notes. Parties may feel good when the mediator is taking down their opening statement or making some notes during the session. However, a mediator whose head is down all the time is not creating an appropriate listening environment.

The mediator should not, of course, persist in passive listening without progressing to active listening because to do so may lead to a lack of direction and a stalemate with parties left to wonder, "What happens next?"

Active listening

Active listening in mediation occurs when the mediator listens to what parties are saying and feeds back in an active way reflecting an appreciation of the significance of what the parties have said, including the underlying emotional content.

The need for accurate hearing in active listening

Effective listening involves actual and accurate listening, not just going through the motions. In addition to demonstrating interest, it involves actually being interested and alert. Mediators who are not actually listening will not be able to summarise accurately and, most importantly, will not pick up the little gems and opportunities for options which emerge during the parties' cross-table dialogue. Often during a training session these opportunities are seen to be missed because the trainee mediator is not listening sufficiently to maximise the use of everything that is being said or may only be hearing the legal solutions and missing out on the non-legal opportunities.

A good example of accurate listening is provided in Chapter 17 — "Practical strategies" (see "Converting a negative into an option"). The party says: "I'm not having him back in the house to finish his botchy job." This statement offers several possibilities for the mediator:

1. The mediator might immediately leap in and remind the speaker of the "no put-down" ground rules.

2. The mediator might reframe and reflect by saying: "You seem to be saying that some rectification is required."

Part 4: Mediation Skills and Strategies

3. If the mediator is alert, this affords a golden opportunity to turn a negative comment into an option by saying: "So, an option for you is to have someone else finish the work."

Alternatively the mediator might use a combination of (2) and (3). The mediator who opts for the first possibility cannot be said to have accurately listened. Item (1) is an example of hearing the words but not the message. The mediator may have listened but not with the aim of making constructive use of what the party has said. (Reframing is discussed more fully later in this chapter.)

During a coaching session a role player party had declined the other party's request for the agreement to contain a clause that certain accident prevention measures be taken to avoid a possible repetition. The declining party actually said: "I'm not agreeing to that. It makes it look as if I was liable." The trainee mediator saw this as a roadblock that required a further private session. The mediator had focused on the party's disagreement rather than the underlying concern. The coach suggested that no private session was required and that the roadblock could be overcome simply by positively reframing the statement to say:

> It seems as if the needs of both of you would be fulfilled if the clause was expanded by saying something like: "A does not admit liability, but nevertheless will take all measures to ensure that the animal will be confined to its enclosure in the future."

This was acceptable to both parties.

The need for an appropriate physical environment

For active listening to occur, it is necessary to create a physical atmosphere conducive to good communication. Furniture can create barriers. Thus, the seating and table arrangements should indicate equity, even though the mediator might be seated at the head of the table for accessibility purposes. The mediator cannot demonstrate active listening if he or she is standing up at the board for long periods at a time and the parties' heads are level with the mediator's waist or chest for most of the session.

Objectives of active listening in mediation

The objectives of active listening in mediation include:

▌ to convey to the parties that the mediator has not merely listened to the parties but has understood them and appreciated the significance that they attach to what they have said;

▌ to reflect back to the parties the intensity of their feelings;

▮ to clarify and minimise miscommunications between the parties;

▮ to make constructive use of what the parties have said in order to facilitate their negotiations and to make more effective their search for a mutually satisfying outcome;

▮ to facilitate problem solving by creating opportunities for empathy and mutual understanding.

How does the mediator make use of active listening throughout the mediation?

An important component of active listening is demonstrating that the mediator has heard and taken account of what has been said in order to make a party feel validated with a view to opening up the dialogue. For example, a party might say: "He can't be trusted to carry out that agreement." The mediator might reframe the statement into: "You are looking for some assurance that everything will proceed as agreed." By making this statement, the mediator is checking back with the parties that the correct meaning has been attached to what they have said.

There is, however, no need to feed back every message, as this can be very irritating to the parties. It can result in negative responses along the lines of "I've just said that, haven't I?"

Progressive summarising

Progressive summarising by the mediator signals active listening to the parties.

Using the parties' language

When the mediator uses the parties' own terminology rather than lapsing into technical or legal jargon, this also indicates active listening.

Other applications of active listening

One of the most important applications of active listening is reframing.

REFRAMING

When and how do mediators reframe — consequences of overdoing it

Reframing has been defined as:

> the process of changing the way a thought is presented so that it maintains its fundamental meaning but is more likely to support resolution efforts.[1]

---

[1] Mayer, B, *The Dynamics of Conflict Resolution. A Practitioner's Guide* (Jossey-Bass, 2000), p 132.

Reframing is one of the most important and productive skills in mediation and is one that is difficult to impart and can only really be acquired through experience. Reframing is not something that should be done just for the sake of it, or because it is a favourite skill. People who have a preference for direct speech may not relate to some over-contrived reframe. Over-reframing, however well intentioned, can be irritating to such a speaker; it can be perceived as patronising as well as creating the impression that the mediator simply didn't understand the meaning of what the person was saying. Reframing may also be confusing to some people who have English as a second language.

The overdoing principles also may apply to a mediator who feels a need to reflect back a speaker's every utterance. The purpose of reflection is to let the speaker feel the mediator has understood the message and to emphasise that the speaker has been heard. Such "automatic pilot"-type reflecting, that is, simply parroting, becomes monotonous and can be counter-productive if it does not also provide an indication that the actual content of the message is being digested and will have some impact on the progress of the session.

The following is an example of a party's statement, which is paraphrased then reframed.

Party's statement: "If only he could understand that I have day-to-day responsibility for the children. He just enjoys playing Father Christmas every second weekend. Can't he do a bit more than that to make my life easier?"

Mediator's paraphrase: "So you're saying that while you have major responsibility for the care of the children, he just enjoys giving them presents every second weekend."

Mediator's reframe: "So you're saying that it would be really helpful if he would play a more active role in caring for the children. Do you have any suggestions as to how he could do that?"

Not only should a mediator's reframe of a party's statement not be a mere paraphrase, but it should also not be too different from the statement. For example:

Party's statement: "I told him the other day that if he wants to have more frequent telephone contacts with the children, he can't ring up at bath time or meal times."

Mediator's paraphrase: "So you don't like him ringing the children up at odd times."

Party's response: "That's not what I said. I just think that his phone calls should be at times when the children are free to talk to him — not at bath time or meal times."

Mediator's reframe: "So you understand that he would like to continue to have telephone contact with the children and you would therefore like to talk over with him about the appropriate times for this to occur."

It is important for the mediator to check back with the party that the reframe does not alter the substance of the party's statement by adding to the reframed statement:

"Am I on the right track?" or "Is that what you would like to see happen?"

Reframing occurs at any stage of the mediation, and can be achieved by changing either the words or the context of a party's statement.

Changing the words of a party's statement occurs when the mediator:

█ paraphrases;

█ summarises, for example, reducing an avalanche of words;

█ puts a series of statements into a more logical sequence or groups the statements into sub-issues;

█ restates an issue in more general terms;

█ neutralises negative statements;

█ mutualises parties' statements.

Changing the context of a party's statement occurs when the mediator:

█ redefines a positional statement in terms of underlying interests;

█ restates one party's interests in terms which are mutually acceptable;

█ stresses the positive elements from one party's communication and plays down the negative ones;

█ minimises the differences between the parties' perspectives;

█ changes the time context from the past to the future.

Why do mediators reframe?

There are multiple purposes for reframing in mediation, for example:

█ to remove the "toxic" content of a statement to make it more palatable;

█ to soften the demands of one party to make them more acceptable to the other party;

█ to harden demands made by a "soft bargainer" who seems content to concede "anything for the sake of peace" and empower the "soft bargainer";

▌ to express statements in more neutral or positive language to make them more acceptable and to avoid additional conflict;

▌ to change the context of a statement, for example, from the past to the future in order to avoid the parties remaining entrenched in their positions;

▌ to redefine parties' perspectives of a conflict in order to set the scene for a more constructive approach;

▌ to extract an underlying interest from a positional statement to facilitate negotiation and the generating of settlement options, for example, by converting a demand into an option;

▌ to mutualise parties' statements to create a more co-operative approach and indicate to the parties that they have more in common than they think.

How can a mediator assist parties to reframe issues and positions?

A mediator can encourage the parties to:

▌ Focus on the situation or the relationship rather than on the person or on positions.

▌ Ask open-ended questions in order to generate qualitative responses.

He or she could ask the questions on behalf of the party, for example, "How would it help you if you could find out from X (the other party) what are the difficulties in ...?"

▌ Formulate joint problem statements, for example, "How can you both avoid ...?" or "What can both of you do ensure that ...?" or "What would be acceptable to you both to ensure that decisions you both make are in the interests of your child?"

▌ Encourage the parties to focus on future relationships instead of past wrongs.

▌ Ask for reasons why a particular position is so important to a party and encourage them to identify underlying interests.

Examples of reframing include:

▌ Neutralising and removing toxicity, for example:

Party's statement: "He breached the contract."

Mediator's reframe: "Your concern is the way the contract was carried out."

Party's statement: "He can't be trusted to carry out the agreement."

Mediator's reframe: "You are looking for some assurance that everything will proceed as agreed" or "What sort of assurance would make you feel more comfortable about agreeing to these terms?"

Party's statement: "It's not going to work."

Mediator's reframe: "Let's look at ways in which it might work best."

Party's statement: "He never listens to me. He doesn't think I have anything important to talk about."

Mediator's reframe: "You would like the opportunity to talk things over together."

▌ Redirecting parties towards a positive and future focus.

Party's statement: "He has never been in the office before 10 in the morning and I'm always there at 8."

Mediator's reframe: "So you are saying that for the future you would like to work on some plan that ensures you are both around at the same time, or which allows for a fair job-sharing arrangement, for example, for you to alternate the early morning arrival."

(Note: The active listening mediator will have identified two possible options emerging from the reframe and the ongoing dialogue may provide the opportunity to nominate these as such.)

▌ Softening demands.

Party's statement: "As far as I'm concerned, I won't accept anything less than access to the children every weekend, otherwise she doesn't get the house."

Mediator's reframe: "You're saying you would like more opportunity to be a parent and that would be possible by more frequent and regular contact with them."

Party's statement: "He just won't admit that what he did was wrong and affected the whole family. Why should I ever see him again? History will only repeat itself."

Mediator's reframe: "You're saying how much this affected you in the past and that things need to change in the future if you decide to see each other again."

▌ Hardening demands.

Party's statement: "Look! Have it your way. Anything you say. You can have all the furniture if you like. Anything for the sake of peace."

Mediator's reframe: "How about listing all the furniture items and you can tell each other why particular items are important to you."

Party's statement: "I suppose you're right. You were always the smart one in our family."

Mediator's reframe: "How about taking it in turn to tell each other what you think should happen in the future, regardless of what happened in the past. Could you start first?" (Question directed to the soft demander.)

▌ Extracting an underlying interest from a positional statement

Party's statement: "I want to end the partnership now and on my terms. He doesn't give a damn about how much work I've put into it."

Mediator's reframe: "So you would like some acknowledgment of your contribution to the partnership to make it worthwhile for you to consider future changes in your working arrangements."

Party's statement: "Why should he (that is, her boyfriend) see my children more often, in fact even live with them, just because he's her live-in boyfriend?"

Mediator's reframe: "So you'd like to discuss future contact arrangements which would allow you to see your children more often."

▌ Mutualising parties' statements

Parties' statements:

Party A: "I'm the one left with the lion's share of the office responsibilities."

Party B: "I'm always out on the road dealing with the subcontractors."

Mediator's reframe: "It seems as if you are both focusing on important aspects of the work and you have an interest in working out how the burden could be lightened for each of you."

RETAINING THE PERCEPTION OF NEUTRALITY

A footnote to active listening, reflecting and reframing is a reminder that the mediator is, and must appear to be, neutral. Acknowledgment should always be through the use of "You" language. It is not neutral in joint session to say to one party: "I can understand how upset you are about this." It is better to say: "You seem to be expressing a concern about the way this occurred. Why don't you tell Bill more about that." Likewise, head nods and other acknowledgments should be of the "I hear what you are saying" non-committal kind and should not indicate agreement. Another common mistake during option generation or settlement proposals occurs if the mediator comments: "That's a good idea." It may be a good idea in the long run, but at that time one party may not think so and may think the mediator is discounting other views.

SUMMARISING

Summarising is a very useful communication tool applied by mediators. It constitutes an important part of the first stage of mediation — the mediator's summaries of the parties' statements. (See Chapter 3 — "Parties' opening statements and mediator's summaries".) As is the case with other communication skills such as listening, paraphrasing and reframing, summarising is used constructively at any stage of the mediation when deemed appropriate. If parties feel that they have been heard and understood it helps to build up their trust in the mediation process as well as in the mediator. What parties appreciate is that the summary reflects not just an understanding of what they have said but an understanding of the underlying situation as well as any feeling which may have been expressed. A summary is not a verbatim, word-for-word, report but is an overview. Quite often a summary is, of necessity, a paraphrase apart from parties' opening statements, which are more by way of précis.

When can summarising be constructive and what are the advantages associated with it?

▌ At the end of both parties' opening statements. (See Chapter 3 — "Parties' opening statements and mediators' summaries".) Although some mediators summarise at the end of each party's statement, we have found it more beneficial to do so when both parties have made their statements.

▌ During the first joint session devoted to clarification and exploration of issues, when parties become negative towards each other and begin to use colourful language. The advantage of a mediator's summary is that it causes an acceptable interruption to their exchange and the mediator can also make use of reframing.

A useful thing a mediator might say is:

> I would like to summarise what we have discussed so far. I noted how you listened to each other about the way the contract got unstuck and I would like to briefly revisit what you both said on that point.

▐ At the end of the first joint session before moving on to private sessions and at the conclusion of each private session. It is useful for the mediator to give a general summing up before moving on to the private sessions as well as at the end of each private session. It should be a summary not a paraphrase.

What are some of the disadvantages of mediators' summarising?

At times the mediator may leave out what a party considers important. Therefore, it is wise for the mediator at the end of a summary to say:

Is there any other matter that you referred to that I should have included in the summary?

Another potential disadvantage is that a mediator may include in the summary what he or she thinks is important due to a hypothesis the mediator might have formed relating to the conflict. This constitutes another reason for checking the summary back with the parties.

The following is an example of a mediator's summary:

What I've heard you say in the past few minutes is that things have not gone well in your relationship as neighbours. You also discussed what worked for you in the past. As far as the future is concerned, you would like to retain what worked well in order to improve your relationship in the future. Would you like to comment on my summary?

Party A's response:

On the whole I think it's a fair summary. However, I can't remember saying anything about our future relationship. As far as I'm concerned there won't be one.

Party B's response:

I agree with her. Neither of us mentioned anything about the future.

The mediator could have avoided these responses had he or she checked on the content of the summary by saying: "Am I on the right track?"

QUESTIONS, QUESTIONS, QUESTIONS

Asking questions is one of the essential communication tools in mediation. Not infrequently newly trained mediators are under the impression that they need to take an active and dominant role in the mediation session and therefore need to ask a whole range of questions of the parties. This is a myth. In the course of mediation, if mediators limit the number of questions asked they will often be rewarded by the wealth of information that emerges naturally during verbal exchanges between the parties. The mediator should encourage parties to ask each other questions. They are more likely to listen to the answer than if the mediator had asked the same question.

1. Why should mediators ask questions?

▮ To clarify what parties are saying.

▮ To encourage parties to provide each other with additional relevant information.

▮ To probe for further ideas to encourage parties to shift the focus to the future.

▮ To facilitate parties' identification of feelings and emotions.

Clarifying what parties are saying

Clarification of what parties are saying can be required at any stage of the mediation. The first opportunity for clarification occurs when the mediator takes notes of each party's opening statement. Questions asked at this stage should not be for the purpose of the mediator "getting the big picture" but in order to clarify some aspect of a party's statement the mediator is not sure about. The mediator could ask:

What did you just say about X? I'm afraid that I didn't quite catch it.

At other stages of the mediation, the mediator should encourage the parties to ask each other clarifying questions. For example, the mediator could ask the listening party: "I wonder if it would help you to get an explanation about X, Y or Z?"

Also, if at any stage the mediator feels that one of the parties (Party A) did not appear to fully grasp what the other party (Party B) has said, and the latter did not ask for clarification, the mediator could say to Party A:

Would it help you if she (Party B) explained what she had in mind when she said X, Y and Z? Is there anything you would like to ask her?

Encouraging parties to provide each other with additional relevant information

At times, parties make statements that are very brief and do not readily lead to a flow of communication. A party might even say:

It simply doesn't suit me. That's all I have to say on the matter.

The mediator could say to that party:

What aspects of the arrangement do not suit you? Would you like to tell him? And when you've done that, would you two like to discuss alternatives to the current arrangement?

Facilitating parties' identification of feelings and emotions

The mediator could ask questions such as: "You did say a moment ago that you have been affected by the new arrangements. Would you like to tell him how you felt about it?"

Probing for further ideas to encourage parties to shift the focus to the future

When the mediator feels that further focus on the past would be repetitive and counter-productive, questions could be asked about what the future might look like for the parties to make life easier. For example:

Would you like to exchange ideas on what you would like to see happen in the future to make life easier for both of you?

Questions can also be asked by the mediator to reality test generated options. For further information see Chapter 17 — "Practical strategies".

2. Different ways of asking questions

There are many different ways of asking questions. The most common types of questions are:

▌ Closed questions.

▌ Open questions.

▌ Hypothetical questions.

Closed questions

Closed questions are generally used for clarifying and checking purposes, for example:

Was the light green?

Are you saying that it will take at least 10 weeks to finish the renovations?

Are you offering $1,000 to complete the repairs?

Is my understanding correct that the figure is $1,000?

These are examples of closed questions, in the sense that they usually require a one-word response, usually a "Yes" or a "No".

They are necessary in particular contexts but they have the potential to close communication down. The reflective or empathic type of questions can also be closed, but they perform a different function, as their main purpose is to demonstrate active listening and mirror the concern of the speaker.

Closed questions may also perform an additional function; to demonstrate active listening and mirror the concern of the speaker.

An example of such a question is:

So you are telling John that you felt distressed when the agreement appeared to be disregarded?

Open questions

Unlike closed questions, open-ended questions have the potential to open up the communication; require a more creative response; and encourage the parties to think more about what their response should be — which in turn may lead to possible solutions emerging from the dialogue. These usually involve the "how", "why", "what", "where" and "when" type of framework. With practice, mediators can acquire the habit of automatically reframing closed questions into open-ended ones.

Examples of open-ended questions are:

What happened then? Tell John.

What was the figure you had in mind?

How long do you think it will take to finish the renovations, bearing in mind that Joe has said he will need six weeks to acquire the cladding?

How important is it for you to come to a decision today?

What would happen if you didn't come to a decision today?

Why do you think that Mary is unable to agree to the settlement your lawyer is proposing?

In what way have you been affected by the past events?

Hypothetical questions

Hypothetical questions are the "what if" questions, and are generally open-ended. These are particularly useful in mediation. They have the multiple potential of opening up the dialogue, performing a reality testing role, refocusing a party on the future and posing a hypothetical solution. These have been discussed in Chapter 17 — "Practical strategies". Examples of hypothetical questions are:

What if A were to offer a $50,000 settlement package? How would you react to such an offer?

What if A could not afford to pay that amount together with all the legal fees?

What if you were to receive the offer that you were proposing to canvass with B?

How do you think your concerns will differ in two years' time from what is a pressing consideration for you today?

3. Pitfalls the mediator should avoid when asking questions

One of the pitfalls mediators should avoid is asking so many questions that communication between the parties becomes almost non-existent. Another important pitfall to avoid is getting trapped into an inquisition framework.

Although questioning may be used to check, clarify or probe, it should be pursued only with the aim of ensuring that each side has a comprehensive understanding of where the other is coming from. A mediator should avoid conducting an inquisition in order to get at the facts. Mediators do not need to know the full facts in order to fulfil their facilitating role. Excessive questioning can be perceived as a cross-examination and can result in a loss of face for one party. It is not the mediator's role to establish the facts and it should be questioned why particular mediators feel they need to do this. This habit most commonly emerges after the parties have given their opening statements, and in some cases the mediator has been known to embark on excessive questioning of one party before the statement has been given by the other party.

The mediator is not an investigator. If the mediator feels any further clarification is warranted, or that the full story has not come out, questions to elicit that information should be kept to a minimum. Usually this type of questioning is done for the mediator's edification, not that of the parties. Anything left unsaid will generally emerge during the joint exploration session. If the mediator feels that there is a so-called hidden agenda, which is jeopardising the smooth running of the session, any clarification or probing should be done during a private session.

Chapter

16

Strategic mediator interventions

KEY TERMS

Active listening. Involves demonstrating to parties that the mediator has heard and understood issues or concerns — including the emotional content — through verbal expression, eye contact, body language, appropriate responses, summarising, reflecting and reframing.

Clarifying. see Questions.

Future projection. Usually involves a hypothesis or invites consideration of the possibility in the future of a different attitude or set of circumstances with regard to what may currently be a distressing or pressing concern, complacency or status quo acceptance. Often involves a type of reality test.

Hypothesising. Involves posing a "What if" scenario to explore or test a party's reaction to certain possibilities should such a situation become a reality.

Identifying. Involves exploring and discovering areas of potential settlement or reasons and interests behind initial positions. Includes identification of options or common ground through active, accurate listening.

Leading statements. Operate in a similar manner to open questions and with a similar rationale. For example, "Tell me more about ...".

Mutualising. Involves identifying and stressing the commonalities in interests, needs, goals, feelings, disappointments and doubts of the parties. Also involves describing an issue (as in agenda setting) in a manner with which each party can identify. This may involve reframing different modes of expression into a mutually relevant and identifiable word or phrase.

Neutralising. Involves framing or reframing comments, statements, issues into neutral language. This is done in order to ensure perception by parties of mediator neutrality or to make a particular word or expression non-provocative or non-judgmental, either in speech or when recording on the whiteboard.

Normalising. Involves a reassurance to a party or parties that their concerns, uncertainties, settlement doubts and surprises at new information are normal experiences, feelings or reactions commonly experienced by parties in dispute.

Option generation. Involves parties in pro-active seeking of options for settlement. May include a brainstorming session.

Option identification. Involves active and accurate listening by mediator in order to identify and raise possible options that emerge from parties' statements, parties' dialogue, comments and suggestions.

Power balancing or equalising. Involves creating and maintaining an atmosphere of equality by ensuring that each party feels equally empowered in the mediation session, for example, by not allowing one party to dominate. May involve ensuring, as far as possible, that one party is not disadvantaged by the superior bargaining power, domineering behaviour, dominating personality features, articulation, or professional advice of the other party.

Prioritising. Involves the mediator encouraging a party to assess what goal is the most important and advantageous to that party out of a stated number of separate goals or demands and what may need to be conceded or offered to the other side in order to achieve the priority. May include a reality test.

Questions.

(i) Clarifying. Involves confirming and checking, through significant and relevant questions, what parties mean or intend by certain statements. Such questions may seek to establish parties' perceptions of background to dispute or to acquire further information. For mediation purposes the questions posed should be non-threatening, non-inquisitorial and non-oppressive.

(ii) Closed questions. These are often used for clarifying and checking. They are commonly framed to elicit a one-word response, usually "yes"

or "no". When used inappropriately may tend to close communication down.

(iii) Open questions. Open questions cannot be answered by one word and are framed to elicit a more creative, thoughtful response and open up the discussion. The questions usually include the words "why", "what", "where", "who", "how" and "when".

Reality testing. Involves the mediator in seeking to explore with the parties the realistic result of a position they have taken or a solution they are proposing and the advantages or disadvantages of adhering to that position. May involve a hypothesis or role reversal.

Refocusing. May involve steering parties away from, or encouraging them to abandon, a preoccupation with past events, a negative attitude, an unrealistic position or unproductive line of discussion. May involve creating a diversion, reframing or picking up on a point made earlier which holds out more promise for productive discussion.

Rehearsing (in private session). Involves encouraging a party to express an opinion or table an offer and exploring ways and means whereby a party may feel confident or comfortable in articulating this opinion or offer to the other party. The mediator might offer to role play the part of the other party to help the rehearsal.

Reframing. Involves changing the construction of a statement to give it another focus or to make it more mutually acceptable by removing the "toxicity"; converting it to a positive focus or neutralising it. Can involve paraphrasing or reflecting what a party has said, such as "so you felt disadvantaged".

Role reversal. Inviting or encouraging parties to put themselves in the position of the other party both with regard to the other party's concerns and possible reaction to any settlement proposals.

Summarising. Involves giving an overview, usually in precis form, of parties' statements, ongoing dialogue, achievements, positions or interests, without losing the essential meaning.

AN OVERVIEW

Mediator interventions are techniques used by mediators throughout the session in order for progress to be maintained. They may be used as routine strategies, impasse preventers or in order to break an impasse once it has arisen.

WHAT IS AN IMPASSE?

The dictionary defines an impasse as an insurmountable obstacle or more colloquially as a blind alley. The word has a ring of extremism. A suitable analogy is that of two tanks coming face-to-face on a narrow bridge. Retreat is impossible and neither can move forward. A more encouraging definition, for mediation purposes, might be that retreat is difficult and one or both cannot, or will not, move forward at that point.

Impasse breaker or routine strategy?

Positional stances taken in a mediation are not necessarily impasses. Such blocks may be troublesome, but are routine features of most mediations. Some of the strategies for resolving impasses discussed below may simply fall into the category of useful techniques to move the session forward. Other interventions may be viewed as special techniques to deal with potential and real impasse situations.

Training issues

Initial basic training can sometimes determine whether interventions are categorised as impasse breakers, impasse preventions or routine mediation techniques. Some training is around 110 hours and is predominantly skills-based. Some of the strategies taught would not be viewed in isolation nor even classed as impasse breakers. In the more comprehensive courses, role reversal techniques, for example, are simply incorporated in the mediation process training as a normal way of proceeding.

However, in the common four-day mediation courses there is simply not the scope for in-depth training in skills and strategies. Many of the graduates from these courses enhance their learning through advanced mediation courses, additional workshops or hands-on experience (including co-mediation). Thus, certain techniques, which some may regard as routine, might appear quite sophisticated to others. All mediators, however, unless they are extremely skilful or extremely lucky, are familiar with the tanks on the bridge.

Expand the repertoire

With experience, mediators usually acquire a repertoire of strategies that they use at the appropriate time. Many mediators have favourites that they have found work best. Focus on the favourites, however, can sometimes prevent a mediator from trying anything new or persevering with a strategy which did not appear to work the first time. New mediators, who are not held back by habit, can sometimes be more flexible than the old hands.

Mediation styles

Some strategies simply do not work for some mediators but work beautifully for others. Personality factors appear to play a part in this. The writers have successfully co-mediated many times. The wavelength is the same and the different approaches are complementary. However, certain strategies and techniques are more effectively employed by one than the other, possibly because the parties have become attuned to and more accepting of the respective personality styles and approaches of each mediator throughout the session. A particular technique may suit the natural style of one person but may appear artificial in the context of another personality. The appearance of artificiality is compounded if the mediator has an internal discomfort with using the technique. It is essential for the mediator to feel comfortable with what they do or say in the course of mediation.

For example, the technique of "mediator abandonment"[1] — where the mediator implies that he or she may withdraw — may sit more comfortably with a more assertive personality type. Suddenly introducing the technique of "mediator silence" is less effective if used by a mediator who has displayed a predominantly passive style throughout the session.

Types of disputes and disputants

The suggested range of interventions is not recommended for all categories of disputes. They may be appropriate in some types only. Mediators should also be aware of the audience. It may not prove useful to employ a future projection technique with a young person who lives from day to day, a short-term thinker or a very elderly person. A predominantly practical thinker may resist hypothesising.

It is also important to take into account the personalities of the parties to a mediation. Some interventions are more appropriate for one party than for both and may, therefore, be more suitable in private rather than joint sessions.

---

[1] See Chapter 17 — "Practical strategies".

RECOGNITION OF THE IMPASSE

Pre-planning

The mediator may perceive a potential impasse situation prior to the mediation and have some strategies in place should this eventuate. This perception may relate to the characteristics of the particular dispute or may predictably arise in certain types of dispute with which the mediator is familiar, for example, family or medical negligence disputes. However, writing the script for the parties or anticipating the parties' script can unbalance a mediator when the parties do not perform as anticipated. A predictable feature of mediation is its unpredictability.

Which features of disputes have a likely impasse potential?

Bearing in mind the above qualifications, early recognition and planning may pay off. Some disputes may be more likely to have impasse implications.

Win/lose situations

These may include contested child residence arrangements; claim to sole ownership of land; some environmental disputes where the issue is to build or not build at that spot; dismantling of a structure or tree demolition; tenancy eviction; or in any situation where a party is mediating solely to preserve the status quo.

Bad timing

Is court a long way off? Is it a recent relationship breakdown, where one party may not have accepted finality? These timing factors are potential temptations to stall for time in decision-making.

Small sum of money

It is generally recognised that the smaller the "pot" to divide, the more positional the parties. This is why million-dollar disputes are often easier to mediate.

Disputes over wills

Of all legal documents, a common feature of disputed wills is that many are prepared as a result of capricious instructions. Each party claims to know the deceased's true intention. This is a classic case of the "empty chair".

The legally aided party

Like the very wealthy client, a legally aided party may not have the immediate financial pressure of legal costs that motivates others to reach a negotiated resolution.

Unrealistic expectations

The win/win propaganda attaching to mediation can, among other things, foster unrealisable expectations among some participants about what is going to be achieved. There is "Trouble in Paradise" when the reality dawns that some pain/pain might be involved in reaching a settlement. This is why it is strategic for the mediator to include in her or his opening statement that in the real world: "No-one ever gets 100% of what they want."

Early sessional identification

In certain cases, a rigidity of position at an early stage of the mediation may foreshadow an ongoing attitude.

How can this be identified?

Rejection

One clue may be the rejection of an issue or agenda item by one party.

Repetition

A party may repeat the same thing several times in their opening statement. Sometimes this indicates an entrenchment of position or an addiction to the dispute — as may early obsession with detail.

Hijack

An attempted hijack occurs if a party or legal representative tries to run the mediation on their own terms. It can involve rejecting the mediation process or undermining the mediator's role in order to control the process. Such comments as "Before we begin I want an apology" or "We don't need that stuff on the board", can indicate a hijack attempt. A mediator response such as "Perhaps I didn't explain my role clearly enough. I will now do so again" can restrain the attempt.

Lack of commitment

It is always useful for a mediator to confirm prior to the commencement of mediation that parties do not have time constraints. Whether this is done or not, a statement about time constraints, "I've got to be out of here by 11.30", can sometimes signal a lack of commitment, and should alert a mediator to certain possibilities. Have they come to see if the other side can be railroaded into a quick-fix solution? Are they testing the settlement anxiety level of the other party? The desire to swing into too-early bargaining can feature in these two possibilities.

A reluctance to discuss the factors from which an offer or claim is derived can signal a lack of commitment among other things. It may, however, be a negotiating ploy or may simply be the result of a lack of preparation. The latter factor in itself is not conducive to settlement and may prove to be problematic. In some cases, attendance at mediation is mandated by statute prior to commencing court proceedings or is a pre-condition to a legal aid grant. The attendee(s) may believe that a token appearance is all that is needed to clear the path for the preferred manner of proceeding.

A lack of commitment may sometimes, but not always, be discerned where opening and subsequent offers fall within what Professor John Wade has described as "the insult zone". These offers are so outrageously out-of-range that the offeror is, in effect, hoping that the recipient may be goaded into an abandonment of the session.

Monumental impasse or temporary bargaining characteristic?

A perceived block may be merely a temporary run-of-the-mill position until the parties get into the swing of the mediation. Parties do not readily move off positions until all the issues have been debated and they have heard the other side. Taking the high, low or seemingly unrealistic ground initially may merely be an opening ploy to provide more scope for future concessions. Parties are entitled to negotiate in their own way. However, there are dangers in taking the extreme ground initially. The mediator may need to alert the particular party to this danger (see Chapter 17 — "Practical strategies").

At what stage does an impasse occur?

Difficulties can occur at any stage. There can be an impasse over an agenda item or the terminology of the Agreement to Mediate. Occasionally a party has been known to comment at the exploration stage "I knew it wouldn't work" in response to a statement made by the other party. But a true impasse usually occurs at the negotiating stage rather than during exploration. However, a mediator experiencing that "settlement tingle" can sometimes be thrown off course by an eleventh-hour impasse, as can the other party, whom it is intended to unsettle.

ANALYSIS

The threshold question is whether it is possible during the session to sufficiently analyse what is occurring in order to deal with the situation in the most appropriate manner. Often mediators are so involved with moving the session along that analysis more realistically occurs in retrospect. This is particularly so with less experienced mediators. There are benefits to be gained from experience, but experience can also lead mediators to make assumptions. In co-mediation there is more scope for recognition and analysis during the session itself.

Sessional analysis is seldom easy, but the authors have found that the questions that may spring to mind on recognition that something is occurring include:

Why is it occurring?

This may be obvious, but is there a hidden factor?

Why is it occurring *now*?

Everything seemed to be flowing so well. Does the person feel he or she has already conceded too much, too easily? Has there been an imbalance in concessions? Is this impasse their *real* issue?

Who is responsible?

This may be obvious, but not always. Who is feeling the most pain in this situation? In whose interest is it to maintain the status quo? Is it in someone's interests to stall? An interest in stalling occurs in some matrimonial property settlements that may oblige a party to vacate the house. Businesses and individuals with cash flow problems can have an interest in stalling. These issues may need to be addressed in private session.[2] Both parties may be "responsible" if each feels they have made superior concessions and the other has not even come close in the tally.

What was the motivation to mediate? Bad faith? Hidden agenda?

A so-called "fishing expedition" may be signalled if one party is not fully participating, or if a legal representative plays a very passive role in the mediation.[3] It can be particularly suspicious where an initiating party shows a lack of involvement. It can be equally suspicious where excessive note-taking or questioning is being undertaken by one party. The

---

[2] See Chapter 17 — "Practical strategies".

[3] See Chapter 19 — "Role of legal representatives".

discussions on "Hijack" and "Lack of Commitment" are equally applicable here. Is a party hoping for acceptance of an unrealistic fob-off offer? A hidden motivation should be considered where someone is sliding away from committing to an agreement or attempting a last-minute sabotage of an agreement in principle.

These issues are generally explored in private session.[4] Sometimes the other side may raise them in joint session, which can force a public incident.

FACE-SAVING

We cannot sufficiently emphasise the impact of face-saving on a dispute. Some mediators put the face-saving need in the hidden agenda category. This is not our view. It is axiomatic that a party will take pains to disguise a potential loss of face. Perhaps the unique factors surrounding the face-saving may be viewed as the hidden agenda because sometimes the mediator has to tease these out. It is not routinely necessary to do this.

In our view a mediator should proceed on the assumption that face-saving factors are involved in most, if not all, disputes, whether or not they are obvious. This is why mediators should desist from too much probing into the facts in an effort to find out who did wrong or to draw out an admission. A mediator can contribute to an impasse by embarking on an inquisition. The mediator inquisition is particularly destructive in the case of a disputant who did something wrong, knows he or she did wrong but, for cultural or other reasons, cannot be seen to be wrong.

A legal representative may need to maintain face with a client and vice versa. The lawyer may negotiate vigorously over the "last gap"[5] prior to settlement in order to maintain credibility with a client regarding an initial forecast of a positive court outcome or to demonstrate that they are doing the job they are being paid to do.

The potency of the absent audience in face-saving

The absent audience of family, friends or business colleagues, who are anxious to hear the result, should always be considered. The perceived duty to report back is a particularly potent settlement disincentive. The

---

[4] See Chapter 17 — "Practical strategies".

[5] See Wade, J H, "The Last Gap in Negotiations. Why is it Important? How can it be Crossed?" (1995) 6 ADRJ 93.

party feels the need to save face with supporters, either because they have been encouraging the party not to give in beyond a certain point, or because the party has informed them that he or she will not relinquish a particular bottom line and will otherwise litigate. This dilemma is intensified where family is the absent audience. It occurs despite the party's full authority to settle. It can also occur where representatives of institutions, such as banks, insurance companies and statutory bodies, are representing their particular organisation. Despite a stated full settlement authority, there can be a concern that overstepping a bottom line may have career implications for that representative. Parties do not face this problem with a court-imposed solution. However, in a mediation, the responsibility for settlement lies with the party.

Importantly, whether or not the absent audience is involved, the party in question needs to salvage some personal dignity in a settlement where they may privately feel their original position or matter of principle has been over-compromised. This is why the offer by one party of a minor concession is so important and should be exploited regardless of whether or not the mediator perceives face-saving to be influencing the dispute.[6]

Case Note

A community support petition was tabled at a mediation. The matter had been aired in the local press. The absent audience numbered hundreds. The party, who had exceeded his bottom line, became very unhappy as settlement approached. The mediator, suspecting that the absent audience was the barrier, raised this privately and asked whether there should be a non-disclosure clause in the agreement, together with a press release that the matter had been settled to everyone's satisfaction. The press release in particular acted as a sweetener, and this face-saver suited the other party, which had been subject to an unsympathetic hearing in the press.

---

6 See Chapter 17 — "Practical strategies".

Mediation as a face-saver

Parties and legal advisers can come to mediation in order to save face. It is interesting that in some cases a mediated settlement mirrors the exact point reached in informal pre-mediation paper or telephone negotiations that have broken down. The offers, counter-offers and settlement proposals are no different from those that have previously been canvassed. These earlier negotiations have often broken down because of a need to maintain face. Acceptance of the last proposals is seen, against all reason and common sense, as "giving in" or the negotiations have been conducted in an aggressive point-scoring manner which has caused bad personal feelings and resultant polarisation. In the cold light of day there is a tacit acknowledgment on both sides that the point reached is probably the best negotiated result likely to be achieved. How often does a mediator hear that the settlement is no different from what has been proposed in the past but that the very presence of the third party neutral — who has guided them through the process in a positive structured manner — has enabled achievement of what they were unable or unwilling to achieve on their own? Also, the mediator is able to point out to both parties in a neutral manner the realities of not reaching agreement. The structuring of the session along traditional mediation lines diverts the discussion into a positive problem solving mode and discussion is more controlled and constructive.

This is why it can be important to inquire whether there have been any previous negotiations or settlement proposals. The timing of this inquiry can be a matter of sensitivity during the mediation itself. Ideally this general inquiry should be made at the preliminary conference if one is held. In other cases the parties might volunteer this information once they have settled into the session. However, even if it appears probable that this was a "face-saving" mediation it does not automatically follow that the negotiators and decision-makers are going to roll over and become purring pussy-cats from the word go or that this will be an impasse-free mediation. There may still be a need to save face even in what has become a face-saving forum and the mediator can still expect some robust negotiating to occur.

TAKING ACTION

Where the mediator is convinced that a genuine "dig-in" is occurring, a strategic intervention is required to prevent entrenchment. The golden rule is not to allow parties or their legal representatives to push themselves so far into a corner that retreat would be difficult or would involve a monumental loss of face. Some legal representatives are particularly prone to making this mistake because of a tendency to indulge in dramatic "all or nothing" statements. The longer the impasse extends, the harder it is to find face-saving ways to move the parties from the position they have adopted.

There is an important footnote to this. The fact that parties are arguing or not agreeing should not be interpreted as an impasse, which requires escape into the private session. Joint discussion should not be cut off prematurely. Constructive ventilation can contribute to clearing the air, thus moving them towards the settlement mode once they have run out of steam. Some of the techniques described in Chapter 17, such as joint session "role reversal" can be used routinely to turn a potentially destructive exchange into a constructive one, rather than merely being employed when real trouble is reached.

Joint session or private meeting?

Some interventions are more useful in joint meetings, but may naturally be also used in private sessions. Some should only be used, or at least expanded, in private session. The threshold issue should be: "Does this strategy apply to both parties?" Each party may need to hear the other's response in order to maximise the effect. If use of a technique, such as some tough reality testing, could result in loss of face to one party, then it should be used privately.

Combined techniques

Some of the techniques discussed in Chapter 17 — "Practical strategies" are not mutually exclusive and cannot be categorised under a single heading. Techniques such as role reversal, hypothesising and reality testing are sometimes combined in the same package.

Practical strategies

PRE-MEDIATION CONDITIONING

At a pre-mediation conference a mediator asked the gathering of parties and legal representatives whether anyone had been involved in mediation before. One of the barristers responded wryly: "No. But I understand it's a process where everybody walks away unhappy." Some mediators, even though emphasising the high mediation settlement rate, make it a practice to alert parties to the possibility that they may feel unhappy on settlement because the ideal settlement is rarely achieved. This pre-conditioning may help parties over the last hurdle or the final pre-settlement impasse. The mediator can then remind the parties of this prediction should the "unhappiness" impasse arise.

DE-EMPHASISE WIN/WIN

As mentioned in Chapter 16, over-statement of the win/win philosophy can create unrealistic expectations in the parties, leading to disillusionment when reality bites. Whilst it is encouraging to the parties when a mediator refers to the settlement success achieved through mediation, creating an expectation that they will both come out as winners may cause problems. This is particularly the case when the mediator has to do some robust "reality-testing" with parties in the private sessions. Achieving agreement usually involves concessions from both sides, which, in some cases, go way beyond the most reluctant bottom line. Focusing on the win/win myth may disadvantage both mediator and parties.

EFFECTIVE USE OF THE AGENDA[1]

Effective agenda use includes allowing or encouraging some discussion on each issue. However, if a particular item is generating a toxicity that is threatening to jeopardise general co-operation, there is a need to move on. Topics are there for discussion, not necessarily agreement. Prolonged unproductive focus on one issue carries the danger of entrenchment and polarisation. Discussion on less contentious topics often has a positive impact, which removes the sting from the difficult one. A mediator may revisit the issue at a less stressful time or merge it in with a topic on which discussions are going well. It may also be useful to revisit a contentious issue during private sessions to explore ways of minimising the difficulties. Sometimes a revisit reveals it was merely a vehicle for early argument.

THE ONE-ISSUE AGENDA

Suggestions for expanding the so-called one-issue agenda are discussed in "Issue identification and agenda setting". A one-issue agenda creates a concentration on positions in the same way as a prolonged focus on a single issue discussed above. There is no prescriptive formula but the mediator can expand the agenda according to "resources" available in the particular case.

USE OF WHITEBOARD

Strategic and practical use of the whiteboard deserves special consideration and is discussed in Chapter 18 — "Effective use of information — note-taking and application of visual aids".

AVOIDING TOO-EARLY SOLUTIONS/ DISCUSSION ON FIGURES

Chapter 5 — "Clarification and exploration of issues: the frst joint session" — discussed the need to allow parties to exhaust discussion before they can proceed to solutions. New information or perspectives more often than not come from such discussions, so that each party's intended commencing offer or position may have shifted. So, the too-early tabling of an offer should be discouraged. Also to be resisted is early

---

[1] See Chapter 4 — "Issue identification and agenda setting".

pressure from advisers or representatives of financial institutions to get down to the figures as "this is what it is all about". When describing the process stages in a mediation where financial considerations are involved, the mediator can emphasise that "in my experience" it is more productive to have some joint discussion prior to focusing on solutions. Sometimes there are personal issues on one side and purely commercial considerations on the other.

Case Note

In a compensation claim involving a death in the family, the mediator had a quiet word with the commercial party beforehand explaining that the family may need some time to speak on some of the personal concerns before they could focus on "how much money". The co-operation and patience of the barrister for the insurance company was a definite plus in bringing the bereaved family to a resolution in a matter which had been outstanding for several years.

DISCOURAGING UNREALISTIC OPENING OFFERS

An initial offer or demand that is too low or too high can give a negotiator room to move, but it can also promote bad faith bargaining, for example:

> Look how far I've moved compared to you. I've cut my original demand right down and you have only upped your offer by 10%.

The danger, unless both are playing the same game, is that one party may feel offended and abandon any attempt at negotiation. This is not uncommon. A settlement-hungry mediator may buy into the "I've moved 90%" game and encourage the slow mover to move further. This may be construed as bias. (The authors generally hold the view that an experienced mediator should be able to mediate in any type of dispute. The other view is that mediators should have some background or practical knowledge in certain types of disputes (for example, personal injury cases) where it might be advantageous for a mediator to recognise that a settlement offer could be entirely out of range and carry the potential for a walk-out.) Where a mediator does not have this background knowledge an agenda item such as "Payment range" can be considered.

When horse-trading is about to begin the mediator may need, either in joint or private session depending on the context, to confront the parties with the danger:

> In my experience, coming in too low/high can sometimes be counter-productive.

The mediator should go on to explain why. This has the twofold effect of alerting a cynical bargainer to the danger of a walk-out and filtering in the message that the mediator is not buying into the 90% game. As discussed, exploration of the range of settlement moneys should be encouraged in the pre-bargaining joint session discussion. This will assist a mediator who is not familiar with the range to bring a sense of realism to the discussion.

CONVERTING WANTS, DEMANDS, POSITIONS INTO OPTIONS

This is particularly effective in taking the sting out of demands and may facilitate a less stubborn approach to a particular demand or offer and avoid a block.

Case Note

At a family law mediation a party said:

> I want 80% of the house. My solicitor says that is the least I will get.

The husband responded:

> 60/40 is the very most you'll get in court and if you insist on 80% I'm going for 50/50.[2]

These demands and threats went on the board under "Options". A mediator might say:

> So Joe's options are 40% and 50%. Mary's option is 80%.

This strategy is effective in all types of disputes whether the parties are demanding that a certain type of fence be erected or that a lease should, or should not, be renewed. By treating the demand as an option, the

---

[2] See "Discouraging unrealistic opening offers", p 225.

mediator encourages the parties not to take up fixed positions. A beneficial side effect of such a conversion is the promotion of an option-generating frame of mind, brainstorming and discussion of variations to the options already identified.

CONVERTING A NEGATIVE INTO AN OPTION

An alert mediator can grasp every opportunity to convert denials and negative comments into the positive by means of options. This involves active listening and reframing.

Case Note

This dialogue occurred in a building dispute.

Plaintiff: "I'm not having him back in the house to finish his botchy job."

Mediator: "So an option for you is to have someone else complete the work?"

Builder: "I insist on finishing the work myself. I want to make sure there are no more complaints."

Mediator: "Then from what you have both said there seem to be three options here: B finishing the job; a third party finishing the job; B supervising the final work."

The initial negative comment could have developed into a block. Instead, it was put to useful effect and promoted creativity. The parties then proceeded to discuss and vary the options.

REMOVING THE SPECIFIC FROM A DEMAND

Another way of dealing with a demand such as "I'll only settle for at least 70% of the profits" is to remove the figure by reframing to "So you are looking for a larger percentage than J?" The removal of a specific opens up the discussion in a less threatening way, in this case on why a larger percentage might or might not be in order. The reframed demand can also go up as an option.

POP-UP OPTIONS

Options can emerge at any time. They do not pop out in an orderly textbook fashion or at a particular stage of the mediation. A mediator who has been trained to hold back on options until the "Brainstorming" phase of their process may risk losing some opportunities. A party's opening statement may contain some negative comments that can be converted into options later. In a banking mediation, for example, a representative's opening statement may include: "I am here to get the debt repaid and have the file off my desk in the next 6 months". This statement is ripe for conversion to an option. Recognising pop-up options is not only a matter of "hearing" such statements for summarising or reflecting, but analysing how they can be used constructively. Even if a mediator is simply collecting the pop-up options for use later, it can be useful to mention at the time: "So an option for you is ...". This assists in injecting the "option" philosophy.

BRAINSTORMING

Whether a brainstorming session is a definite stage in a mediator's practice or is used as an optional strategy, inviting parties to contribute as many ideas as they can for resolution is a very creative way to get them working together. Brainstorming works best when there is an arrangement to be mapped out, whether personal or commercial. It may not work so well where parties are, say, arguing over a sum of money. Brainstorming has specific ground rules:

▌ All ideas, no matter how bizarre, are welcomed.

▌ No comment or criticism is allowed.

▌ Parties can build on each other's ideas. They can also contribute an idea which might "snip off" a part of another's idea, resulting in two ideas.

▌ No evaluation of options (that is, that wouldn't work) is allowed.

Where a brainstorming session is held, the mediator can kick this off by contributing the pop-up options that have been identified, thus demonstrating how many of their ideas have already been noted. The real value in brainstorming lies in getting the parties, whether blocked or otherwise, to see that there may be more than one way to resolve the matter.

A negative response to someone's idea should prompt the mediator to remind the parties that their initial task is to get out all the ideas no matter how unacceptable or unworkable they may at first appear. When early evaluation of options is discouraged, it can result in an initially rejected option becoming varied or partially accepted.

AVOIDING MEDIATOR JARGON

A mediator who automatically trots out words which have a specific meaning in the ADR industry, or in the particular profession the mediator might practise in, should not assume knowledge on the part of the parties. Such assumptions may risk undermining the parties' comfort and losing their confidence. The word "Options" is one such word. It may be necessary to decode the word for the benefit of some parties. Although "options" implies a range of choices, a simple explanation can be that "Options are ideas, your ideas or ideas that I have heard you mention". Similarly with "Brainstorming" one actual dictionary definition being "A sudden violent mental disturbance". A more comprehensive description is required for the activity as it is used in mediation sessions and workshops than just the word itself.

SUMMARISING IN ORDER TO AVOID OR DEAL WITH BLOCKS

The mediator summarises on an ongoing basis. Ongoing summaries are part and parcel of a mediation session and serve many purposes. When an agenda item is completed, the mediator might summarise before moving on. This reinforces each person's thoughts on the matter and injects the idea that it's okay for parties to have different viewpoints. Summarising is discussed in more detail elsewhere.[3] If it appears that a heated exchange is leading to a block, the mediator can, rather than jumping in to read the riot act, summarise the parties' exchange when they have run out of steam or at some other appropriate point. As with the mediator's summary of the opening statements, a summary later in the mediation has the effect of assuring the parties that they have each been heard and goes some way to preventing repetition. A wrap-up summary pulling it all together prior to the private session can be a springboard to private session discussions.

....

[3] See Chapter 15 — "Communication skills and their application in mediation".

REINFORCING CONCESSIONS

Summaries should also include any concessions that have been made. It is quite common for each party to genuinely perceive that they alone have been the one giving all the concessions, although the mediator might have a different view. Trivialising a concession from the other party is also not uncommon. In a financial matter, for example, parties will often point out how much they have "moved" compared to the other party and there is a tendency to see their own "movement" as monumental and to diminish that of the other side. A mediator who has been "keeping the score" can use this information in private session: "You may not realise it, but the bank has actually moved on interest rates and is considering releasing the guarantee."

MUTUALISING — FOCUSING ON INTERESTS

Mutualising can occur at the end of a summary. It involves identifying and including the needs and interests of both sides in the same summary or comment in order for the parties to gain an appreciation that it is not only their own needs which require consideration. For example:

> So, Mary, we are looking for a solution which enables you to spend less time at the office but helps you, Bob, to achieve an earlier repayment of your loan.

or

> It sounds like you both have an interest in relocating within a certain period. Let's look at the options for achieving this.

When summarising or reframing, the "sounds like" comment is very non-threatening and neutral.

USING THEIR OWN NEGOTIATION PRINCIPLE

Where parties have agreed upon a common principle for their negotiations such as "fairness"; "children's best interests"; "out-of-court solution"; or "settling today", the mediator should not hesitate to use it. It should not be merely cosmetic. As well as keeping it in mind as a guiding background principle, the mediator can use it pro-actively. To prevent them digging in, a mediator should remind them of their agreed objective. A more interventionist approach is to ask them to comment on a proposal or demand in the context of the stated objective. For example:

> Looking at your agreed principle of a fair solution, tell Bob how what you are proposing is fair to you.

then

> Now could you explain how this is fair to Bob?

This method incorporates a role reversal. In joint session the mediator must put both parties through the same exercise. In a family context the script could be:

> I'd like you to both think about how the property division you are each proposing will further the children's interests.

Likewise in a workplace context: "I wonder if you could give some thoughts about how you think your proposals will help improve the atmosphere at work, as I noted this was the main aim of you both."

MUTUALISING THE TASK

Mutualising can also telegraph joint responsibility for finding a solution. Prior to a private session a mediator can say: "So Bob and Mary, what we have is an issue about loan repayments. This is one of the things you can both think about (talk about with your advisers) now that we are having a break."

RECOGNISING NEEDS

> We tend to think of needs as concrete things and often they are. These can include the need for shelter as in the cases of a separating couple or a proposed tenant eviction. They can include survival needs such as assistance with a mortgage or reduction of interest rates. On a personal level they can include the need to save face, to maintain dignity.[4]

However, needs can be identified in a more abstract manner and can be the subtext of the parties' dialogue, such as the need for "certainty" (that the loan will be repaid); "time" (to pay/to get a new job); "finality" (this situation can't go on); "commercial realism" ("we are running a business"); "opportunity" (to keep running the business); and so on. Often the more creative options flow from identifying needs. Competing needs are more easily reconciled than competing positions. Where Party A is saying "This can't go on" (the "finality" need) and Party B is saying

---

[4] Charlton, R, *Dispute Resolution Guidebook* (LBC Information Services, 2000), p 70.

"I can't pay right now" (the "time" need), there is a possibility that both needs might be reconciled. If B is given time to finalise payment within, say, six months, A may be assured of "finality" at that time.

It is not often useful to ask parties what are their needs. The mediator is more likely to get a rehash of wants and demands. It is far better for the mediator to identify needs and before writing them up on the board (often a corner will do if using single words) checking them with the parties by reframing: "So A, you are seeking an *opportunity* to stay in the area near to your place of work, and B, you need some *finality* to the current arrangement because of the job opportunity in London."

REMOVING THE SETTLEMENT PRESSURE

The drawbacks of getting into solutions and figures too early have been emphasised. Quite often, in the normal flow of a mediation, settlement pressure has built up after about three hours and if an impasse is looming, or a proposal has been tabled but not yet acted upon, this point can be a good time to take a break.

Case Note

After three hours of mediation in a dispute over a lease, the parties had accepted the option of the lessee vacating, subject to an acceptable settlement figure being negotiated. They then started to argue over the amount. In order to crystallise the agreement in principle, the mediator discouraged any immediate horse-trading on the basis that this could jeopardise what had just been achieved. "You have reached agreement on a way to proceed. I don't want you to discuss figures right now. It's lunch-time. Think about it over lunch or have a walk." Distancing the parties temporarily from the negotiations had the effect of consolidating the agreed option, thus making it difficult to go back over old ground. It also provided the participants with a chance to clear their heads and to consider how to tackle the next negotiating stage.

An added advantage of everyone having a break at the same time is that, unlike private sessions, the absent party does not feel suspicious about what is being discussed.

Removing the pressure by taking a break is most usefully employed where the agreement in principle has been reached after several hours of mediation. Taking a break can work at other times, such as where a party is quivering about a final decision, or where a legal adviser needs time with a client to reassess the position or receive further instructions on the basis of new information emerging at the mediation. Furthermore, an unmet need for a break, in the case of a smoker, for example, can distract a party from full participation.

On the other hand, some mediators believe in maintaining the settlement pressure without a break in case the momentum is lost. It is a play-by-ear situation.

MEDIATOR SILENCE

Mediator silence is most usefully employed by mediators who are fairly interventionist. If the mediator is less so, the "shock effect" of this is lost. In a scenario where the parties are deadlocked or have run out of steam, they may be looking to the mediator to play the rescuer. The mediator could just sit there, looking from one party to the other. Someone invariably says something to get things moving. The interventionist mediator has effectively engaged in role reversal.

SUMMARISING THE INDIVIDUAL CONCESSIONS OR OFFERS

Summarising the individual concessions reinforces how much a party has, or parties have, moved from their original position(s). It also allows the mediator to put a proposal in a more marketable style. For example:

> Let's look at how much you have both moved from your original positions. A, you made the opening offer. B, you responded with a concession to extend the lease. A, you are prepared to repaint the premises yourself when the lease expires.

In financial bargaining, this may only be appropriate where the opening offers or claims were perceived to be within range (or were more or less equally unreasonable or unrealistic).

As discussed under "Mutualising", a mediator should always make a note of concessions to assist in summarising and in private sessions.

NEGOTIATION EDUCATION

In some cases Party A will make an offer or put forward a proposal which will be rejected by Party B. Party B will then ask Party A to put another

234 I Part 4: Mediation Skills and Strategies

proposal. Party B is, in effect, asking Party A to "bid against" herself or himself.

Some mediator-writers maintain that parties may need to be educated in the correct ways to negotiate. Deadlocked or particularly difficult parties can be reminded that they are present to negotiate a settlement and then advised that:

> This is not the way to negotiate. In a negotiation if someone says "I will do such and such", then the correct response is "Well, if you do that, then I will do this".

Where concessions have been more or less one-sided this negotiation philosophy can be explained in the private session with the "light-on" party. It is a form of reality test. A note made of each party's concessions or number of moves can be compared. The mediator might ask this party where any gap in concessions can be equalised.

THE ROLE REVERSAL

One of the underlying aims of mediation is to place each party in the other's shoes by allowing each side to ventilate their individual viewpoint and by encouraging each side to acknowledge (but not necessarily agree with) the other viewpoint. Thus, the egocentric viewpoint is often filtered out as a normal result of the mediation process. There are various ways in which a mediator can more pro-actively encourage role reversal, depending on assessment by the mediator both of the parties and whether the timing is right.

Some role reversal techniques are quite sophisticated and their success may depend on the sophistication and ability of the parties. Some people are quite incapable of reversing roles for personality reasons. Others may resist doing so for tactical reasons. A half-hearted role reversal such as, "Yes, I can see how Mary could have become upset" is commonly followed by a revert-to-role comment such as, "But, as I explained, I was trying to get some efficiency going". The mediator needs to anticipate the self-validation comment.

If role reversing takes place in joint session, it must be done with both parties, not just the person perceived to be causing the blockade. The mediator might say:

> I'm now going to ask you to step into each other's place for a minute.

Case Note

A mediation took place between a freight carrier and a user of the service. There was potential for maintaining an ongoing relationship. The complainant alleged that the goods, which were needed for display at an overseas trade fair, arrived late and damaged. The mediator said:

> Bill, now that you have heard how John felt about the non-delivery, how do you think you would have reacted if you had been in John's position when the goods did not arrive?

Bill then launched into a further dissertation on the reasons for the non-delivery and resisted validating John's frustration. The mediator then reminded Bill that at this point he was being asked to look at it purely from John's perspective. This reminder resulted in Bill acknowledging that he would have felt very angry had he been in John's position. The next step was to invite John to put himself into Bill's shoes regarding his efforts to locate the missing goods and to experience his dismay when he found that no local carriers were working because of a religious festival. When both had role reversed the mediator summed up the role reversal, noting that each had demonstrated an understanding of the other's viewpoint and that it was a frustrating time for both of them (see "Mutualising"[5]).

CREATING AN ANALOGY

If parties have difficulty role reversing on the particular facts it can be useful to create a hypothetical analogous situation. This may involve saying:

> Let's look at an analogous situation. Bill, what if you had taken the whole day off work because the carpet layer was expected. How would you feel when he didn't arrive and you couldn't make any contact?

then:

> John, if you had arranged an urgent appointment and your car broke down (or the train was held up for an hour) and you couldn't make telephone contact, what would you be feeling at that time?

---

[5] See pp 230–1, 245.

ROLE REVERSAL SUMMING UP

A sophisticated extension of normal role reversal is to ask each side to sum up on behalf of the other party, in effect taking over the mediator's role. The mediator might suggest:

> John, having heard what Bill has been saying all morning, I'd like you to give a summary of Bill's position as you have heard him tell it. And Bill, in a minute I'm going to ask you to do the same thing for John.

Again, the mediator should preface the invitation by stating that they are not being asked to comment on the validity or otherwise of the other's position.

A blunter form of a role reversal summary can be used where one party refuses to listen to or acknowledge the other's position, or is constantly interrupting when it is the other's turn to speak. The mediator might say:

> Bill, please tell us what you heard John say.

LEGAL REPRESENTATIVES' ROLE REVERSAL

At a mediation workshop a barrister commented: "Surely you wouldn't ask the legal representatives to sum up the case from the other's viewpoint." We acknowledge that it would be a brave mediator who would issue such an invitation to opposing counsel. There is, however, a useful exception to this, that is, where it becomes apparent that both legal representatives are being reasonable and realistic about their own client's strengths, weaknesses and vulnerabilities, but are having difficulties in "reality testing" their entrenched clients. Sometimes a legal representative will approach the mediator privately about such difficulties or the mediator may see fit to approach the lawyer. Where entrenched clients are a common difficulty, it can be in order to invite the lawyers to sum up for each other in joint session, or if it is a unilateral difficulty, the mediator can encourage the lawyer to sum up the other party's case in private session.

ROLE REVERSAL IN A POTENTIAL WIN/LOSE RESULT

Role reversal is particularly useful where there is potential for a win/lose result. Contested child residence is an example. This role reversal combines the techniques of hypothesising, reality testing and future projection. Thus:

> Jane, if Jodie went to live with Harold what sort of contact with Jodie would you expect for yourself?

A predictable response is that Jane wants the most liberal contact possible. After putting Harold through the same exercise with hopefully (and usually) the same result, the mediator might comment that it "seems that" the parties would grant the same contact to each other as they would seek for themselves. This exercise has, at times, resulted in virtually a shared parenting arrangement. It can make the crucial point of who gets priority parenting merely academic.

The same exercise can be undertaken where the parent with the majority parenting proposes to take the children interstate or out of town.

> Jane, if it was Harold, rather than yourself, who was moving to Adelaide with the children, what would you like to see happen regarding joint parenting? How much would you expect Harold to contribute to your fare to Adelaide or the children's fares to Sydney?

HYPOTHESISING

The value of the hypothetical cannot be over-estimated. Hypotheticals are used to approach an issue on a "What if" or "If this were to happen" basis. Hypotheticals have multiple potential. They can open up the dialogue, perform a reality testing role, encourage a refocus on the future, or pose a "hypothetical solution".[6] Hypotheticals tend to be non-threatening as they operate only in the realm of ideas or possibilities. There is no commitment involved and certainly a minimising of settlement pressure. It has been noted how the discussion can be opened up when parties receive the relaxing assurance that they are not committing to anything, for example:

> We are discussing this proposal on a purely hypothetical basis. Posing something as a hypothetical is another way of exploring options, but one which is less likely to be dismissed by the other party on the ground that it was not their idea.[7]

Let us imagine that Party A has put forward a settlement proposal that contains several items. When writing up on the whiteboard, and in order to take out the possible "sting" for Party B, the mediator might say:

---

[6] Charlton, n 4, p 86.
[7] Charlton, n 4, p 62.

Let's consider this on a hypothetical basis. Party B, hypothetically if you were to consider this as a possible settlement option what are your ideas on how it might work?

or:

Bill, hypothetically, what would you like to inject into that proposal to make it work for you?

The hypothetical settlement method can be used in any negotiation where a proposal is made by one party but is seemingly unacceptable to the other.

The technique of hypothesis may combine a role reversal and a reality test. The hypothesis can include such comments as:

If you were in Joe's shoes, how would you feel if this proposal were made to you? Would you accept it? Given what Joe has been saying all morning, do you really think he will accept it?

What if Joe were to accept only part of your proposal, would you be able to accept his ideas regarding the other items?

FUTURE PROJECTION

Hypothesising can involve projecting someone into the future. This does not work with people who, for various reasons, cannot project past the immediate. However, where it is appropriate the mediator can say:

Let's play the "what if" game. What if it's two years hence? How important will the $10,000 gap be then? You can assess this by thinking of something that was a burning issue for you two years ago, but which is completely insignificant now.

How do you think you'll feel when the hearing comes on in 18 months, knowing you won't have to go, knowing you won't have to be cross-examined, knowing you can spend the cost of the hearing on yourself rather than on the lawyers?

What if the tribunal decides there was a valid lease after all? What sort of settlement moneys would you be responsible for? How would you pay them? If in fact the lease is valid, what sort of reasonable settlement today will save you carrying all the responsibility if the case goes against you?

The last mentioned hypothesis incorporates a reality test.

"PART OF MY ROLE IS ... "

This simple prefix to a statement can assist the mediator in making the session run more smoothly or to get a party to understand why he or she is being asked searching questions in private session. The underlying message is "Please help me do my job". Thus, if one party is trying to dominate:

> Part of my role is to try to ensure that you both have an equal say as far as possible.

In using the whiteboard:

> Part of my role is to put matters on the whiteboard for all to see.

If reality testing:

> Part of my role is to help you each test out what you are proposing.

REALITY TESTING

Reality testing most commonly occurs in the private session for face-saving reasons. The mediator needs to stress that "part of my role is to play devil's advocate", otherwise a robust reality test might be seen as support for the other party. In order to avoid the perception of being an advocate for the other party, the mediator should give the assurance that the other party will be taken through a similar exercise.

A reality test should be preceded by clarification of the position the party has apparently taken and its importance to the party. This also puts the party on notice that the mediator is aware a position has been taken. This awareness is not always as obvious to a party as a mediator may think.

Reality testing questions may include:

> What would happen if John stopped paying the mortgage?

> How certain are you of winning, on a scale of one to ten — nine; five; three? What are the risks for you?

> How certain do you think the other party is of winning, on a scale of one to ten? How do you think they would respond if I asked them this question?

> What if you don't come to some accommodation today. How would this affect your financial position? Who else would be affected? How has this affected you/your spouse/your business up to now?

> Do you think X will accept that offer? Would you accept it if you were X?

Reality testing may include having to raise inconsistencies, for example: "In the joint session you were saying you would be prepared to do Y and now you are saying X. How do these fit together?"

Creating a climate of realism may include modifying a person's expectations. Where a party is holding out for an admission of wrong-doing, he or she may have to be reminded that:

> In my experience it is not common for a person to admit they have done something wrong, but that does not mean you cannot reach an acceptable resolution.

Where a party is still hanging on to past events, even though these have been thoroughly explored prior to the private session, the mediator might ask if realistically there is anything in the past that can be changed. Or may say:

> We have talked quite a bit about the past incidents and it seemed that you both acknowledged that we can't change the past.

"Honey catches more flies than vinegar" as the saying goes. Where a party has persisted in an antagonistic attitude towards the other person, it is in private session that a mediator can point out that:

> Bill, in my experience challenging Joe on everything he says may result in him resisting giving the concessions you are seeking.

Reality testing — a caution

In recent years the mediation experience of lawyers and other advisers has grown considerably. A favourite reality test promoted in training courses involves drawing attention to the ramifications of court costs and legal expenses in a non-settlement. This has lost some of its sting, particularly with the repeat players. In some cases reality testing on these aspects can come across as patronising or naïve or as the only tool in the toolbox. Conscientious lawyers will have advised their client of these aspects. Sometimes they are reserving the costs aspect as their bottom line in a negotiation. In such a case it is better for a mediator to say in private session: "Look, I know you will both have considered the costs aspect, but shall we have a chat about it in any case?" It is then that the lawyer will often confirm that if all else fails the bottom line is to concede to the other party what it would cost to go to court and what it might cost if the case is not successful.

THE COST OF DISAGREEING

The above observation cautions against naïve reality testing in private session. However, a public airing has proved to be useful in certain matters, particularly where there is a small sum of money to be divided, sometimes among several people, such as occurs in disputes over wills. It can also be useful where it seems the parties are resisting their lawyer's advice. Some mediators have a template of these questions that they take along to the mediation or write up on the board at the time. Mediators can design their own template.

This may include such things as:

▌ How much time spent so far?

▌ What are financial costs to date?

▌ What are the personal costs in stress/worry?

▌ Estimated out of pocket expenses?

▌ How many preparation meetings?

▌ How many letters/telephone calls, documents required?

▌ Estimated time/costs of a hearing (highest/lowest)?[8]

This is a form of brainstorming as everyone can participate — including the lawyers.

PROBLEM SOLVING QUESTIONS

As mentioned in Chapter 4 — "Issue identification and agenda setting"— some mediators prefer to set an agenda in the form of problem solving questions. The advantages and disadvantages were discussed in that chapter. It is the writers' view that these questions can also facilitate problem solving at a later stage when problems have been aired and exposed. Whether these questions are mutualised or not they can be written on the board so that all parties have the opportunity to respond:

▌ What are the advantages and disadvantages of a sale?

▌ How can the partnership be structured in the future?

▌ How should the 15% difference in the valuations be dealt with?

▌ How can the work relationship be smoothed out?

---

[8] See also Chapter 18 — "Effective use of information — note-taking and application of visual aids".

SLEEP EASY TEST

There is another form of reality testing that a mediator should pursue. This is the mediator's "sleep easy" test. It involves testing the "livability" of the proposed arrangement.

> If you accept $20,000 and in two months you hear that Mrs Jones up the street has received $50,000 for exactly the same injury, could you live with that?

The writers' view is that a mediator might feel an obligation to test out the accepting party in this regard, particularly if the mediator holds the view that the party may be feeling short-changed or possibly resentful.

THE ONGOING RELATIONSHIP

What would you like to have happened?

When parties with an actual or potential ongoing relationship have explained the problem from their own perspective, it is extremely useful to invite each side to relate what they would like to have happened (moving on from complaining about what did happen). This is so, whether the relationship is trading, commercial, community, doctor/patient, workplace, family or public authority/customer. The usefulness of this technique lies in setting the seeds or promoting suggestions or options for the manner of proceeding in the future.

What would you have done differently?

Another technique to preserve the ongoing relationship by promoting an understanding is to say:

> Now that you have heard how you were each affected by the situation, what do you think you might each have done differently?

Express this as an open question rather than asking: "Is there anything you would have done differently?" These are routine mediation techniques but are particularly pertinent with the ongoing relationship.

THE SWEETENER

One form of sweetener involves giving some acknowledgment to the other party. This needs to be more than a passing reference, a throwaway line or involve an instant qualification. It should be an emphatic isolated statement. In customer service complaint handling contexts it has been demonstrated that in 70% of cases complainants want an apology or some acknowledgment that they have received unsatisfactory service. The complaint often dies once this acknowledgment is received.

The sweetener can work wonders. The mediator can lay the groundwork and give some encouragement for it in private session if no acknowledgment has emerged in the earlier joint session. The mediator can encourage such comments as:

I really valued our past relationship.

I know in the past you always paid the rent on time.

I felt we had an excellent professional relationship before this occurred.

You were always a good father/provider.

I really am sorry that the accident affected you so badly.

Such sweeteners or validations are not guaranteed to work a miracle, but the writers have seen them turn the mediation around in the most positive fashion.

A tangible sweetener can enable a party to save face and find more acceptable the bitter pill (that is, the least favoured option) that they may, of necessity, be forced to swallow. If a party has little choice but to accept a below-range offer or otherwise litigate, it is a good idea to encourage the other party to give a small concession or several small concessions to soften the blow. The mediator might say:

Is there something you can offer to make settlement more attractive to the other party or make them feel they have not given up so much?

Face-saving sweeteners have included offers to pay the mediator's fee — or so many hours thereof — pay for the room hire or to pay post-mediation settlement costs such as drafting or lodgment fees. One of the authors once offered to voluntarily forego the last three hours of her fee, which operated as a sweetener for both parties.[9]

---

[9] See also "The last gap", p 253.

Case Note

In a mediation over a notice to quit a fish and chip shop, the tenant did not achieve her preferred option of a lease renewal. In the interests of settling, she was offered compensation by the lessor and, after much haggling, both parties were unhappy about the amount one had to give and the other was to receive. Both were wavering about finalisation. The sweetener from the lessor involved the lessee remaining on the premises for two months subsequent to the notice taking effect, which partly covered a holiday trading period. The fixtures and fittings installed by the outgoing tenant were granted to the lessor, who was able to on-sell to the incoming tenant. The landlord had previously demanded that they be removed upon the tenant's vacating the premises according to the terms of the lease. Because of the mutual unhappiness about the settlement moneys, both had been maintaining positions on matters they subsequently conceded. To encourage the sweeteners, the mediator asked the parties to consider whether these concessions were minor in the whole financial context.

Case Note

In another case, a mis-communication had resulted in a sick person going to the emergency department of the wrong hospital across the other side of town. In private session the aggrieved person said: "She didn't even comment when I said the taxi ride cost me an extra $55." The mediator spotted this as a possible sweetener and requested permission to raise it with the other party privately. After exploring Party B's issues, A's dissatisfaction was conveyed to B, who immediately responded: "Oh, I will pay it." When the unnecessary journey was raised in the following joint session, Party B made the offer without any prompting. This was accepted. From then on, all the other issues still in contention paled into insignificance. It was interesting in this case that Party B had not thought to spontaneously offer the money during the joint session, nor had Party A requested it, but had hung on to her grievance. It was the mediator who spotted a possible sweetener and sought to act upon it.

ISOLATING AN ACKNOWLEDGMENT OR APOLOGY

It has been noticed that sometimes an apology, acknowledgment or expression of regret becomes drowned among all the other conversational waves that are occurring at the same time. Maybe it is delivered in a low-key manner. Perhaps the recipient is still struggling with a range of factors and does not hear it in isolation from the rest. This calls for the mediator to isolate it or to include it in a summary. Certainly it should always be noted down so that if a party is still feeling aggrieved in private session, the mediator can make a point of reminding the party of the statement and, if necessary, adding that, "in my experience it is not always easy for a person to apologise".

MUTUALISING THE UNHAPPINESS

If both sides are unhappy, the mediator should point this out to each one, having first obtained permission to do so if the unhappiness has been expressed in private session. Whether the unhappiness is mutual or unilateral the mediator should encourage the offer of a sweetener.

PRIORITISING

There are several situations that call for a party to consider priorities. One is where a party has become so involved in a long-standing dispute that every issue takes on equal and monumental importance. Fighting over the property settlement ratio ranks equally with who will get the wedding photos. Another is where a party, although not necessarily dispute-addicted, is trying to achieve several goals.

If factors such as these are preventing overall settlement, the mediator should, usually in private session if only one party is involved, request that party to state the most important thing for them to achieve out of all the possibilities. The mediator can even take the party through the exercise of ranking the possibilities in order of importance, perhaps including the reality test that it seems unlikely, given what the other side wants, that they will achieve everything. When the priority has been identified, the mediator might say:

> What can you offer A in order to get the thing that is most important to you?

or:

246 Part 4: Mediation Skills and Strategies

What can you think of that will make what you are proposing attractive to A?

This is an appeal not only to reality, but to creativity.

DEALING WITH ENCROACHMENTS (OR THE ELEVENTH-HOUR ADD-ON)

It sometimes occurs that a party will state particular goals or one priority in their opening statement and the mediation proceeds on that basis. The party will then make additional demands. Additional demands do not threaten the proceedings where the other party is prepared to enter into negotiations on the subject matter of the encroachment. In the following case they were not.

Case Note

In a mediation involving a defamation action, the plaintiff stated at the outset that his only goals were to secure a public apology and to recover legal costs to date. After some time, the other side agreed to the apology and the negotiations revolved around the wording of the apology and to whom it should be published. An arrangement was reached about legal costs. Just as pens were poised to sign the heads of agreement, the plaintiff demanded financial compensation. This caused the defendant to threaten to abandon the settlement achieved thus far.

Such a case calls upon the mediator's analytical skills. Did the other party concede too easily and give the impression of being weak? Was this an acknowledgment of guilt? Sometimes a last-minute demand is symptomatic of an unwillingness to let go of the dispute. So much involvement and energy may have been expended on the dispute over the last couple of years that it has taken on a life of its own. When settlement is imminent, no matter how attractive the terms, there may be a gap emerging in the disputant's life. A great deal of mediator tact is required.

First, the settlement pressure needs to be removed. A break of up to an hour could be suggested. This takes away the excitement of the session for an addicted disputant. More dramatically, the encroacher could be privately confronted with what has happened and asked for an explanation. A last resort method is to become angry, and this may be quite genuine:

We have been sitting here in good faith for X hours — so has everybody else. You were the one who defined the boundaries here and we all operated within them. Where do you suggest we go from here?

The add-on can, of course, be the result of a genuine oversight. If this is the case, after the fur has stopped flying, the mediator needs to explore with the outraged party their willingness to discuss this issue and to encourage the first party to explain the oversight. Another way is to pre-empt the situation by asking parties if they have any other issues to raise when discussion of agenda topics has been completed.

CONFRONTATION

The above example is extremely confrontational, but it can work. One of the writers, who had conducted a nine-hour mediation on a pro bono basis, used this blow-up technique to encourage a ditherer to settle, pointing out the pro bono nature of the service given and the time and energy expended in the session.

We believe that in certain circumstances it is appropriate to privately confront a disputant in this fashion because we have a right as mediators to know what is going on or to know why that person is there. In a case such as that described above, the mediator might comment that all appeared to be satisfactory until the extra demand caused things to break down. The party might be reminded of his stated settlement preferences and be asked what was his particular reason for jeopardising the agreement with the eleventh-hour demand. Depending on the response, the mediator might take this a step further by exploring whether the thought of settlement is upsetting in some way, or whether going home to report to family and friends on the settlement terms would cause a loss of face. If the latter is the problem, the mediator should try to reassure the person that this is quite a common pre-settlement experience in a long-standing dispute and that party evaluations have shown that a few days after settlement the parties feel an enormous sense of relief.[10]

Where a party has been blocking or unco-operative from the outset, the mediator could say:

I am not sure why you came to mediation because you appear to be sticking with the position you came in with. As we discussed at the preliminary conference, mediation works best when parties are able to demonstrate some flexibility. Can you tell me if it is worthwhile continuing?

---

[10] See "The normaliser", p 253.

Another form of confrontation involves raising the question of whether the disputants only participated in mediation because they had doubts about the certainty of their position should the matter go to court.

Confrontations can jolt the party into a more realistic frame of mind. It should be emphasised that confrontations need not be of the jolting kind. A great deal of tact is required in some cases and mediators should develop both the hard and soft approach.

Confrontational techniques can also be used where a person is not encroaching but reneging.

Case Note

In a dispute between separated parents over children's issues, the parties attended the mediation without their long-standing legal advisers. Both were negotiating very successfully and things were proceeding well. The ex-wife began to withdraw and then renege on the agreements in principle that had been recorded. The private session confrontation took the form of explaining in a non-threatening way what had been observed and gently persuading her that she could tell the mediators what the problem was without fear of them judging her actions. It transpired that her legal instructions had been not to negotiate on certain things, or to ensure that she conceded certain points only in return for particularised concessions. The "hidden agenda" here was that she was afraid to admit to her legal adviser that the agreements formulated were quite different from those she had been instructed to achieve. Not only had she developed an over-dependency on the lawyer through the long-standing solicitor–client relationship in the face of many personal and legal tribulations, she had also come to view this person as an important power figure. The mediators then encouraged her to stick with her agreements on the basis that she had felt they were right for her. They then assisted her to rehearse ways in which she could explain to her lawyer why she preferred the agreement that had been reached.

This example is another version of what happens with "the absent audience" and is a twist to the authority to settle issue.

APPEALING TO FAIRNESS

Sometimes the demands from one party appear to be top-heavy or one party has been moving but the other party is sticking. This calls for a gentle but simple reality test. The mediator can say to the blocker:

> In mediation, the other party may feel it's unfair if you are asking them to do something you are not prepared to do yourself. By asking for 80% of the valuation you are asking him to be happy with 20%.

or:

> If you are only prepared to offer 20% you are asking the other party to concede 80%.

or:

> You are asking him to move off the position he came in with even though you are not prepared to do this yourself. In mediation it's very difficult for you as one party to ask the other party to do something unless you demonstrate equal willingness.

MEDIATOR ABANDONMENT (OR CALLING THE BLUFF)

Mediator abandonment is another case where the mediator reverses roles. This is most effectively used by a fairly pro-active, interventionist mediator. Timing is vital. It is best employed where a mediation has been proceeding for some hours without much progress being achieved, or where the parties cannot make a settlement decision. If both parties have been equally unco-operative, the mediator can imply abandonment in the joint session in the following manner:

> Perhaps you may feel you are better off going to court. There is no doubt that some people do feel more comfortable with an imposed solution, even if it turns out to be one which goes against their interests.

A harder line would be:

> Some people find the responsibility of decision-making uncomfortable and want someone to make the decision for them. Perhaps this is not the right forum for you.

The shock effect can positively refocus the parties. It has also been used successfully where a client has been holding the mediation to ransom with constant threats of walking out. A bluff is being called. A collateral risk is that the mediator's bluff may be called instead. However, mediators do report that this shock tactic is often received with consternation and a hasty reassurance of a desire to continue.

A softer line of approach is for the mediator to show frustration and to say: "I really don't think we're getting anywhere and I honestly don't know what to do next. Do you have any ideas?"

DEALING WITH "YERBUT"

"Yerbut" is the "Yes, but" syndrome. The "Yes" acknowledgment is instantly qualified with a "But", in the same manner as a qualified apology.

"Yerbut" is a recognisable participant in many mediations. Sometimes both parties will "yerbut" their way through the session. Chronic "yerbutting" most often occurs in four situations:

1. where a party is reluctant to let go of the dispute;[11]

2. where a party perceives a lack of acknowledgment by the other party or feels that there has been insufficient time given to the exploration session and the mediator has allowed a too-early focus on settlement;

3. where the parties, as happens quite frequently, are concentrating more upon what the other party is gaining than on the advantages to themselves;

4. where a party or parties enjoy the continuing conflict more than the prospect of settlement.

Ongoing "yerbutting" calls for a confrontation and a refocus. In joint session you can note that:

> I have been observing that every time an option comes up or a suggestion is made one (or both) of you will focus on the downside. No option will be perfect or suit both of you 100%. It's unrealistic to seek this. Every option will generally have a drawback. Let's look at the positive aspects of each option and see which is the least difficult or most mutually satisfying.

"Yerbut" can call for a "normaliser"[12] such as:

---

[11] See "Confrontation", p 247.
[12] See "The normaliser", p 253.

What seems to be happening is something we have often observed in mediation. Parties do sometimes tend to focus on the advantages to the other party and risk ignoring their own gains.

REFOCUSING

Parties will sometimes resist assessing their own worst case scenario by seeking comfort about what it will cost their opponents to go to court. The mediator should again remind parties that at this stage their worst case scenario is being considered and this may be the other party's best scenario. Sometimes both parties may be engaging in this comforting activity.

The other-party focus can take the form of an ongoing preoccupation with what the opponent has or has not done in the past, despite sufficient exploration and despite the mediation having reached a mutually acceptable pre-settlement stage. This preoccupation often involves the "yerbutting" party querying why such an offer or proposed action was not made at an earlier time. There can sometimes be mutterings that a proposed settlement is "unjust enrichment" as far as the other party is concerned, even though the proposed settlement addresses both parties' needs.

Where this preoccupation appears to be the result of obsessive thinking, the mediator might appeal to the party by saying:

Please think about your own needs. That is what is most important.

Legal representatives have sometimes been observed to be harsher with their "yerbutting" clients by saying:

What John might do with the fixtures if you leave them is irrelevant, particularly when you consider the concession you have gained by agreeing to leave them behind.

or:

What does it matter whether he will be using the third bedroom as a studio if he gets the holiday house? You are getting the city apartment.

The other-party focus may also, and often in joint session, take the form of sarcastic remarks denoting distrust of the other party's future intentions, for example: "How can I ever trust you to keep your word about X? I never could rely on you in the past." The mediator could say: "Perhaps you'd like to think about adding a clause in your agreement to outline what should happen when something that has been agreed upon does not eventuate?"

REHEARSING

Rehearsing involves empowering a party to put forward a suggestion or reframe a proposal in the most advantageous way. It can involve discussing ways to table a first offer without the mediator acting as the agent. The mediator can discuss with the party in private session exactly what is sought to be achieved and then say:

> How would you feel most comfortable doing this? What would you like to say? Rather than saying, "I can't afford to lay the pipes, you will have to do it", have you thought of saying "Thank you for your offer to allow relocation of the water supply. I would like to accept that offer, but unfortunately I can't afford to pay the whole cost of digging out the trench and wonder if you could contribute as you own the earth moving equipment."

The party can be encouraged to use the mediator as a sounding board and try out the script as if the mediator were the other party. However, don't expect a word-perfect performance when the joint session resumes, or in some cases a performance of any kind without some encouragement by the mediator. In the latter situation, it has been found best to avoid plunging the party into the rehearsed speech, but to encourage some general comments on the topic before saying: "Richard have you any further thoughts on relocation of the water supply?"

TABLING AN OFFER

Quite frequently a party may feel there is a loss of face involved in being the first to put an offer on the table — usually after a private session. A party will frequently express the desire to be the recipient of an offer from the other party. The mediator can assure a party that there is no loss of face involved in making the first offer and that in fact it has been known to work to the advantage of the initiator because the other party is then put in the position of having to respond. Another way is to encourage the party to include the offer in a range of offers and present them as options. The mediator can rehearse the party, when the joint session reconvenes, to say:

> Well my options at this point are: (a) to proceed to court; (b) to make an offer if you will guarantee that it won't be encroached upon; (c) to meet you half way (or 35% of the way) on the amount of your claim.

The latter option is the real offer. Tabling a conditional offer works best when the client is represented by a lawyer who can then present it as a conditional hypothesis to the other party's representative:

How would you react if I were to persuade my client to consider $X? I am not willing to suggest a settlement figure to my client only to have you cut it in half.

Quite often a proposal is tabled in a broad brush fashion, such as:

I will allow some time to pay (without stipulating the time) but there should be a new valuation (without stating who should pay for it).

These feelers are quite normal and do not involve a loss of face. It can be quite easy for the other party to agree in principle. Once the agreement in principle is captured, fine tuning can then occur.

THE NORMALISER

Normalising involves putting parties' feelings into context. It addresses their feeling of helplessness or of being in a unique bind by reassuring them that what they are going through is quite normal. It can break that final impasse when parties are dithering about settlement terms. To dispel that final doubt, the mediator can tell the parties that people are commonly uncertain as the settlement decision becomes imminent. It is useful to explain that it is common to feel disappointment having seen their expectations whittled down, but that this feeling disappears within a few days and is replaced by relief at the finality of the whole proceeding.

Early disagreement can also be normalised as can parties' feelings of anxiety. However, care is needed in the timing of a normaliser so that it doesn't imply the matter is merely run of the mill. It should not be done in such a way, or at such a time, as might trivialise what the parties see as their "unique" dispute. This is why it is usually more productive down the track.

THE LAST GAP

Professor John Wade of Bond University, Queensland refers to that final bridge to be crossed before settlement as the "last gap".[13] Often that settlement tingle is in the air but the parties are not quite there. It's not yet sewn up — will they or won't they?

The last gap can often yawn in a financial context but it can involve a lack of agreement on a chattel, on contractual terms or a variety of matters.

---

[13] See Wade J H, "The Last Gap in Negotiations. Why is it Important? How can it be Crossed?" (1995) 6 ADRJ 93.

The last gap often involves money. A financial discrepancy sometimes cannot be easily closed because each side has quite genuinely gone way beyond their bottom line. If the parties cannot agree to split the difference, the gap must be tackled in some other manner, such as exploring the possible alternatives to a negotiated settlement. This could then be followed with: "Is this the best/worst alternative for you?"

Case Note

A money gap was closed in a most unusual way. The corporation had made a final offer which was about $50,000 above its bottom line. This sum was about $50,000 below the plaintiff's bottom acceptance line. It was crunch time for the parties. It was tingle time for the mediator. A joint session was reconvened.

P's lawyer: "My client is very unhappy."

C's lawyer: "Your client could not possibly be as unhappy as my client."

The parties had each been concentrating on the other party's potential settlement advantages and legal disadvantages throughout the session. On jointly hearing that the other side was equally unhappy, they felt much better. The mutual unhappiness broke the impasse. They agreed to settle for the stalemated amount and then began co-operating harmoniously with regard to some other undecided fine tuning issues, which involved conceding some sweeteners.

There are other mutualising ways of crossing the last gap, including those where the lawyers are willing to convey to their respective clients their opponent's difficulty in convincing her or his client to settle. This can produce a common softening of client attitudes.

Offering a sweetener to close the gap has been discussed earlier. Sometimes when a person is feeling insecure about accepting a settlement it can be useful to ask the offerer how soon they can pay the money to the recipient. If payment can be promised within a few weeks or sooner, this is often an attraction which can be a deciding factor, or can operate as a face-saver.

THE GARFIELD FACTOR

The Garfield factor arises where agreement has been reached and goods and assets assigned, but at the last minute a party demands a re-negotiation on something that has been assigned to the other. The Garfield factor can feature in what John Wade calls "the last dance".[14] The "last dance" most usually occurs in matrimonial disputes or in those disputes that have involved a personal relationship including one in a commercial context. The "last dance" also features where, for example, there has been no acknowledgment or apology[15] and frantic end-of-session negotiations involve focusing on a relatively minor point or chattel which may not have been in issue before. Such negotiations involve statements such as: "It's a matter of principle."

Case Note

Garfield was one of three family cats. In the course of a family mediation over property and parenting Garfield had been assigned, along with the other cats, to the legal custodial parent who was remaining with the children in the former matrimonial home. Just as the settlement was about to be ratified the non-custodial parent suddenly demanded that Garfield be reassigned. This blew up into a major issue that threatened to jeopardise all the other settlements which had been achieved. It turned out that Garfield was the cat who been acquired early in the relationship before the children were born. He had suddenly become symbolic of the end of the relationship. He became the focus of a way of disputing established by the couple, who had learned to loathe each other, and at least one of whom was reluctant to abandon the enjoyment of that poisonous way of relating. In this case, the "take a break" technique was used (see "Removing the settlement pressure", p 232-233), the parties agreeing to meet for a second session, but only on the basis that the other arrangements were to be ratified at the present session. This was agreed. Subsequently, the second session was cancelled. The break and the financial implications of a future session broke the negative chain.

---

[14] Wade, n 13.

[15] See "The sweetener", pp 242-3.

NO GOING BACK

The above case study involved a decision to freeze the agreement or concessions achieved up to the point of impasse and have a separate negotiation over the gap. This is a most useful technique. The effect of a break from the negotiations often puts the gap into perspective and magnifies the achievements. The agreement to freeze can also incorporate an arrangement to address the gap by a certain deadline.

EARLY WARNING ALERT

An early warning or pre-mediation alert can assist in closing the last gap or even prevent it from arising. Mediators might consider the benefits of mentioning the last gap possibility at the preliminary conference or in the mediator's opening statement, such as:

> You may find that as the mediation is moving to its final stages there is a gap that you both find difficult to close. Think about how you are going to deal with it or ways in which you might co-operate in its closure.

This may assist a disputant to reduce the sense of panic or anger when the last gap is reached.

INFORMING PARTIES OF WAYS OF CLOSING THE GAP

John Wade suggests that the mediator might then, or at some later appropriate point, recount ways in which other parties have closed gaps such as: splitting the difference; delayed or instalment payments; tossing a coin; drawing from a range of solutions; deferring a decision on the gap while ratifying in principle the other agreements; or transferring the gap to a third party. Tossing a coin or selecting from a range of solutions are dependent on the luck of the draw. They relieve parties of the responsibility of a decision in terms of further concessions and allow them to save face.

Drawing from a range of solutions

A simple example involves the money gap. Where the gap is $20,000, ten slips of paper can be placed in a container beginning with $2,000 and ending with $20,000. The amounts on each slip go up in increments of $2,000. The drawer receives the amount on the drawn piece of paper. The residue goes to the other party.

Transferring to a third party

With this option the parties agree to transfer the last gap to a child, a charity, a grant, or to pay the mediator's fee.

Splitting the difference

This is a common way of dealing with the gap. There is a footnote to this. Where the standard process of narrowing the gap by concessions has left the range of offers biased towards the "exaggerated" opening offer, the reasonable person will often feel punished for her or his reasonable behaviour and decline to play.

The Garfield warning?

An experienced family lawyer warned a client in advance about a possible last demand for a reassignment as a way of avoiding ratifying the settlement terms. As predicted, the Garfield factor arose. Garfield in this case turned out to be a camera. Forewarned was forearmed:

> "You can have the bloody camera" said the wife. "If we spend another two hours arguing over it we will have wasted enough money to buy six of the things, and far better ones than that one."

In this case it was the lawyer who placed his client on the alert. It is difficult to see how mediators can warn parties about the Garfield factor without jeopardising their neutrality because the warning implies bad faith on the part of one or the other party. If taking this chance, the mediator should give the warning in joint session and present it as an anecdote which happened on another occasion, such as:

> Everything was agreed upon but just as they were about to finalise settlement this person made one demand for reassignment. It is not the first time I have seen this. It may be over quite a small thing. The solicitor had warned his client about this and told her to think about how she was going to deal with it.

VALIDATING THE GAP

In a mediation conducted by one of the authors, the gap was closed in an unexpected way. One of the parties was a public authority which had requested the mediation as a last ditch attempt to pacify a chronic and threatening complainant. An attempt to pacify is a common feature of mediations involving complaints against public authorities. In the interests of finality and peace and quiet, the authority's representative had conceded to most of the complainant's demands, but in the closing

258 Part 4: Mediation Skills and Strategies

stages was left with a feeling of disquiet about the unevenness of the proposed settlement terms. The complainants had conceded very little. Because of the gross imbalance, this was one case where the mediator, in private session, felt compelled to express some solidarity with the authority's representative and in fact gave some encouragement not to settle in view of the strong reservations which were, quite rightly, being expressed. The mediator's "permission" to not settle had an unintended opposite effect. Having his concerns validated by the mediator appeared to work as a personal face-saver for the authority's representative and made him much more relaxed about what had been conceded.

"YOU DON'T HAVE TO SETTLE"

Settlement rate reports vary. Depending on the agencies and types of matters involved settlement rates range from 65% to 80%. What constitutes a "settlement" can sometimes be open to interpretation. No long-practising and experienced mediator can claim a personal 100% settlement record. Where a party simply cannot settle or where the mediator perceives that a proposed non-settlement would be perfectly valid, as in the above example, then the parties' decision should receive endorsement. They should not be made to feel they have failed because a settlement did not occur. In fact the mediator should say:

> Although mediation has worked well for many people, at least 20% of matters do not settle. Someone has to make up that 20%.

With the public authority representative mentioned above, endorsement of the non-settlement decision put him at sufficient ease to allow him to proceed to settlement. In quite a few cases, the mediator's "permission" to not settle seems to galvanise a party into giving the negotiation another shot, in a similar way to "mediator abandonment". It has become a challenge. This, of course, will not always occur.

However, sometimes where parties have not settled at the mediation session they have been known to do so a few days or a few weeks later. This may be due to having had the opportunity of a cooling down period and more considerations given to the implications of not settling.

18

Effective use of information – note-taking and application of visual aids

In any mediation, a mediator faces a barrage of new information. While not called upon to advise any party, nor decide the outcome, a mediator still needs to manage that information in a way that provides:

1. an understanding of the background to the dispute and, in order to facilitate discussion, the parties' perspectives including their views on matters to be resolved;

2. a record of the parties' needs and options for settlement in order to facilitate a resolution; and

3. documentation of any settlement.

Additionally, mediators need to impart information to mediation participants in a user-friendly manner.

Mediators make use of a number of tools in the management and dissemination of information they collate during mediation. When used appropriately and strategically, they enhance opportunities for both the mediator and parties to participate actively and productively in the mediation, therefore optimising the potential for reaching a mutually satisfying agreement.

The most basic tool is the humble notepad used primarily for note-taking either for private use or as a precursor to later verbal reminder or transfer to a visual aid. Visual recording tools and aids include whiteboards, flip-charts, diagrams and posters. Notebook computers have reportedly been used by mediators proficient in typing, either to keep notes or to convey information on process, formulae or structures through a projector.

NOTE-TAKING

Purposes of note-taking

▌ To record the names of participants and to help locate them at the table, therefore avoiding a mediator having to rely on their memory, particularly with a crowded table. Name tags can serve the same purpose where there is a large number of people present (although people often are reluctant to be tagged). Particular mediations have a standard set of basic information needs, and mediators in such fields often have a template for this information, which provides easy understanding. When combined together, the top sheet of a mediator's notepad, in a child residence/contact case, may look like:

Janice P (solicitor)	Jacob K (barrister)
Ruby A (mother)	Francis C (father)
Barbara P (maternal grandmother)	

(Peter 8, Paul 6, Mary 3)

Period of relationship:

Period of separation:

Children live with:

Mother lives (area):

Father lives (area):

Last contact:

Existing orders/pending hearing:

▌ To provide a basis for accurately summarising the parties' statements during the first joint session. The notes act as a basis for identifying matters for discussion between the parties, which matters then form the agenda.[1]

▌ To help identify common ground between the parties and each party's needs and options.

▌ To record progress achieved by the parties, which can then be summarised progressively by the mediator.

▌ To record any other information which may be used strategically to facilitate mutual understanding and future settlement.

A major advantage of note-taking is that, when parties' statements are repeated by a mediator some time later, it conveys that the mediator has been listening to them and that what they have said or are saying is significant enough to be noted. Quoting from notes can also be most effective if a party is beginning to back-slide on an earlier statement or cannot recall saying it:

> Maybe I misunderstood you at the time Mary, but my notes indicate that you proposed XYZ. Could you please clarify.

Note-taking complements the use of visual aids because, once verbally identified by the mediator, matters for discussion, common ground and options can be transferred from the mediator's notes to a whiteboard for all participants to refer to constantly.

Pitfalls relating to note-taking and how to avoid them

Although note-taking is a very useful tool, it can be inappropriate or excessive.[2] Unless notes have a high expectation of being used, mediators should question the utility of taking extensive or ongoing notes and be wary of the following common pitfalls:

▌ Mediators might be distracted from performing the primary role of being both facilitator and strategist and, in some cases, from actively listening.

▌ The mediator's eye contact may be compromised, hindering the observation of parties' body language, and their effect on each other.

▌ It might also impede the mediator from assessing their own impact on the parties.

---

[1] A more detailed discussion on note-taking of opening statements is contained in Chapter 3 — "Parties' opening statements and mediator's summaries".

[2] See Chapter 6 — "Private sessions".

▌ Extensive note-taking might convey a false impression to the parties that, whenever note-taking ceases, what they are saying is not significant enough to be recorded.

▌ Indiscriminate or disordered note-taking hinders the ability to retrieve or summarise pertinent statements made some time previously. If this cannot be easily achieved, why take such notes?

▌ Some mediators report that they take notes on a lap-top. This may imply to the parties that the notes will have a use outside the mediation, or be kept for posterity, rather than destroyed at its conclusion. It may also imply a mechanical approach, rather than the personal touch. (However, a computer can be useful to record draft agreements, which are then printed out for all parties to peruse and fine tune prior to recording the final agreement.)

It is important for mediators to be conscious of the precise reasons for note-taking. It may also be useful to inform the parties of those reasons, for example:

I am taking notes to help me summarise your statements accurately rather than rely on my memory.

or:

I am taking notes of the agreement you're beginning to reach so that you don't forget important elements when we are ready to document it.

If a mediator is unable to articulate a reason relevant to the process for incessant note-taking, then the extent of the practice should be questioned. Apart from parties' opening statements — when detailed notes are both appropriate and needed — simple and occasional jottings of significant statements or clarifications may well suffice for the purposes of reminding or summarising later, and for private session discussion.

In complaint conciliation, for example, one of the writers has found it useful to note the agenda item being discussed, jot down an acknowledgment, clarification or apology (for example, R regrets any miscommunication; or B requests clinical notes). The jotting is placed on whichever side of the page has been mentally allocated to a particular party. A line is struck across the page when the discussion moves on to the next item. This is an easy aide memoire and can be accomplished quite unobtrusively.

It is important to resist taking notes during a private session in order to avoid any of the information being sighted inadvertently by the other party during their own private session. Certainly there should be no writing on the whiteboard. It is more useful to encourage the parties to take notes in preparation for final negotiations. However, if during horse-trading, a party requests the mediator to convey an offer to the other party together with the rationale behind it, the mediator should write down this information and double check with the offerer for accuracy.

Destroying Notes

To maintain the confidentiality of what transpires during a mediation, notes taken by the mediator should be destroyed. Given litigation involving destruction of documents, a prudent mediator might consider:

1. Including in the mediator's opening statement something to the effect of:

   At the end of the mediation in order to preserve confidentiality, I will be destroying any notes that I take.

2. Dramatically, and in front of the parties, tearing up the notes at the end of the mediation.

3. Providing in the Agreement to Mediate a clause requiring the destruction of the mediator's notes.

Where a computer has been used to keep notes, deletion of the file is less dramatic and the parties need to take it on trust that the mediator has not created a duplicate file or that a deleted file is not capable of being restored. For this reason alone, the use of a computer by a mediator to keep notes is at best problematic.

Often legal representatives of parties and sometimes a party will be seen to take extensive notes. This can be inhibiting for the free exchange of ideas where a party sees that everything he or she says is meticulously recorded and so becomes guarded in speech. When this is observed, a mediator should explore, possibly in private, the purpose of meticulous note-taking, particularly when such discussions are usually expressed in the relevant legislation or clauses in the typical mediation agreement to be confidential and privileged.

WHITEBOARDS AND VISUAL AIDS

Visual aids constitute a public form of note-taking or record keeping. They enable simultaneous viewing by all persons taking part in a mediation session. The public sharing of data has been described as a "power-balancing strategy".[3]

The mainstay for mediators has been and remains the whiteboard and/or flip chart. Portable whiteboards (in the form of plastic white sheets that adhere to walls and windows via static contact) serve well where a whiteboard is not available at a venue or, if available, is very small (as Mae West might have said: "a person can never have enough whiteboard space"). The attraction of these sheets, which can be obtained from most law stationers, is that they can be cleaned off and used many times. They are more user-friendly and certainly more easily transportable than rolls of butcher's paper.

In recent times, the range of visual aids has expanded to encompass electronic whiteboards, overhead projectors, computer screen displays and even, it could be said, mediation through the Internet.

Nothing surpasses the utility of a whiteboard. An electronic board, when available, meets most needs and has the following features:

▌ it never runs out of space as there are usually several screens that can be rotated to avoid rubbing off the board (for example, when the mediation has moved beyond agenda discussion to the stage of examining options);

▌ if a screen needs to be cleaned, copies can first be printed for use by the parties and the mediator;

▌ at the agreement stage, the agreement can be fine tuned over the several screens of the board, with changes readily achieved. When completed, it can be printed out (albeit in landscape format) for photocopying and signature.

Frequent users see a whiteboard as indispensable in their mediation practice. However, it is recognised that some mediators do not feel at ease using a whiteboard. The reluctant ones often have a feeling of awkwardness both in regard to the idea, and in the actuality, of standing up before parties and their advisers: "standing at a whiteboard makes me feel like a school teacher". This goes hand in hand with a reluctance to create an impression with the parties of behaving like a school teacher.

....

[3] Haynes, J M and G L, *Mediating Divorce. Casebook of Strategies for Successful Family Negotiations* (Jossey-Bass, 1989), p 143.

For this and other reasons, there is often a tendency to avoid whiteboard scribing.

And yet a visual aid, whatever form it takes, can bring numerous advantages to the mediation session, both for the mediator and the parties. Apart from this general proposition, extensive whiteboard use is recommended where there is a history of verbal or physical abuse, or where there is absolutely no ability, or desire, to engage in productive joint dialogue.

The mediator can explain at the outset that:

> I will probably be using the whiteboard from time to time. I have found that this is useful for all of us and that it can be very helpful to record the discussion topics and your ideas and options as we go. You also are free to use it to demonstrate a point or to list a proposal.

Why use a visual aid?

Creates a focus on the problem, not on the person

Mediators' "case books" are filled with reminiscences of where a visual aid has created a focus on the problem, diminishing the concentration on often hostile personal feelings towards the person across the table. When parties have reached an impasse, making notes on the board is particularly useful in distracting them from a potentially unproductive exchange by focusing them on the problem rather than on each other.

Whiteboard recording not only draws the parties' attention to common ground between them or provides opportunity for focusing on the future, but also allows them to draw breath. It provides an opportunity for the parties to pause and focus on a constructive joint activity: that of looking at the board and correcting any mistakes or inaccuracies.

The mediator might say:

> While you've been talking I've made notes of some of the things you've said (options I've identified) which will be useful a little later in the mediation when you're ready to negotiate and seek agreement about future arrangements. I'll just jot them on the board and I need your help in getting it right. Let me know if I've heard you correctly.

Acknowledgment

The listing of a party's discussion topics, needs and options enables that party to see their respective views acknowledged and dignified.[4]

---

[4] Haynes, n 3, pp 23, 142–3.

Although recorded in summary form, the listing indicates to a party that the mediator has captured the essence, and perhaps importance, of what they have said. Whilst they are not as positive about the recording of the other party's statements, they at least are forced to acknowledge their existence and the need to address them. At the same time as the parties are preening themselves through the acknowledgment of their separate statements, the public recording of information allows the mediator to attribute the contributions to the respective parties (without being seen to endorse the contribution).

Promotes objectivity

A whiteboard message, particularly one that is instigated by the mediator, is a clinical recording. When written up by the mediator, the message cannot so easily be blamed on one or other of the parties as might a message verbally delivered by either of them. A written message does not contain a speaker's nuances or tones of voice that someone may find objectionable, nor does it carry the same (objectionable) weight as it may with a verbal delivery.

A constant reminder of progress

Whilst verbal reminders by way of summarising keep track of what was discussed in the immediate past, a whiteboard can be a constant visual reminder of progress. If a mediator uses a break in discussion to tick off agenda items already discussed or to list options, this indicates to the parties how much has been achieved and "where we are at".

Enables prompt capture of options

As ideas for resolution emerge, a mediator can preserve an option for consideration by noting it on a whiteboard. The time taken by a mediator to articulate, clarify and check the option with a proposing party provides the other party with space to consider the idea and avoids immediate rejection. Even if rejected at that stage, its listing on the board enables a return to that idea for reconsideration at a later time. As well, once an option is noted, the pressure is on the other party to bring forth their own ideas. This then promotes creativity and encourages further options to emerge.

Promotes clarity in offers and prevents reneging

Where offers are recorded (and checked) just after they are verbalised, this activity lessens any misunderstandings which may arise from the spoken word, such as when someone is "thinking aloud" or is formulating their ideas. Additionally, it is very difficult to resile from a proposal that has been recorded for all to see, even if it was mere "kite flying". The recording can inhibit any impulse to go back on a previous offer because of some annoyance subsequently felt with the other party.

Essential tool for brainstorming, work-shopping proposals and fine tuning

The whiteboard or flip chart is an essential tool for a brainstorming session. Additionally, work-shopping options can be more easily achieved with whiteboard work. A proposal by one party that is recorded for all to see can be mutually "work-shopped" to ascertain the common ground. Modifications, omissions or additions suggested by the other party can then be recorded. The other party's ideas can be recorded on a line beneath the original proposal or in a different coloured marker pen.[5] This is known colloquially as the Red Pen/Blue Pen method. Ultimately, visual recording and corrections identify which parts of the original proposal are agreed, which can be rubbed off and which parts have still to be resolved.

Involves parties and advisers: promotes teamwork

All participants can contribute to what is written on a whiteboard whether in compiling an agenda or some other contribution, and can do it more productively than when, for example, a dispute resolver is noting down agreements or options on a notepad which is then verbalised.

Sometimes overlooked is the fact that the whiteboard marker belongs to everyone in the room. Parties can be invited to contribute something to the whiteboard story. To promote teamwork, both parties, or their advisers, can be invited to draw a subdivision or position of an easement. Each can mark up their own version of where they believe a boundary is situated or demonstrate how a building alteration might prevent overshadowing. Many an adviser has been converted from an advocate to a problem solver when invited to illustrate a technical point on the whiteboard.[6]

A reference point for changing tack or saving face

It has been frequently noted that the whiteboard is often used as a face-saver. Even in circumstances where a party has tended, or pretended, to not consider what is written on the whiteboard, that party will

---

[5] The "red pen/blue pen" method described in "Options as Hypotheticals", in Charlton, R, *Dispute Resolution Guidebook*, (LBC Information Services, 2000), pp 61-5.

[6] See also "Lists and charts", p 273; "The cost of disagreeing", p 241; Chapter 16 — "Strategic mediator interventions".

subsequently study the whiteboard quite intently in order to create a "thinking" space for themselves, to resile from an impulsive sudden death statement or to seize the whiteboard details as a reference point for a change of mind or for renegotiating a point.

People are more visual than auditory

Most people are more able to take in information and process it more productively than is the case with the spoken word. This is why conference speakers, unless they are particularly confident or dynamic, will generally use overheads or computerised aids to illustrate a point. It is also the case that people will recognise a face but forget the name that goes with it. People naturally relate to visuals over the spoken word or at least have equal appreciation.[7]

Overcomes hearing or listening impairment

The following case study involved a party who was hearing impaired and had, of necessity, come to rely on visual aids almost 100% in order to "hear" and respond verbally to what a speaker was saying.

An analogy might be drawn between this scenario and those in which some mediation participants might be described as "listening impaired". We are all "listening impaired" to some extent, in the sense of selective listening, interrupting or just switching off. Whether or not a party agrees with what is written on a whiteboard, it is not so easy to selectively listen to or interrupt the written word.

Case Study

The participation of a hearing-impaired party involved a new and positive "whiteboard experience" for one of the writers. A visual dialogue was the only practical way for this person to be able to meaningfully participate. A guardianship order had been made because the natural mother had been, and was still, considered to be unable to care for her child. She was, however, seeking increased contact. The parties' acrimonious history had been exacerbated because they were all members of the same extended family, the natural mother having the gut feeling that the guardians had "stolen" her child. Because of the mother's impaired hearing, extensive whiteboard use was a necessity. This procedure was assisted through use of an electronic whiteboard.

---

[7] This of course does not apply to vision impaired persons who need to rely on the spoken word.

Initially, in order to provide an outline of the process and the courtesy rules, the whiteboard was set out this way —

Process stages	It is agreed that
# Opening statements & Summaries	# All will be treated courteously
# Agenda setting	# All will work to achieve a practical arrangement in
# Issue discussions	Patrick's best interests
# Possible private meetings	# Patrick's interests have priority
# Problem solving	over the personal interests, desires
# Agreement terms	or convenience of anyone else

This sheet was run off and clipped to a flip chart stand.

The procedure that followed involved a support person writing up on the board the main points from the guardian's opening statement. This was not an agenda at this stage, but simply a scribing of the main points in substitution for the normal practice of the mediator summarising the party's opening statement. The party with the hearing disability was not speech impaired and so could respond verbally to the whiteboard record.

Despite the existing animosity, and the fact that some of the points in the guardian's statement were pretty hard-hitting, the whiteboard use drew the mother's attention away from her physical focus on the "opposition" across the table. It resulted in a more arm's length analysis by the mother of what the guardian had been saying than might otherwise have been the case if a verbal summary had been undertaken.

The whiteboard procedure was continued throughout the meeting and included scribing of the agenda, the points made to support and summarise the preferred outcomes of each party, the options, and the actual outcomes. This worked out satisfactorily and, surprisingly, the whole process took a shorter time than had been envisaged.

In this case, the main "dialogue" scribe was the mother's support person. His skills enabled capture of the information in a neat and user-friendly manner. These skills had been developed through working with hearing impaired people and were certainly superior to those of the mediator, not only in their conciseness but also in legibility and information organisation. In this regard it was encouraging to see a demonstration of how whiteboard skills can be developed and can be improved.

The pitfalls with visual aids — what to avoid

▌ A visual aid is to visually aid. This key purpose is sometimes forgotten by an over-enthusiastic user who insists on recording as much detail as possible. Over-crowding of information, particularly initially, indicates that the purpose may not have been grasped, ensures that the value is lost and may lead to early whiteboard burnout. Crowding, particularly with a small fixed whiteboard, does not leave space for emerging options, among other things.

▌ Too much time spent writing up goals and headings at the start of the session can be irritating and embarrassing to participants particularly where they are left with nothing else to do but look at each other.

▌ To avoid the parties' concentration on the mediator's back, or each other, the mediator should "talk to" any inclusion as it is written up. Down-the-track recording should be linked to what has been recently said.

▌ Neutral and non-judgmental language applies not only when setting the agenda, but throughout the mediation. As mentioned elsewhere,[8] adjectives are usually slanted in favour of one party and should be avoided.

▌ Writing can be too small and/or illegible. This is a "practice makes perfect" exercise.

▌ Avoid cursive writing. The support person in the Case Note above confirmed that he had trained himself to perfect printing in small capitals as this was less problematic to readers because of the consistent style. He also mentioned that printing is less likely to meander up and down the whiteboard than cursive writing.

▌ How tall are you? The support person in the Case Note above was quite tall. He explained that, as with most tall people, his recording became untidy towards the bottom of the board. He thus preferred

---

[8] See discussions on neutrality and agenda setting in Chapters 4 and 20.

to avoid the "bottom line" where possible. Similarly, short people should avoid the "top line" if it means they need to stretch. He advised that it is better to work at a comfortable height.

▌ Prioritising agenda items or options by numbering them should be avoided as probably should numbering generally unless requested by the parties. Numbering, particularly without consultation, may telegraph that the mediator thinks some items are more important than others.

▌ Ongoing standing at the board tends to reinforce the school teacher image and detracts from cross-table communication between the parties. Equally, ongoing jumping up, jack-in-the-box style, can detract from the smooth running of the session. Like all mediation activities, use of the whiteboard should be done selectively and in some cases for strategic reasons (for example, to create a diversion).

▌ If the whiteboard is fixed and small, it will be necessary to clean it from time to time to avoid clutter and to ensure clarity. The parties should be asked if they still need the recorded information. If they do and the whiteboard is not an electronic one, parties could be asked to assist in transferring the data to flip charts or to their notepads. If they do not require the information to be retained, it can simply be erased.

How to use constructively: avoiding the "whiteboard from hell"

An example of a hellish whiteboard is featured below.

Our goal today is to reach an agreement that is in the best short & long term interests of your children: Peter, Paul & Mary		
ISSUES	NEEDS	OPTIONS
• Residences	1. Mother needs children	1. All issues to be
• Contact	to reside with her and	decided by a Judge
• Normal	not see father	
• Holidays	2. Father needs to have	2. Get a life!
• Xmas	contact with children	
• Birthdays	regularly and more	(common ground)
• Telephone	frequently, and children	
• Mother's drunkenness	to reside with his parents	
• Father's violence	3. Each wants to decide	OUTCOME
• Child abuse	schools & religion	

The whiteboard from hell results from its over-employment at an early stage. Overload usually involves clutter. Clutter is counter-productive as it is not visually aiding anyone. The normal-sized fixed whiteboard cannot cope with all the information some mediators may see as important, particularly where the user favours dividing the whiteboard into column headings such as "Issues", "Needs", "Options" and "Outcomes". Such an approach at the time of agenda setting can result in a scrambled mess, and no room for later addition of emerging options and agreement. Remaining within the columns necessitates such tiny writing that binoculars are needed to decipher the message. Balloons and arrows pointing to additional information have the same effect.

A laborious statement such as "Our goal today is to reach an agreement that is in the best short- and long-term interests of your children, Peter, Paul and Mary", while high-sounding, is hardly space-saving. Similarly with statements of "Needs" — "Father needs to have more regular contact with children, for longer periods and for children to reside with his parents during school holidays". Leaving aside that these are really options or wants rather than underlying needs, the whole statement is too long and overbearing and does little to aid visually, which is the whole point of the exercise. Dot points are more succinct and act as triggers. Bite-sized communication applies to the written as well as the spoken word. Detail is required only when listing offers or recording agreements.

There are of course other problems with the "whiteboard from hell", neutral language being one. A better approach is captured below:

GOAL: Best interests of Peter, Paul and Mary	
ISSUES	**OPTIONS**
• Residence	• Children live with Mother/paternal
• Contact	grandparents
• Normal	• Mutual non-substance abuse
• Holidays	• Joint long term decisions
• Xmas	
• Birthdays	
• Telephone	
• Welfare	
<u>NEEDS</u>	
Security	
Certainty	

This is an example of the use of a small, fixed whiteboard. Recording of mutually satisfying options or ultimate agreements will require the board to be wiped or the information transferred to a separate sheet.

Other uses of visual aids

The process model

One mediation agency has, as part of its procedure, a poster-sized sheet displaying its mediation model. This has been found to be helpful to show parties where "they are at" and the progress that has been achieved ("We have now reached the problem solving phase"). This assists in avoiding back-tracking.

When using a formula

Some people in their everyday lives, particularly at work, are used to working with formulae and with lists. "Getting the parties to agree to a formula in a particular context can work in a number of respects whether it involves a financial formula or lists dates and events."[9] This is where simple column headings, with simple insertions can work. Where a formula is agreed upon the various headings can be written up in consultation with the parties so that each has the opportunity for some input. This method triggers feelings of familiarity and encourages the co-operative problem solving environment that all dispute resolvers hope to achieve. Where, for example, a contractor has been paid at hourly rates and there is some disagreement over the work undertaken, the mediator can use the board or flip chart to insert certain headings such as:

Activity	Claim	Client's time estimate
24.5.03 Review architect's plan	5 hrs @ $100 per hr	3 hours
26.5.03 Document drafting	7 hours	3–4 hours

Lists and charts

In a complicated matter, the board or flip charts can be used to record a chronology of events to which both parties can contribute and generally reach agreement on. This can extend to such things as a simple flow-chart on corporate group structures or a family tree to define complex relationships. Even in those cases where such information is primarily to aid the mediator's understanding, it still can be used to create a diversion or to allow parties some face-saving breathing space.

"The costs of disagreeing" can be a useful visual aid.[10] Some mediators have a "costs of disagreeing script" already written on butcher's paper

---

[9] See discussion on impasses in Chapter 16 — "Strategic mediator interventions".

[10] See Charlton, n 5, p 90.

that can be displayed as written up or transposed to the whiteboard. This "costs" template can include about ten queries including "What are costs to date?"; "How much time off work?"; "How much time spent so far?"

Closing the gap

In an appropriate case, the whiteboard or flip chart can be used to record "the gap" between so-called final offers and counter offers. This simple act can visually demonstrate how small the gap is and how close the parties are. Once again, the visual aid is far more powerful than auditory communication, particularly where parties are fixated on the fact that there is a gap, or that "the opposition" is not agreeing with their so-called bottom line.

In personal injury matters, precedents usually identify a range of figures that have been awarded by the courts for certain types of injuries. It can be useful to invite parties' lawyers to have whiteboard input into such things as:

"Highest payment in range for X type of injury";

"Lowest payment in range for X type of injury".

Naturally, different perceptions of "highest" and "lowest" will be offered. Nevertheless, using the board as a visual aid can "immediately demonstrate the gap and may inject the idea that a suitable compromise may lie somewhere in between.[11]

Reality bites

Converting ratios into actual figures works as a reality test. In a property division for example, parties and particularly their lawyers often speak in terms of ratios 40% and 60%. But the gap in, or disagreement over, these ratios often looks less formidable when converted into dollar terms and written up for all to see. This is particularly so when the joint property of many relationships is insufficient to cater for individual needs (let alone, wants).

Some visual aids are less useful than others at different stages of the mediation session. For example, overheads may be helpful for parties when the mediator's role and the mediation process are outlined. However, they are of little use for the ongoing information collected in the course of the mediation. Conversely, at the end of a mediation, a projector that enables a computer screen to be displayed, will assist with the negotiation of a settlement agreement.

---

[11] Charlton, n 5, p 183.

Part 5

Special Mediation Issues

Role of legal representatives

In this chapter the role of legal representatives in mediation is divided into two sections. The first section deals with the legal representative's role from the mediator's perspective. The second section is designed to provide assistance to a legal adviser representing a party in mediation.

THE ROLE OF THE LEGAL REPRESENTATIVE FROM THE MEDIATOR'S PERSPECTIVE

Legal representatives can play a very constructive role in mediation. Equally they can hinder. Mediators need to be aware of different dynamics that may operate in a mediation depending on whether or not the parties are legally represented.

Legal representation has been known to move forward a mediation in which, despite difficult parties, the representative has been encouraging and realistic. On the other hand a legal representative's input may have prevented a fair and reasonable agreement which the parties may have independently reached but for the representative's unhelpfulness or adversarial attitude. However, as mediation representation becomes more familiar to members of the legal profession there are increasing reports of the helpfulness of legal representatives in the session.

Mediators may be familiar with the situation where an agreement in a court-based mediation, held without legal representation, has been jeopardised or sabotaged when the party presents it for legal ratification. In some cases the lawyer is doing no more than fulfilling the obligation of acting in what are perceived as the client's best legal interests. Had the lawyer been present at the session and been able to observe and participate in its progress, there may have been a more realistic appreciation of how and why the agreement was reached. This is another result of the absent audience.[1]

The legal takeover

It has been common in the past for mediators to report that the mediation either did not succeed or was made more difficult because of the presence of legal representatives. A common complaint is that one or other of the legal representatives attempted to "hijack" the process, did not understand or ignored the philosophy of mediation as a co-operative, problem solving operation, and thus turned the session into an adversarial courtroom-style contest.

The passive legal representative

Very occasionally, a legal representative might play a somewhat passive role in the mediation. Warning bells should sound if such a situation occurs.

Case Note

One of the authors was involved in a mediation where the legal represen-tative made no contribution at all. Prior to conducting private sessions, a private meeting was held with the legal representative to inquire into the reason for his passive role. He admitted quite openly that he was not at all interested in settling the matter through mediation. He had every intention of advising his client that the matter would be pursued through litigation. The only reason why he agreed to mediation was to see what sort of witness his client would make in court. Not surprisingly the mediation came to a halt at that stage in view of the complete absence of good faith.

The need for the mediator to focus on empowering the parties

In evaluating one of the "Settlement Week" mediation initiatives in the early 1990s,[2] it was noted that 422 out of the 502 opening statements were delivered by the legal representatives rather than by the parties.

----

[1] See Chapter 16 — "Strategic mediator interventions".

[2] See Dewdney, M, Chinkin, C and Sordo, B, *Contemporary Developments in Mediation within the Legal System and Evaluation of the 1992–3 Settlement Week Programme*, Annexure J, p 152.

The evaluators commented that "it was disappointing to find that the parties were not more actively involved in giving the opening statements". Whilst there is no doubt that parties sometimes prefer their lawyers to do this, this high figure promotes speculation that in some cases the mediator invited this procedure or did not emphasise strongly enough the parties' role as central to the dispute. If, in fact, the mediator hands this role to the legal representatives, then the mediator is setting the scene for a hijack and is elevating the lawyers' role above that of the parties. The mediator may, in fact, be disempowering the parties and at the same time losing sight of their own role or indeed their obligation to control the process. It cannot be over-emphasised that the mediator should resist a takeover by the legal representatives and should set the correct scene at the preliminary conference, which is normally attended by the parties' lawyers. It should be noted that many mediators do emphatically set the correct scene but report that an attempted hijack occurs nevertheless.

Case Note

At a preliminary conference the mediators requested the parties to come to the mediation with their opening statement prepared. One of the legal representatives announced that he would make the opening statement for his clients. The mediators responded that, in accordance with the underlying philosophy of mediation, "we always encourage the parties to take the central role and it is desirable that the mediation begins on this basis". The mediators pointed out that this did not prevent a representative adding something to the statement if there were matters that the party had not covered.

Some mediators report that a power struggle can develop between the mediator and one or other of the legal representatives as to the manner in which the session is to be conducted. Some barristers have a tendency to regard a mediation as similar to a pre-hearing conference. In the case described above, the mediators sensed at the preliminary conference that there was a potential for this. When writing to the legal representatives to confirm the mediation details they referred to the agreement that the parties would make the opening statement and attached a pro forma information sheet setting out the legal representatives' role. Furnishing an information sheet is a good idea in any case, whether or not there is an apparent potential for a hijack.

Maintaining focus on the mediator's central role

> ### Case Note
>
> During the initial stages of a mediation, a legal representative attempted to usurp the mediator's role of guiding the parties through the agreed process. This involved an attempt to circumvent the stages the mediator wished the session to follow so "we can get to the figures". In this case the mediator responded, "Perhaps I did not explain my role clearly enough, in which case I will do so again". After repeating her explanation of her own role she added that each participant had a separate role to play in making the mediation a success and that fulfilment of an individual role often depended on each participant helping the others. This had the effect of re-establishing the mediator's authority and allowing the mediation to proceed in accordance with the agreed plan.

Gaining the co-operation of the legal representatives

Setting the scene

As a significant number of lawyers have now been trained in mediation, it is more likely than not that legal representatives will be an asset rather than a liability in mediation.

A prerequisite for encouraging co-operation is the need to emphasise the underlying principles of mediation and the nature of the meeting. The mediator should state that the parties are central to the dispute and that the mediator will direct most of the attention to them as it is their dispute and it is they who will need to live with the outcome. Further, the mediator should explain that mediation is an informal meeting between the parties which is conducted in a non-threatening, non-legal context.

The number one rule is that a lawyer should not, under any circumstances, attempt to cross-examine the other lawyer's client. This message can be delivered as bluntly as that or the mediator can say: "The best practice is for lawyer to speak to lawyer." However, sometimes a party will address a remark to the other party's lawyer, in which case it would be natural and courteous for the lawyer to respond, so there should be some flexibility in this regard.

Maximising the benefits

After emphasising the parties' central role the mediator might say to the parties:

> We have Mr B and Ms X QC here to help us today and they will be able to contribute a great deal to solving the problem, which is what this meeting is all about.

If necessary at the beginning, or even during the session, the mediator can provide some anecdotes of how legal representatives have positively contributed to past mediations, such as joining in option generating, acknowledging the other party's concerns and so on.

Drawing attention to the representatives' settlement onus and ability

Although emphasis is placed on the parties' role, in some cases it has been found useful to refer to the lawyers' settlement onus and ability and even to say:

> I am sure that Ms X QC and Mr B have had a lot of experience in settling disputes.

Just as mediators will often recite their high settlement record, the writers have indeed heard some legal representatives boast about "My 100% mediation settlement record". The following case note is on this point.

Case Note

A legal representative for an insurance company had shown adversarial potential at the preliminary conference. During this meeting, he had mentioned that he would be involved in a couple of other mediations prior to the one in question. When he arrived at the mediation the mediator asked lightly whether he had "managed to settle the intervening cases". This produced the response that "of course" he had settled his matters and furthermore he had brought terms of settlement along in anticipation of settling this one.

Inviting a contribution

Where the party has made the opening statement, the representative should be invited to add anything her or his client has left unsaid. Where the brainstorming strategy is being used, the legal representatives should be invited to contribute to the options that are being generated.

Similarly, if a party has preferred their representative to make the opening statement, the party should be asked if they wish to add anything. This is important because the adviser's focus might be, and often is, quite different from that of their client.

However, if it is the party's choice that the adviser make the opening statement then that should be respected. The party may regard the adviser as the expert who is after all being paid for the work.[3]

A lawyer's contribution can involve encouraging their clients to observe the courtesy rules.

Where, for example in a family law matter, the parties are equally difficult, argumentative or even abusive, the mediator can request the lawyers to curb their clients' excesses. Legal representatives trained in mediation will often help divert their client's attention to a more fruitful discussion.

Case Note 1

A situation involving verbal abuse arose at a preliminary conference. Both lawyers sat there helplessly. The mediator rang both lawyers before the mediation and requested some intervention from them if the verbal abuse continued at the mediation itself, which it did. The combined efforts of the mediator and the lawyers went some way to focusing the parties on the future and preventing the continual excursions down the bitter memory lane.

Case Note 2

In a mediation where a legal representative was taking an adversarial rather than problem solving approach, the mediator drew the representative aside. She advised him in private that he was not helping the parties reach settlement but rather that his attitude was contributing greatly to the increasing polarisation of the parties. She then discussed ways in which they both thought he might contribute to softening the positional stance. She reported that this discussion took the form of "how can we help each other", and effectively engendered a much more co-operative approach.

---

[3] Charlton, R, *Dispute Resolution Guidebook* (LBC Information Services, 2000), pp 22–3.

Seating arrangements

The mediator should be pro-active regarding the seating arrangements both at the preliminary conference and at the mediation. The parties should be seated on each side of the mediator, with the legal representatives on the far side of their clients. If the legal representatives have already seated themselves at the closest point to the mediator, the mediator should tactfully request them to move. The mediator might say:

> John do you mind moving up a space? Perhaps you didn't realise that it's the usual practice to seat the party next to the mediator and this always works quite well.

Case Note

On one occasion the above request produced an announcement by one legal representative to the other that "she's trying to sideline us". The mediator used humour on this occasion by laughing and stating, "I obviously can't fool you, Jane. I bet you have seen this happen before today". This broke the tension which might have been created and produced smiles all round.

The tendency of lawyers to bring along thick files and "evidence" to the mediation is obviously their prerogative. Some mediators discourage it as being not conducive to the spirit of mediation and promoting tension in parties on the other side (which indeed it may be intended to do). In practice, these files are rarely consulted once the mediation gets underway. They can be the lawyers' security blanket and the representatives would be failing in their duty if the files were left in the office when there may be points that require checking. However, the lawyers should certainly be requested to refrain from delving into the files or shuffling papers (which they are prone to do in order to check or refute a point) while the parties are making their opening statements. The mediator should emphasise that this is a listening exercise for the non-speakers.

Case Note

In a mediation over a disputed will a legal representative entered the room and with great deliberation plonked on the table a file clearly bearing the words "Fraud and Undue Influence". This was spotted by the mediator while the others were settling down. The mediator walked around the table, placed a sheet of paper over the file and quietly asked the lawyer whether she would remove the file or whether she wanted to discuss the matter privately.

Situations arising

The new mediator might need to be aware of certain characteristics and the dynamics of legal representation in a mediation session.

▐ A legal representative may feel the need to put on a show for the client. This can involve the need to display to the client that the lawyer is in control and acting in the client's best interests in the legal sense and the need to vindicate the advice the lawyer has given the client to date and to prevent any perception that the advice was over-optimistic.

▐ Related to the above, there may be a need for lawyers to save face in front of their clients. As discussed in Chapter 16 — "Strategic mediator interventions" — the mediator can develop strategies to prevent a legal representative from taking an initial hard line position from which retreat may be difficult without a loss of face.

▐ A legal representative may be using the mediation session as a mechanism to reality test an entrenched or unrealistic client. Or the session itself may be a face-saving mechanism where initial legal advice has been over-optimistic. Such a situation is obviously helpful to the mediator. However, if the client's lack of realism is based on early advice from the legal representative then the mediator can assist the legal representative to prevent making the about-face too obvious. One way to do this is to invite the lawyer to contribute to options. During the brainstorming, the lawyer's contribution is often the one that the parties now consider to be a realistic settlement proposal. Disguising it among the other options allows the lawyer to save face.

▮ At some stage during the mediation it may be feasible for both legal representatives to consult with each other without their clients. Mediators can suggest this.

▮ The mediator may perceive it as useful to have a joint session without the lawyers. If one or other of the lawyers has been too much in the adversarial mode, the mediator might say:

> As you X and you B seem to have some burning issues to discuss with each other, why don't you have a session together while I continue with Bill and Ben. This may progress the matter much quicker than otherwise.

▮ It is not unknown for one lawyer to suggest to the other that clients may make more progress in their absence. This situation usually occurs where one of the legal advisers: (a) is a trained mediator; (b) is used to mediation; and/or (c) perceives that the other lawyer's input or presence is having an impeding effect. A mediator can suggest to the more tuned-in lawyer that this strategy be canvassed with the other lawyer.

▮ It has sometimes been noted that a lawyer who makes adversarial or positional noises at a preliminary conference may be doing this for negotiating effect and often comes to the mediation with an entirely different attitude. This may sometimes be the result of the mediator's pre-mediation "pep talk".

▮ Barristers are often accustomed to being the centre of attention and may feel the need to engage in the theatricals of the courtroom. One mediator report highlighted a barrister quoting Shakespeare at the preliminary conference and airing his knowledge on Greek philosophy during the mediation itself. Despite the literary subject matter, this actually contributed to the informality and humour of the session. However, other theatricals may not be so productive.

▮ Parties may be overawed by the legal representatives' presence and, despite mediator encouragement to participate, may not feel comfortable in letting go of the lawyer-reliance. The situation is difficult where one party is prepared to negotiate on their own behalf but the other party cannot. This has the potential for creating a dialogue between a party and the other party's legal representative which: (a) may create a power imbalance; and/or (b) may encourage the lawyer to embark on a cross-examination which, as mentioned earlier, should not happen. This situation should be carefully monitored by the mediator who may need to intervene if a disempowering dynamic is developing.

Case Note

The absent mediator: In one mediation, the legal representatives and their parties actually benefited from finalising their negotiations in the absence of the mediator. This happened after the mediator intuitively felt that they would be more comfortable doing so. It was a government department workplace mediation where all the parties and their representatives were men and it became obvious that they were using "polite language" out of respect for the female mediator. They were very relieved when the mediator offered to absent herself from the final negotiations and return to help formulate and finalise the agreement.

THE LEGAL REPRESENTATIVE'S PERSPECTIVE

The role of the legal representative in mediation is essentially that of adviser or consultant to the client, not of negotiator or advocate. The presence of legal representatives can be extremely helpful in providing client support, encouragement and advice. They are not present to engage in an adversarial courtroom-style contest either with each other or with the opposing party. Courtroom-style tactics such as cross-examination or embarking on an inquisition to prove or disprove certain facts are completely out of place in the mediation forum. Sir Laurence Street has observed "A legal adviser who does not understand and observe this is a direct impediment to the mediation process".

If a preliminary conference is held, the mediator will usually explain their own neutral role, the process to be followed and will often request that the lawyers prepare an advice of the legal costs which have been incurred to date. The legal representatives can reinforce some of the principles of mediation with the client prior to the mediation itself. Regardless of whether a preliminary conference is held, a useful pre-mediation checklist for legal representatives in preparing their clients is suggested by the Law Society of New South Wales in the "Guidelines for Legal Representatives in Mediation".

Checklist for legal representatives

▮ Explaining the mediator's neutral role and that the mediator will not be making a decision.

▮ Explaining that a process will be followed which has been found to work successfully.

▮ Assisting clients to identify their needs, interests and issues.

▮ If necessary, assisting clients to prepare their opening statement.

▮ Discussing issues that would be considered by the court.

▮ Exploring what could be the worst, best and possible outcomes.

▮ Discussing ways to achieve the client's desired outcome or priority.

▮ Discussing the likely reaction of the other party and ways to overcome any objection.

▮ Explaining the nature of a without prejudice and confidential discussion.

▮ Explaining to the client that mediation should be approached with an open mind and that the other party will also be trying to achieve the best possible result for themselves.

▮ Explaining that the mediator will not be making a decision on the matter but that the settlement decision must be their own .

▮ Advising of the legal costs which have been incurred to date and the potential costs to the hearing, as well as the time to the hearing.

To this could be added that settlement usually involves a compromise for both parties and that essentially the agreement will be one that the parties can live with, rather than one which results in a "win" for one party only.

Where legal representatives can help

Assisting the client

Essentially the legal adviser is present at the mediation to provide support and assistance to the client. The underlying philosophy of mediation is that the parties are central to the dispute and that the ultimate settlement decision is theirs. Lawyers can assist by actively encouraging the clients' central participation and by empowering clients to involve themselves as much as possible in the discussions and in the decision-making process. Even though the legal representative is taking a lower profile in a mediation than is the case in the legal forum, the client will be pleased to be assured that the representative is there for support and consultation. This assurance of support gives the client confidence to take the central role. The legal adviser can assist in the smooth running of the session by assisting the client to assess any settlement proposals realistically. The lawyer can also assist by contributing to settlement options where it is appropriate to do so. It is not appropriate to attempt to cross-examine the other lawyer's client.

Assisting the mediator

The mediator's role is to encourage and empower the parties to take a central role, to facilitate direct communication between them and to guide them through the mediation process. Although it is the parties' dispute, the mediation process, with its various stages, is controlled by the mediator and is one that has been developed to maximise settlement prospects in a non-adversarial context. With this in mind, legal representatives can assist in the smooth running of the session by allowing the mediator to guide the parties through the procedural aspects of the mediation.

Further, lawyers can support the mediator's role to empower the parties by means of encouraging and controlling parties' direct communication, by raising matters for their consideration and by ensuring that each party has equal input as far as possible. As well as the legal issues that may need to be addressed for settlement to occur, parties come to mediation with issues and concerns that are not necessarily within the legal context. The legal representative may be hearing these for the first time. The mediator may identify these and encourage the parties to have some discussion on them. It has been found that parties sometimes cannot go forward to settlement unless there has been an airing of all concerns, both legal and non-legal, which are important to them.

As mentioned previously, one useful way of assisting both the mediator and the parties is for the representative to contribute to the range of options for settlement based on their professional experience.

Consultation

Where it is appropriate, the lawyer may discuss with the mediator, with the other lawyer and with the client such legal, evidentiary, practical or personal matters which the parties or the mediator may raise.

Adjusting advice

It may be necessary for legal representatives to adjust original advice on hearing the other party's version and perhaps take some further instructions from the client in the light of changed perceptions. It is not uncommon that information emerging may promote a different perspective.

Preparing the settlement terms

The legal representatives will usually prepare the terms of settlement or heads of agreement in accordance with the settlement reached at the end of the mediation for signature by the parties before they leave.

Good faith participation

If a legal representative forms the view before or during the mediation that the other party is not participating in good faith this issue should be raised with the client and/or the mediator. As previously noted, in very rare cases it may be the legal representative who is not participating in good faith. This should be raised by the mediator in a private session with the legal representative.

Mediation standards

There is a high standard of conduct required of a mediator. It is not the mediator's role to give advice or opinions, make suggestions that may disadvantage a party, propose or endorse possible outcomes or support either party's view. If a legal representative is of the view that these standards, particularly relating to neutrality, are not being met a private meeting with the mediator should be immediately requested.

Note: Contributions to the above discussion on the role of legal representatives by Sir Laurence Street, Bernadette Rogers and the Dispute Resolution Committee of the New South Wales Law Society are acknowledged.

Chapter

20

How neutral are we?

THE CONCEPT OF NEUTRALITY

Defining neutrality and impartiality

The terms "neutrality" and "impartiality" are often used interchangeably. Both terms commonly appear in Agreements to Mediate. Some writers have attempted to define different applications for the two terms. In other cases, there is no attempt at separate definitions, nor agreement on what the differences are.

Dictionary definitions[1] describe the terms in this way:

Neutral — Taking no part with either side, especially not assisting either of two belligerents; indifferent, impartial; a person that stands aloof from a contest.

Impartial — Not partial; not favouring one party or one side more than another; equitably disinterested.

Regardless of whether there is a separation or blending of the two terms, one writer has stated:

I, for one, do not believe Mediation is a process involving neutrality and as far as I am concerned, the only neutral mediator is a **DEAD ONE** (authors' emphasis).[2]

....

[1] *Concise English Dictionary* (1985 edn), pp 772 and 586 respectively.

[2] Tillett, G, *Domestic Violence Mediation Workshop* (Sydney, 26 October 1991).

291

Is the only neutral mediator a dead one?

Dr Tillett points out that we human beings by definition are not neutral. All have values and personal preferences. All carry the whole baggage of our past with us whether we are mediating or participating. All are susceptible to social pressures, cultural norms, sex roles and stereotypes.

Perceptions

Despite Dr Tillett's statement, he acknowledges the need for mediators to be, as well as to be seen to be, neutral.[3] The authors agree with this approach. Another writer points out that the loss of impartiality is as much a matter of party perception as it is of a mediator's objective behaviour.[4] A mediator or co-mediators may be unaware that parties may perceive them as being biased from the outset because of factors outside their control.

Case Note

Many years ago, the authors were co-mediating a family matter between a male and a female. The male party appeared increasingly tense and became verbally aggressive towards one of us. The co-mediator attempted to restrain his attitude towards her colleague but this only exacerbated his hostility. The other mediator then asked if he was feeling uncomfortable being the only male person there. He confirmed that he was uncomfortable and would prefer not to continue. The mediators referred the matter back to the agency to arrange for a gender balanced mediation team.

This particular scenario highlights the need to check with the parties about potential difficulties relating to neutrality perception arising from gender or culture, preferably at the intake stage.

The neutrality contract

Neutrality is one of the central philosophical concepts of mediation. It underpins the practice of mediation and sets it apart from most other

---

[3] Tillet, G, *Resolving Conflict. A Practical Approach* (Sydney University Press, 1991).

[4] Boule, L, *Mediation — Skills and Techniques* (Butterworths, 2001), p 258.

forms of dispute resolution. The Agreements to Mediate (that is, contracts) which include the rights and responsibilities of mediator and parties invariably include a clause stating that "The mediator will be neutral and impartial". A mediator's opening statement stresses the practitioner's neutral role. But what is the speaker thinking of as he or she makes this statement? What are the different shades of meaning for individual practitioners?

The neutrality assurance in the mediator's opening statement is so automatic, so standard. Some might argue it is also self-serving in the sense that such automatic assurance, of itself, may be seen as sufficient to take care of whatever follows, regardless of any subsequent impression that the mediator might create.

Breaching the contract

A breach of neutrality may arise from factors involving the subconscious or unawareness, including unconscious bias. The neutrality breach is identified most easily where the mediator strays into the advice, opinion-giving territory. Other areas of breach can be more subtle and yet have still been identified by mediation clients. Contributing factors may be simply a lack of skill, including the inability to reframe or to "reality test" in a non-threatening manner; communication deficiencies; unequal opportunities; attitude; temperament; or where poor initial training compounds problems arising in subsequent practice.

There is enough anecdotal and, in some cases, empirical evidence to suggest that some mediators consistently either breach the neutrality contract or fail to create a perception of neutrality. More worrisome is that they can be blissfully unaware of this. With some, there may be a very narrow concept of what is encompassed within the term neutrality. For example, that it merely relates to refraining from blatantly taking sides, or providing legal advice on how parties should settle.

A practitioner may have never been exposed to the big picture through training, debriefing methods or other forms of quality control or have an understanding of all the nuances which can contribute to a perception in the parties of a lack of neutrality. Such lack of appreciation can have a profound effect on one or both parties resulting in a loss of trust and sometimes the failure of the mediation process.[5]

---

[5] Boule, n 4.

The psychology of neutrality

Achieving neutrality is essential if the trust of each party is to be gained and maintained. When gained, a mediator may confidently use the full gambit of skills to facilitate a resolution. If trust is lost with a party because he or she perceives a lack of neutrality on the part of the mediator, no amount of skills or strategies is likely to encourage resolution.

Case Note

The mediator was an experienced arbitrator and expert in his field, who occasionally was asked to mediate. One "technique" was to express his opinion in joint session as to which argument he favoured. This caused the representatives of one party to preen themselves, while the representatives of the other party cringed and lost face. At least the mediator was "even-handed" in that he tended to alternate his opinions between the parties. Perhaps that was his idea of neutrality. The result was that he lost the trust of both parties and the mediation became a contest as to which adviser was right. After one day, the decision-maker for each party refused to mediate further and instead met separately from advisers and the mediator to resolve the dispute.

This mediator did not understand the psychology involved in facilitating a resolution. It did not depend on trust in his learned opinions, as he may have thought. It required him to create doubt in both parties' minds in private session, not to reinforce one party's belief in its case at the expense of the other at any one time. Loss of the parties' trust spilled into the private session. Neither could trust him not to reveal all to the other party should a sounding be taken in private session. His actions rendered him peripheral to the dispute, one other reason being that the parties did not believe they were getting what they expected in terms of mediation.

Where a point of view is offered, "at least one party would lose trust in the mediator, if they would not stand to benefit from the expressed view."[6]

---

[6] Boule, n 4, p 266.

> **Case Note**
>
> "A businesswoman I interviewed reported on an unsatisfactory mediation experience where the mediation was run on the adversarial lines she had sought to avoid when seeking mediation. The mediator did not adhere to the neutrality principle and at an early stage gave an unsolicited legal opinion. The opinion was biased towards the other party."[7]

THE DIRTY DOZEN (AND COUNTING) — WHAT TO AVOID

There are at least a dozen identifiable areas where mediators stray into the no-go zone, and have been observed to breach the neutrality contract. These areas have been identified by trainers, service providers, co-mediators and parties. Some parties, who are repeat players, have a "black list" of mediators whose services they will no longer use for reasons of perceived bias. There is thus a professional and financial inducement to avoid the "dirty dozen".

1. Treating parties differently

This is multi-faceted, but it can include an intense concentration on one party for a long period of time, such as prolonged questioning or allowing one party to dominate or monologue. With a one-party focus, the other party is (and will feel) blotted out and may perceive this as mediator bias. Alternatively, the party being questioned extensively may feel belittled.

> **Case Note**
>
> Party A stated that she would like to arrange a particular parenting program for one year and then another for the following years when the child started school. She was invited to give her proposal for Year 1. Having allowed the tabling of this proposal the mediator then invited her to give her proposal for Year 2. The father quite rightly protested that he would like to give his proposal for Year 1, or at least respond to his ex-partner's proposal, before she tabled her Year 2 proposal. This manner of proceeding not only gave precedence to one party, but in the eyes of Party B displayed a gender bias in favour of the mother.

[7] Garwood, M, "Managing Quality of ADR for Commercial Disputes" (1999) 10 ADRJ 173.

This one-party focus was a simple slip on the part of the mediator and yet the other party felt effectively sidelined and peripheral to the exercise. It was interpreted as a gender bias, when none actually existed.

As mentioned in Chapter 3, another very common observation is the mediator asking the second speaker to "respond" to the first speaker's opening statement, thus putting them on the defensive. Further, such an approach may result in the second speaker directing their statement to Party A rather than to the mediator. This can often lead to hostile exchanges where there is disagreement with what is being said. Moreover, the first speaker will not subsequently have the same opportunity to "respond" to the second speaker's opening statement.

2. The complacency factor — does familiarity breed contempt?

Case Note

A program director made this comment in a newsletter:

> We [need] ... to make sure that familiarity and complacency don't allow us to give less than the best attention to each session. This involves ensuring that we are not only impartial, but are clearly seen to be impartial ... It is hard sometimes to find the line between option generation and reality testing (which we need to do) and becoming an adviser/expert/counsellor (which other people need to do) ... Clearly, if advice is being given the quality of the mediation is questionable.

Complacency and familiarity resulting in not giving "the best attention to each session" may involve conducting each case in a stereotyped manner and forgetting that each case is unique, even if the topic (for example, neighbourhood conflict) may be commonplace. Complacency may involve a foregone conclusion that one party should change its position. The Director of another mediation program became concerned that, where a party sought to change parenting arrangements or to increase/decrease child support payments, the mediators tended to focus primarily on the initiator's story. Further, they failed to give an equal airing to the issues and concerns of the party who wished to maintain the status quo.

Similarly, videoed simulations have sometimes revealed the trap of practitioners taking up one person's line and running with it. This was most usually the plaintiff's line, the initiator's line or the complainant's line. The sessions were then conducted on the basis that it was for the respondent party to admit, concede to or accommodate the other party. How often might we all do this, albeit unwittingly, overlooking the fact that a party has the right, and in some cases, the obligation (for example, for child safety reasons), to mediate to maintain the status quo.

3. Judgmental language

Language use applies to both the written and spoken word. Mediators' lists of issues have included such expressions as:

"Late delivery";

"Harassment";

"Money owing";

"Poor communication";

"Defective work".

All of these expressions are capable of being reframed into neutral language. One basic whiteboard rule is "forget about adjectives". Adjectives are almost always slanted in one party's favour.

Similarly, with the spoken word:

How do you think Party A will react to your offer of only $50,000?

The use of the adjective in a private session immediately created an impression of judgment, pressure or mediator disapproval. Did this "small offer" create difficulties for the mediator in achieving early resolution, or any resolution? Further, the mediator was unwittingly telegraphing to Party B some of the discussion with Party A, namely that the proposed offer was a long way apart from the offer that Party A had discussed with the mediator in the first private session. What about confidentiality in all its aspects?

Even an innocent comment in joint session such as "That's a good idea", may produce discomfort in one party. The latter may not think it's a good idea and sees the mediator as supporting the opposition. Further, the party whose idea it was, is reinforced in its position and may become reluctant to compromise. Another simple comment such as "of course" might also be seen as a value judgment as it is likely to indicate that the mediator agrees with a party's statement whereas the purpose of the comment may have been to convey, "of course, I have heard you".

4. The temperamentally unsuited

The idea of being a mediator is so appealing that it attracts persons of both suitable and unsuitable temperaments. "Like acting or playing in a rock band, there is a certain glamour associated with being a mediator."[8] Whatever its attractions, maintaining neutrality is the most difficult and the most exhausting area of mediation practice. One of the most important attributes of a mediator is patience. Those who advocate that advice giving or suggestion making is okay (as a short-cut to resolution) may be temperamentally unsuited to mediation practice in all its facets.

In reality, many professional people are not used to working with two people in conflict in the same room at the same time. The comfort zone is the one-to-one adviser-client situation. There may be a low tolerance for debate. Even-handedness proves to be problematic. The early "escape" into private session is usually rationalised on the basis that the parties were arguing or, at any rate, not agreeing.[9] The value of parties speaking directly to each other is not grasped. Nor is the value of getting all the views on the table prior to undertaking private sessions. Unfortunately, private sessions, because of the overriding principle of confidentiality, often provide a shelter to the mediator who cannot resist giving advice, and this leads to loss of neutrality.

Untoward pressurising or getting too involved in decision-making may represent an easy way out for the temperamentally unsuited. There have been several Supreme Court cases that contain an allegation of duress being applied by a mediator. In *State Bank of NSW v Freeman*,[10] Freeman had alleged that the mediator had placed him under "sustained and unconscionable duress" during the afternoon session of the mediation.

5. Debating the facts or establishing "proof"

It is not a mediator's role to enter into a debate with one of the parties, even if the latter is contradicting themselves or an untruth has been revealed. Nor is it appropriate to seek proof of what one person is saying or inappropriately encourage production of evidence. Such actions may provoke an argument over an issue in which the mediator has no stake. It is up to the parties themselves to challenge any statement in joint session and for the mediator to carefully weigh up whether the matter should be raised in private session. An exception to this caution could be where there are allegations of child abuse in a parenting mediation, for example. In such a case it might be prudent to ask privately whether the matter has been reported to the police.

---

[8] Lewis, P, "Lots of Planes but no Hangar" (1997) 8 ADRJ 154 at 155.

[9] See Chapter 12 — "Shuttle negotiation and shuttle mediation".

[10] (Unreported, NSW Sup CT, 31 January 1996).

6. Questioning techniques

In role plays, it is not uncommon to see a mediator embarking on an inquisition with one party after their opening statement in such a way as to produce a complete loss of face in front of the other party. Other joint session questioning can also severely disadvantage one or other of the parties.

Case Note

In a mediation which involved the issue of the timing of delivery of goods, one of the parties complained later that the mediator had said to the opposing party: "Oh, and how many other times did he deliver the goods late?"

This is not only an example of an interrogation but also displays a lack of skill or practice in other techniques which might have been used to elicit this information if it had been considered to be important. Usually, any inquisition is conducted for the benefit of a mediator who is experiencing discomfort if he or she does not know all the facts. This can be irritating to the parties, as well as unfair to one or other of them. Questioning, whatever form it takes, should be done sparingly and only to give the parties a greater understanding, not enlighten a fact-hungry mediator.

7. Party B's private session

A tendency to run with one person's story in joint session (see above) can carry through to the private sessions. Video simulations have shown that the person who had the first private session has been the more advantaged party. Mediators tended to thoroughly explore that person's issues and concerns and what that person was seeking. Commonly, mediators did not go through the same procedure with Party B. Often Party B was confronted with an attitude implying that: "This is what Party A wants, what are you going to do about it?"

Adopting a practice of giving an assurance to both parties, that the content of the private sessions will as far as possible be the same for both of them, may also be a reminder to the mediator to ensure that this will be so. The mediator can do this prior to the private sessions, or give this assurance at the start of each person's private session. Party B is usually waiting patiently for the private session with Party A to come to an end, perhaps uneasy or suspicious of what Party A is saying to the mediator.

If, during Party B's private session, the focus tends to be on conveying what Party A wants, these suspicions will be confirmed. Further, the image of mediator neutrality becomes easily tainted, with Party B ready to form the impression that the mediator either agrees with, or has been influenced by, Party A.

8. Co-operating in a hijack

A mediator who allows one party to flaunt the courtesy or non-interruption guidelines on an ongoing basis may be perceived as favouring that party or at least disadvantaging the other party. A similar situation might arise if the mediator gives in to a party threatening to discontinue unless they are granted an instant private session with the mediator.

Case Note

The second situation arose where a co-mediation was being conducted by teleconference. An aggressive party was making demands about how the process should be conducted. The less experienced mediator, without consulting her colleague, agreed that he be accommodated, her motivation being that he would continue to disrupt the process, and make life difficult for the mediators unless his demands were acceded to. This may well have been the case, but what was not appreciated by the less experienced mediator was the effect the mediators' compliance might have on the other party.

In such cases, some other strategy[11] should have been considered to overcome any perception of the mediator co-operating in a hijack.

9. The mediator's agenda

A common scenario arises where the mediator is tunnel-visioned on their own idea of what settlement should be, commonly known as "The Mediator's Agenda".[12] It is often very obvious to a mediator how a matter might be settled, particularly if a similar problem has been settled a certain way before. A temptation arises to steer the session along tracks that lead to a particular solution, selectively employing interventions to this end and ignoring other factors. One or both parties may be

---

[11] See Chapter 22 — "Party- and mediator-driven problems".

[12] See Chapter 22 — "Party- and mediator-driven problems".

disadvantaged. In this case, the "mediator's agenda" can incorporate the "complacency factor" discussed above.

The mediator's agenda can also involve an "I know what's best for you" element, thinking "This is how it should be settled". This is compounded where a mediator not only acts on their own agenda, but in fact compiles their own list of discussion topics on the basis that "These are the issues I think are important for you to discuss". Further, a problem that might seem complex to the parties may seem very simple to a repeat mediator.

Case Note

In a recent "fishbowl" simulation, the mediator began by saying "Now this is a very simple dispute".

This comment raises two issues. First, it implies a judgment on the part of the mediator and possibly telegraphs a view that the dispute should have been resolved earlier or that not too much time need be expended on it. Second, very rarely do parties see their dispute as "simple". If that was, in fact, the case, it may very likely have been resolved without the need for mediation. Such categorisation of a dispute by the mediator prior to a session is another facet of the mediator's agenda.

10. Dislike of a party or representative (or when to hold your breath and sit on your hands)

Where a mediator recognises that he or she is experiencing a feeling of dislike or annoyance towards a party or representative, that practitioner will be on guard about allowing this to show or impact on even-handedness. However, dislike or frustration can manifest itself in other less obvious ways that may be unrecognised by the mediator.

Case Note

A mediator felt he had overcome a body language problem that he had become aware of some years before. However, more recently an observer at a commercial mediation drew him aside at morning tea break and said, "Do you realise that every time so-and-so spoke you rolled your eyes?"

This is an example of where, no matter how scrupulously impartial a mediator may try to be, the body language give-away may be severely embarrassing. Leaning, eye-balling, impatience or restlessness may all mirror an attitude towards one or other of the participants. Certain hand movements, such as finger jabbing, can be very offensive. A videoed session can be a useful check. Another may be to ask a co-mediator, if there is one, to take note of any repetitive body language that may be either distracting or offensive. A family member can also provide feed-back on these habits.

11. Settlement hunger

This has been identified as the most chronic, problematic and commonly reported area where neutrality and mediators part company.

Feedback from the repeat players consistently raises a concern about settlement pressure. This is different from the "mediator's agenda" which carries with it the temptation to pursue one's own idea of what the settlement should be. Here the mediator is just "settlement hungry" in the sense that the hunger for a settlement, any type of settlement, overrides other important considerations.

It is inevitable that mediators seek a settlement as the normal outcome of their practice. After all, our role is to assist in facilitating this. Isn't this what mediation is all about? Settlement enhances our job satisfaction whereas non-settlement can make us soul-search about what might have been, what else we could have done or what could have been done differently. Such soul searching is far less likely to occur when a settlement has been achieved.

What can happen when the settlement drive becomes over-powerful or all-consuming? In videoed assessments, it has been noted that even in situations where an accreditation candidate has been reassured that a positive assessment will in no way depend on whether the matter settles, some pursue settlement as if their lives depended on it. Conversely where a simulated settlement is achieved, it can be puzzling to the candidate if the performance was assessed as less than average, because "after all, I settled it".

Settlement hunger has been observed to produce what amounts to harassment of a party who was not agreeing to the settlement that was being proposed by the other party and often robustly endorsed by the mediator. In cases where neutrality had been scrupulously observed up to the settlement option stage, a sensing of "settlement blood" appeared to result in all objectivity flying out of the window in pursuit of a resolution.

There is no doubt that some mediators experience the doldrums over a non-settlement. There is a tendency to take this personally, particularly in the early years of practice. There may also be a concern about repeat work. How often do we hear a mediator say "I have a 90% settlement rate". The idea of a high settlement rate being the measure of a "good" mediator is alive and well, as some CVs will attest. However, in a journal article, an author[13] drew an analogy between a real estate agent and a mediator. He said:

> I would be cautious of a real estate agent who boasted about a high "success" rate. It would suggest to me that the agent may be using pressure tactics to get vendors to sell cheaply or purchasers to rush into purchasing. Similarly, I would be cautious of a mediator who claimed a high "success" rate.

On the other hand, a sequence of non-settlements can be disheartening for even the most hardened practitioner and might also provide some scope for analysis. This sequence may be due to bad luck or coincidence; to a practice method that has become a recent habit; or to an indifferent or complacent attitude which has developed. Perhaps the person is simply going through a stale period. It happens. Whatever the reason, mediators should not necessarily feel they are to blame, particularly in cases where parties remain entrenched because they have a greater need to disagree than to settle.

A bonus for mediators, in contrast to some other dispute resolvers, is that we are liberated from a settlement decision. Indeed, some negotiators who represent themselves or parties have commented on mediators who unduly interfere in the settlement negotiations, and yet do not seem to have the skills to do so without ruffling feathers.

At least 20% of matters do not settle at mediation. All mediators are part of that 20% or, according to the writer quoted above, they should be if they are sticking to the neutrality contract.

Case Note

A respected mediator rang the agency that had allocated a matter to him. He reported that the matter had not settled and added "I'm afraid I failed". The agency person responded: "No, they failed."

---

[13] Davenport, P, "What is Wrong with Mediation" (1997) 8 ADRJ 133.

Settlement hunger has been encouraged by statistics emerging from organisations, agencies and courts on settlement rates. These statistics are often produced to demonstrate the success of the program or, in some cases, to justify its existence. In some such cases, employed staff have been known to comment unfavourably to a mediator when a settlement does not result. Might some mental reframing lead to a change? For example, instead of "I settled it", perhaps the reframe should be "They settled it". Instead of thinking "Oh dear, I failed" the thought might be "I did my best but they decided not to settle it". Instead of "I got them to settle", substitute "We all worked hard and they got there in the end".

12. The too hard basket

It is an exquisite confidence boost when our first and early mediations settle. However, in the following illustration Mr X QC, in common with some other high profile or successful professionals, fell into the trap of thinking that professional expertise was instantly transferable to mediation expertise.

Case Note

The very first mediation of Mr X QC did not settle. The person who debriefed with him reported that he was quite devastated. However, he took steps to ensure that his subsequent mediations, allocated under the particular program, did settle. In fact, two serious complaints were received by the program administrator about the way he operated, and which led one insurer to abandon participation in the program.

A rude awakening for some trainees and new practitioners is that mediating can be difficult and far different to lawyering, negotiating or counselling. Maintaining neutrality is part of this challenge.

Several myths attach to mediation practice: one is the "Anyone can mediate" myth; and another is "I've been mediating all my life". The latter is particularly prevalent among negotiators who have represented parties and among relationship counsellors. "Tuned-in" trainees soon recognise that perhaps they haven't been mediating all their life after all and that mediating involves much more than just settling a matter, one task being to neutrally manage discussions between two disputing parties rather than just providing advice to one.

Trainers have observed that when professional people articulate their awareness of the difficulties they are experiencing in changing hats, this sensitivity is often a pointer to them becoming a switched-on mediator. Where difficulties are observed that a trainee does not acknowledge or will not accept, does it point to the reverse? Some trainers may think so.

When Mr X QC fell into the black hole, he resorted to his comfort zone. He recommended how parties should settle and told them the actual figure. The neutrality principle, with its need for patience and balance, was just too hard for him to follow, particularly accompanied by the risk of failure to resolve.

13. Advice giving

One of the outcomes of the "too-hard" basket is that an unskilled lawyer mediator may resort to unsolicited legal advice that can also extend to settlement suggestions. Apart from the "too-hard" basket, it can sometimes be difficult for a mediator to keep a rein on their legal expertise particularly where they are familiar with the subject matter and its court outcomes:

> She wouldn't get 80% in court, so it's foolish to maintain that position in mediation. She should take her ex-partner's offer of 60%, and run.

It should not be denied that these thoughts have passed through the mind of many an experienced lawyer/mediator, particularly so with unrepresented parties. Most take great pains to not articulate them, despite the doubt about a particular position held should the matter proceed to court.

14. The Flat Earth Society — a personal challenge

Members of the Flat Earth Society are convinced, contrary to all scientific evidence, that the Earth is flat. To argue otherwise amounts to heresy. Thus, a party may push a button for a flat-earth mediator when she says in her opening statement:

> As sure as the Earth is round, he doesn't even know when the kids' birthdays are.

Two points emerge from this tongue-in-cheek example. First, the mediator doesn't even hear the substantive statement about the kids because a tightly-held personal belief has been challenged and has become the focus of the statement. Second, the mediator may start judging the speaker. So, even if the statement has been heard in its entirety, the mediator may discount what is being said as a result of discounting the speaker as a person who holds an opposing (or even bizarre) view.

We may all be flat-earthers in one way or another in the sense that a challenge to our personal beliefs may cause a reaction that impacts on the mediation or a party.

15. Conscious and unconscious personal values

The Flat Earth syndrome represents a challenge to a personal, political or philosophical point of view. Mediators can guard against these reactions when experience has led us to become aware of our conditioned responses. With awareness, we take pains to ensure our reactions do not intrude into our mediation practice. But what happens when a button is pushed for the first time or when our reactions result from something in the subconscious? It is where we are not consciously aware that trouble may arise.

Case Note

A number of co-mediators had identified a bias by a community mediator against dog owners. This puzzled the mediator in question when it was first raised as he had always considered himself to be an animal lover. On reflection, he realised he had become more annoyed of late when local dog owners did not clean up after their pets in his own neighbourhood. He conceded that this annoyance may have subconsciously extended to those people who allowed their dogs to bark through the night unchecked, even though he personally had not been disturbed by night-time barking. He subsequently acknowledged that he might always find it difficult to be even-handed with insensitive dog owners, whatever form the insensitivity might take, and so made the decision to decline any neighbourhood disputes which involved dogs, barking or otherwise.

---

16. The power balancing factor

Power balancing, so called in support of a perceived weaker person, may be dangerous and may in itself lead to a loss of neutrality. Boulle states that mediators do have some responsibility over the power issue but that responsibility should revolve mainly around their control of the process of mediation. "Mediators", he states, "are not the advocates of the less powerful party, nor the champions of the poor and oppressed."[14]

---

[14] Boulle, L, *Mediation Skills and Techniques* (Butterworths, 2001), p 225. See also Chapter 21 — "Power issues".

POOR TRAINING/BAD PRACTICE

Many of the "Dirty Dozen" stem from poor training that leads to bad practice. In many mediation courses, the issue of neutrality is dealt with in a somewhat perfunctory way. Because of time constraints, the focus tends to be on defining it in an academic sense rather than demonstrating how it operates in a practical way. Where a role-playing trainee may be advised of the more blatant infringements, the more subtle aspects may not be raised or even recognised. This lack of recognition may particularly stem from those cases where a trainer has little or no coal face mediation experience but is basically training on paper knowledge or anecdotal information. It would assist trainees if they could at least be given a written outline on the practical aspects of neutrality and on those subtleties that are frequently overlooked.

Table 20.1: Dos and Don'ts for Creating a Perception of Neutrality

Dos	Don'ts
1. THE CONCEPT of NEUTRALITY	
• Be aware of the need to be seen to be neutral by the parties.	• Don't take it for granted that the mediation process or assertion of neutrality will ensure the parties' perception of neutrality.
2. TREAT PARTIES EVEN-HANDEDLY	
• Focus equally on each party during joint sessions.	• Don't devote more attention to one party than the other.
• Apply interventions equitably to both parties.	• Don't summarise only one party's statement or dialogue or role reverse with only one party.
• Maintain a balance between the parties' verbal exchanges.	• Don't allow one party to dominate the discussions.
• Provide parties with alternate turns in proposing options for settlement.	• Don't ask one party to list all their options before asking the other party.
• Recognise there may be power imbalances.	• Don't seek to correct power imbalance by favouring the less powerful party.
• Explore in the second party's private session, the interests of that party in the same manner as for the first party.	• Don't commence second party's private session with what came out of the first private session.

Dos	Don'ts
3. USING APPROPRIATE LANGUAGE AND ASKING APPROPRIATE QUESTIONS	
• Use non-judgmental language in spoken and written word.	• Don't use judgmental or non-neutral words, and avoid adjectives.
• Avoid affirmative expressions of support.	• Don't use expressions like "of course" or "that's a good idea".
• Focus on asking open-ended questions and keep closed questions to a minimum.	• Don't adopt an inquisitorial or cross-examining approach.
• Be aware of reasons for asking questions, and avoid fact finding.	• Don't ask in joint session questions that put a party on the spot.
4. MEDIATOR'S ACTIONS	
• Be aware of and control personal values and prejudices.	• Don't make statements that include your personal opinion.
• Use the content of parties' statements to determine agenda.	• Don't adopt mediator's agenda or define what you think the parties should discuss.
• Encourage parties and advisers to exchange opinions.	• Don't offer opinion or advice, even if asked by a party, as one party will be disadvantaged compared to the other.
• Allow parties to propose options for settlement and remember the mediator has no stake in outcome.	• Don't tell the parties how they should resolve the matter and don't pressure them to accept a settlement.

THE LAST WORD

This discussion began by identifying that a key neutrality factor is how the mediator may be perceived by the parties. It is probably far easier to define what is not neutrality, based on parties' perceptions, than to explain what it is.

By analogy, most people know what a hippopotamus looks like, but many would be challenged in describing it and most would have difficulty drawing one.

Chapter

21

Power issues

THE CONCEPT OF POWER IMBALANCE

No one really doubts the existence of power imbalance or inequalities between parties that have the potential of affecting the mediation session and final outcome. The problem is whether or not power can be balanced between the parties by the mediator's faithful adherence to the mediation process.

Some mediators, especially newly trained ones, believe or are encouraged to believe that the process itself looks after pre-existing power imbalances. However, the situation is far more complex. To rely on the "magic of the process" and waving the mediator's magic wand can be naïve to say the least. It is always necessary to be creative and apply appropriate strategic interventions.

It should always be remembered that power is a dynamic, not a static, concept. The balance of power tends to shift from one party to the other depending on the issue being explored, discussed or negotiated. It is extremely rare that only one of the parties is the most powerful at every stage of the mediation.

A great deal of literature on mediation focuses on inequalities of power and what mediators should or can do to redress any imbalances. Imbalances can be identified in terms of gender, culture, generation; one-shot and repeat players; the individual and the big institution; the legally and non-legally aided; the inarticulate and the assertive; the wealthy and not so wealthy; and knowledgeable and the ignorant or ill-advised.

Another potential area of inequality can be created when only one of the parties pays for the mediation session. That person may be perceived by the non-paying party as being more powerful and be in a position of getting the mediator on-side. (This of course does not apply to organisations that provide mediation or conciliation free of charge to the parties.) On the other hand, the non-paying party may be in a powerful position, as they have staked nothing financially and may treat the matter in a less than committed manner.

Although mediators do not doubt the existence of power imbalances, the concept of the balance of power has attracted differences of opinion. For example Bernard Mayer[1] believes that the balance of power concept is somewhat confusing if not meaningless. He considers as misleading the idea that power can be balanced so as to produce some equality or even equivalence of power. The concept of power he maintains is elusive as it is manifested in so many different ways.

What Mayer says has some validity. However, it is still important for mediators to attempt to ensure that a party is not placed at a disadvantage when communicating, negotiating or attempting to reach settlement by applying the process equitably. Any perception on the part of the mediator of power imbalance or inequality needs to be tested, preferably in private session. It should be kept in mind that it is unrealistic in a few hours to remedy pre-existing inequalities which become evident not only during mediation but also in the course of litigation as well as other dispute resolution processes.

Power imbalance and domestic violence

A number of authors have commented on the controversial matter of whether mediation or other non-judicial forums of dispute resolution are appropriate when dealing with the issue of domestic violence. It is always important to check with the party who was (and may still be) a victim of domestic violence whether he or she can take part in a mediation without feeling at a disadvantage or overpowered. Preferably, this should be done prior to the mediation. However, the information relating to domestic violence may only become evident in the course of the mediation, usually during a private session. If it does become evident, the mediator should determine whether it is affecting the party's participation in the mediation in any way. The party who was the victim of domestic violence may feel more comfortable continuing the mediation in the form of shuttle mediation. In the authors' experience, possible power imbalance has not constituted a major or even a minor problem. This is largely due to the fact that there has been little to no contact between the parties for some time.

[1] Mayer, B, *The Dynamics of Conflict Resolution* (Jossey-Bass, 2000), pp 51 and 53.

The complications of the power topic deserve more comprehensive treatment than can be allocated here. The question frequently raised is whether mediators can or should redress power imbalances and still maintain their neutrality.

Power of the mediator

It has been observed that it is the mediator who holds most of the power in mediation. This practitioner guides the parties through the process, frames the questions and initiates the interventions, draws out the silent party, reality tests the fairness of the agreement and the comfort level of the parties with options and proposed settlements.

Drawing on the experience of many hundreds of mediations we have found that power is seldom what it seems. A new mediator who enters the arena with preconceived notions of power imbalances may receive some surprises. Power in the outside world does not necessarily translate to the mediation forum. Therefore, because of the nebulous nature of the concept of power balance, it is wise for the mediator not to act on the basis of preconceived ideas.

Contrary to some preconceived or theoretical notions:

1. If either party is convinced that they could do better in another forum they are free to choose that forum.

2. Silence can be more powerful than articulation in certain situations.

3. Children and adolescents have tremendous power over their parents.

4. Big institutions and individual managers have as much at stake in finding a cost and time effective settlement as the "one-shot" player.

5. Domestic violence survivors have often been found to be very positional in mediation. Far from the intimidated woman cowering in the corner of the room, so often portrayed in some of the literature, this person has often become empowered through the very act of leaving the destructive relationship and has progressed in confidence and awareness of her rights since that time.[2]

6. The so-called weaker party can be as manipulative as any other participant — although in a very disguised manner. It is sometimes manifested in the form of ready tears to gain the mediator's sympathy.

---

[2] See Charlton, R, *Dispute Resolution Guidebook* (LBC Information Services, 2000), pp 164–6.

7. Legally aided clients have advantages over their non-legally aided opponents.

In some cases where it is perceived that one party is feeling intimidated by the other:

❚ the dialogue is better conducted in the triangular fashion, that is, through the mediator, rather than directly;

❚ the mediator should give frequent summaries;

❚ the mediator should ensure that each party has equal floor space; and

❚ the mediator should intervene where one party tends to monologue.

In some other cases an early private session may be in order to redress any imbalance and give confidence to the party perceived as the weaker.

Lack of knowledge is a prime source of power imbalance. Parties should always mediate from a position of knowledge, whether it be legal, financial or with regard to other future implications. If they do not have this knowledge the session should be postponed or terminated until such advice is obtained. It is essential that parties are ready to make informed decisions in the course of reaching settlement.

Where a gross power imbalance appears to exist, the parties should be given the option of sleeping on their decision and a deadline should be negotiated for acceptance or otherwise of settlement proposals, or arrangements should be made for a second session.

In the end, the decision to mediate, to continue, or to settle must rest with the parties. Mediators are there to guide the parties through the process in the most equitable manner possible. They are not there to function as members of the "we know what's best for you" brigade.

Party- and mediator-driven problems

PARTY-DRIVEN PROBLEMS

The hidden agenda and bad faith participation

Mediators should be wary of making an early decision that one or other of the parties has a "hidden agenda" and then proceeding on that basis. There is sometimes too much emphasis placed on this rather catchy-sounding concept in training courses and in the mediation literature. An early reluctance to settle or to disclose all relevant information should not automatically be interpreted as signifying that the parties are hiding, or at least refusing to disclose, something of significance. This is more likely to be a negotiating strategy. In practice hidden agendas are rare. Parties' motivations are more likely to be all too obvious.

Face-saving is not a hidden agenda and is a factor in most disputes (see Chapter 16 — "Strategic mediator interventions"). A reluctance to settle, where both have been stating that settlement is their aim, is often due to some issue not having been given sufficient ventilation, the omission of an acknowledgment or some other emotional factor. Or that a proposed settlement offer is simply not commercially viable.

If mediators become convinced that motivations are suspect and are affecting the mediation, they should raise their concerns with the parties in private session. The following case note is an illustration of what is sometimes referred to as the "fishing expedition".

Case Note

One of the authors became suspicious where an initiating party appeared to be taking an uncharacteristically passive role in a mediation. The party took copious notes while the other party was talking, and generally appeared to be evasive with regard to the mediator's encouragement to communicate with the other party. A private session was called. The mediator then advised of her concern about what she had observed and asked if anything was amiss. She advised that she was finding it extremely difficult to continue in the circumstances where one party was being forthcoming and the other party was not.

After some more gentle probing and an elaboration of the mediator's observations, the party admitted that he had initiated the mediation on the strength of legal advice to find out whether there would be any surprises with regard to a forthcoming Supreme Court case. The mediator advised that she was not prepared to continue in such circumstances and further that she no longer felt bound by the confidentiality of the private session. She asked the party how she should best explain the termination to the other party and he indicated his consent to a proposed explanation being given. Although he said he was willing to continue in good faith if the other party was prepared to go on, in this particular case the mediator exercised her right to terminate the session.

Generally, confronting one or other of the parties with the bad faith issue is difficult because the mediator might be wrong or might receive a hostile or defensive response. The best practice is to proceed on the basis that the mediator has observed certain reactions of the parties to the mediation or observed the form the mediation has taken and "in confidence" ask whether there is something he or she needs to be told. Another way is to conduct a private session with the good faith party, ascertain their reaction to the way the session is going and, if they have observed the same behaviour, ask their permission to raise their concerns with the other party. Generally, in this situation the mediator needs to proceed with caution.

Case Note

This was a case where the other party's solicitor reacted angrily in joint session as a result of receiving what he perceived to be an insulting offer after three hours of mediation. All issues had been explored and enough doubt had been created to encourage parties to move substantially off fixed positions.

In private session the mediator was able to take up the point of the solicitor's anger and said, "Do you think the other side was indicating that you didn't come here in good faith?", followed by "Would you like the other side to leave this mediation with the perception that you didn't participate in good faith?" This relieved the mediator of the responsibility of having to raise the matter on the strength of her own observation. This confrontation resulted in a substantially increased offer, albeit one which the other party did not consider sufficient.

In this case the bad faith lawyer appeared to be shamed by having his ulterior motive exposed by the mediator. The matter did not settle at mediation, but settled a few weeks later on similar terms to those discussed following the bad faith confrontation.

Requests to the mediator for advice, opinions, to witness documents

Parties will sometimes ask a mediator how they should settle or what the mediator thinks they should do. Naturally the mediator responds by reinforcing their non-advising role. Mediators who are tempted out of their role in the interests of settlement should make it quite clear that they are no longer acting as a mediator and cannot go back to being a mediator once they have accepted some other role.

One of the writers, when asked to witness a real property transfer resulting from a mediation, obtained a written acknowledgment from the parties verifying that the mediation was concluded and confirming that she was witnessing the document as a private person and not as a mediator.

Accusations of bias against the mediator

It is the mediator's nightmare to be accused of bias. Such accusations are rare, but sometimes do occur no matter how careful the mediator has been. It can happen where a party is particularly wound up and the mediator is either trying to emphasise the ground rules or is trying to give the other party a fair input into the dialogue.

The accusation of "You are not giving me a fair go" is very intimidating. It usually stems from a party's distorted perception in the following way. A naturally verbose person may be a talker rather than a listener and, in general interactions with people on social or other occasions is used to dominating the conversation. In mediation he or she is being requested to share the talking space equally. This is a complete change in the natural order of things for that person, whose subjective view, quite understandably, is of not being given a "fair go" because a "fair go" is to be the centre of attention. One mediator responded to this accusation by saying:

> The reason I intervened at that point was because I noted that you had interrupted B at least eight times in the last five minutes. You may not have been aware of this. I was also becoming concerned that with so many ideas being expressed by you, we needed to break these down and explore each one separately.

Where a perception of bias may possibly have a genuine basis, the mediator should consider saying:

> Thank you for drawing that to my attention. It does sometimes happen in mediation that the mediator sees a need to balance things up and I may have been trying to do that at that point.

Demands for a private session

The mediator should resist one party's demand for a private session. Instantly accommodating this demand means that the party may have successfully hijacked the process and usurped the mediator's role. Where a party resists continuing in the joint session or appears unwilling or unable to continue unless a private session is promised, the mediator should ensure that the other party does not feel disadvantaged. A number of possibilities are open to the mediator, including:

▮ suggesting a coffee break to be followed by a private session with each party starting with the initiator;

▮ consulting with the other party to establish whether they would also appreciate a private session at this stage of the mediation;

▮ suggesting breaking into private session with the other party first.

The directive party

A party may sometimes demand that the mediator write something up on the board in a certain way (for example, an agenda item). If accession to this demand will lead to a judgmental or non-neutral result, the mediator should reiterate that the mediator's role is a neutral one and that he or she would be acting inappropriately if they wrote something up in the manner demanded.

The writers have often coped with such demands in this way, and the demanding party appears to accept that they are putting the mediator in a compromising or unfair position, which they may not have realised when the demand was made. This intervention can be used successfully in other circumstances, such as when a party is monologuing or claiming too much of the floor.

Dealing with angry people

Parties may be difficult to handle because the process method is not to their liking for personality reasons. In most cases where parties are being difficult it is because they are angry or frustrated with the dispute or the other party for historical reasons and this frustration may spill over to the mediator.

Mediator patience and perseverance usually pay off. Generally a personal response, such as debating with the party or retaliating because the party has criticised the mediator, should be avoided. No response is better than a defensive response.

Allowing ventilation of feelings has been discussed throughout this book. The mediator can acknowledge and give recognition to parties' feelings through paraphrasing, summarising and reflective listening.

Genuine misunderstandings about what the mediator is trying to achieve should be cleared up and this can be done without the mediator becoming defensive. Agreement and apology, where appropriate, are time-honoured methods of diffusing anger. Rather than launching into a defence, no matter how justified, the mediator can say:

> I agree, that may have been confusing. I am sorry if I didn't make myself clear.

Where parties are angry with each other, as they often are, intervening too early can sometimes escalate the anger and increase the demands. Interventions are more productive when the anger level has dropped.

The threatening party

Threats of retribution or violence

Threats of this nature should not be tolerated. In such cases the mediator should call off the session. In some extreme cases the mediator should advise the parties that the confidentiality of the session is breached by such threats and that consideration will be given to informing the appropriate authorities. Most Agreements to Mediate contain a confidentiality clause that states that there is no obligation to maintain confidentiality with regard to certain criminal offences. Mediators should obtain information as to whether the threat constitutes a criminal offence.

Other types of threats

These can occur where one party has some information about another party and may be using it as a coercive negotiating tool. Quite often the information involves taxation evasion, social security fraud or hidden partnership assets. Sometimes a party will threaten to go to the media about their complaint if the other party does not succumb to their demands. Usually these threats are not made directly but are raised by a party in private session.

Case Note

In a mediation concerning a property settlement following the demise of a de facto relationship, the property owner revealed that the other party had been receiving social security benefits by portraying herself as a single person during the relationship. He intended to use this information to make her forego a substantial part of her claim. In this case, the mediator, who was a lawyer, asked him whether he had thought of seeking legal advice about his own position in this regard. The alleged fraud had apparently been perpetrated with his knowledge and consent, even though the ex-de facto partner was the official recipient of the benefit. This "reality test" promoted better faith bargaining. The mediator's comment in this case was not legal advice, but rather an alert to the possibility that more legal information might be required.

Where an opportunity such as that outlined in the above Case Note does not present itself, the mediator needs to consider whether the best way out of the moral dilemma is to ignore it and continue the mediation regardless, on the basis that the parties should sort it out themselves.

Another option is to call their bluff. In the case of, say, the media threats, the mediator might reality test by asking why they have not already approached the media, what they think might be involved in media contact and what would happen if the media were not sympathetic. A role reversal might entail asking whether, if they were the other party, they would have come to mediation if they had known they were going to be threatened, or whether, if they were the other party, they would concede ground in response to a threat.

Another way is to ask them to hypothesise about what their position would have been if they had not had the information in question and whether they would have taken a softer position.

Insults and other destructive communication

Occasional insults can be part and parcel of a session. Bad language and even aggression may be a normal communication pattern for both parties. Just because a mediator is personally discomforted by four-letter words or insults does not mean that the parties are. This way of communicating is quite common in certain trades and industries, and may be generally so with people in other circumstances.

Ongoing insults, particularly from one party only, should not be tolerated. Even if it is the parties' normal way of communicating, the mediator should make it clear that the time has come where it is not possible to move forward in such circumstances. The mediator can also make it clear that he or she has no interest in being a participant where such destructive communication is overwhelming the session.

In some cases the mediator can remind the parties that they are spending money and time on rehashing fights they have fought a thousand times before and they might like to consider a more cost-effective way of continuing the fight.

An occasional swear word can usually be ignored. If recurrent swearing or other forms of antagonism are upsetting to the other party the mediator should intervene and point out that the aim is to convince the other party to settle and that favourable settlement is rarely achieved by antagonising the opponent. This advice can be given in joint session if both are point-scoring or privately if it is predominantly one individual who is doing so.

The walk-out

A threatened walk-out can be a manipulation or can signal a lack of commitment. It can indicate that a party is not coping well, the mediation is not proving favourable to that party or the doubt that has been created has resulted in a devastating loss of face.

Rarely are threatened walk-outs carried through. Even while moving towards the door the party may be entertaining the hope that the mediator will intervene to prevent the action.

The mediator should usually try to prevent a walk-out and keep the needs of the other party in mind. The mediator should suggest a coffee or comfort break. If possible the mediator should resist running into private session to counsel the person in the first instance as this may create a power imbalance and may be perceived as a successful strategy on the part of the one making the threat.

Where a party is continually disrupting the session by threatening to walk out, but does not do so, the mediator should call their bluff and actually invite the party to do so if the session makes the party uncomfortable. This "reverse psychology" usually has an instant impact.

A real walk-out, in contrast to a threatened one, sometimes occurs where there has been bad faith participation by one or other of the parties. In either case, there is little point in continuing the mediation as the element of good faith no longer exists to strike an agreement. Sometimes a bad faith participant will manufacture an excuse, such as mediator bias, to abandon the session, or a party who feels the other side has abused the mediation process may walk away in genuine disgust.

MEDIATOR-DRIVEN PROBLEMS

Problems can occur during mediation not just as a result of parties' conduct as outlined above, but directly as a result of what the mediator does, especially if the mediator is recently trained. The following examples illustrate how mediators can create unnecessary problems for themselves, and some suggestions are offered for avoiding the problems or at least correcting them.

The mediator acts as an advocate or adviser rather than a neutral third party

The mediator offers advice to a party

The mediator may be tempted to abandon the facilitating role for that of the professional adviser to a party be it that of a lawyer or counsellor. The facilitator's role is in fact far more difficult and it requires great skill and experience not to deviate from it. The mediator often spontaneously assumes the adviser's role without waiting for a request or a demand from the parties. The party might have said:

> What do you think I should do? You've had a lot of experience in this area.

If the mediator is aware of having erred, this should be communicated to the parties. For example:

> Joe, I'm aware that I've told you what you ought to do about your problem. I shouldn't have said that. My role is not to advise you. Can you think of other ways of dealing with it? Could you both suggest options?

If the mediator is not aware of having lapsed into an advisory role, he or she risks antagonising one of the parties while at the same time ignoring one of the important principles of mediation. (See Chapter 20 — "How neutral are we?")

The mediator defines the issues

The mediator defines the issues rather than acknowledging that they were derived from the parties' opening statements and may even add new ones not mentioned in their statements

For example, the mediator says:

> The issues as I see them are X, Y and Z. And it's quite obvious to me that you ought to discuss A, B and C as well. It's most important you do so.

Instead of saying:

> From what you've both said in your opening statements, the issues appear to be X, Y and Z. Did I hear you correctly?

Once again the mediator risks losing neutrality and antagonising one or both of the parties.

The approach the mediator should adopt is outlined in more detail in Chapter 3 — "Parties' opening statements and mediator's summaries".

The mediator appears to take sides or actually takes sides with one of the parties

In joint session the mediator may appear to be taking sides with one of the parties. For example, the mediator might comment on Mary's opinion that she has carried the total responsibility for the office management and that Bob has never acknowledged her efforts, by saying, "I really think you have a point there", thus risking losing neutrality and creating a perception of bias. Instead of offering an opinion, it would have been a better strategy to ask Bob to comment on her statement. For example:

> You've just heard Mary say that she really thinks she's assumed the total responsibility for the office management and that you have taken her for

granted and never acknowledged her efforts. Can you tell her what you think of what she's just said?

The mediator allows herself or himself to be seduced by one of the parties

The mediator might get too caught up with one of the parties who tries to curry favour through flattery or by other means. The mediator should refocus the party's attention on the mediation and politely divert the party's attention to the issue under discussion. If not, the other party will perceive preferential treatment.

One of the parties may try a form of "emotional blackmail" on the mediator by bringing on the tears. Certainly, it may not necessarily be a strategy on the part of the party. Whether it is or not the mediator could pass the packet of tissues to the party. The tears may cease without further disruption to the mediation. If they do not it may be better to adjourn the session briefly and have a brief private session with each party, beginning with the distressed party.

The mediator speaks and negotiates on behalf of one party, acting more as the party's agent

This may create the impression for the other party that the mediator is advocating for that party and actually agrees with the offers made. It is far better to discourage the parties from making use of the mediator in that way.

The mediator treats the parties differently

The mediator might at the end of Party A's opening statement ask Party B to respond to it rather than outline what brought Party B to mediation. As Party A has not been given equal opportunity to do the same, having been the first to begin, the mediator is promoting an accuser–defendant dynamic.

The mediator might only summarise Party B's statement and forget to summarise Party A's statement. A mediator's checklist is important to avoid these inconsistencies.

At the end of the first private session the mediator might suggest that he or she convey offers from the first party in private session to the second party. Thus, the second party has not been given the same opportunity to make the best use of the private session in terms of exploring further settlement options, expanding on the issues and evaluating options which might be mutually satisfying. Instead the mediator has forced one party merely to react to the other party. (See Chapter 6 — "Private sessions" to avoid creating this sort of imbalance.)

Mediator acts on her or his private agenda

The mediator makes judgmental statements about what the parties say or do, especially in private session

For example: "You'll get absolutely nowhere with that approach", or "I'm glad you've admitted that", or "I'm glad you've conceded that", or "Don't you think you should agree that your case is a weak one?", or "You'd be far better off if you stuck to your guns and did not accept anything less than ... ", or "There's no chance he'd win in court, so you can afford not to be so generous in your concessions". This is not appropriate mediator behaviour.

The mediator should, of course, avoid giving personal views on anything, even when asked. The way to avoid this is to foster a collaborative problem solving approach by the parties and elicit their views, asking them to comment on each other's opinions. In joint or private session, the mediator could ask: "Can you think of ways you can get X and he could get Y?"

The mediator stops listening to the parties and directs the mediation to obtain a result based on a private agenda formulated early in the session

When the mediator stops listening to the parties, any opportunity to empower the parties is wasted. Additional difficulties that need to be overcome are created as the parties are forced to deal with issues that have no relevance to them, thus resulting in a monumental impasse.

Mediator adopts a controlled rational approach and avoids dealing with the parties' feelings and emotions at all costs

The mediator refers regularly to the ground rules to control the parties at the first sign of a negative and heated exchange between them.

As discussed in more detail in Chapter 5, the mediator should allow all the parties to ventilate, then, if it goes on too long, intervene strategically without constant reminders about the ground rules. It is very useful to let the parties have their day in mediation. Again, the freezing out of feelings often leads to a final impasse because of parties' frustration at not being allowed to ventilate.

The mediator points to parties' contradictions in the course of mediation

For example: "But didn't you just say the very opposite?" or "But just a moment ago, you actually denied that."

The mediator should avoid pointing out any contradictory statements by the party who might as a result be discouraged from making any further statements. It should also be remembered that parties are entitled to change their minds. It serves very little purpose to draw any attention to such contradictory statements and may cause that party to lose face. Even if parties contradict the mediator, the mediator should ignore it and say: "Yes, and ..." rather than "Yes, but ...".

Mediator is overly concerned with premature settlement thus jeopardising the prospect of productive negotiation and a mutually satisfying outcome

Mediators who are overly concerned with premature settlement are either demonstrating their lack of experience or do not possess some of the appropriate personal qualities, namely patience and perseverance, which make for an effective mediator. The mediator should ensure that all issues have been explored and clarified, then encourage option generating rather than an immediate solution, even if one of the parties insists on immediate horse-trading often based on an entrenched position. The danger of seeking settlement too early may result in an impasse actively created by the mediator and which cannot be overcome.

Procedural problems

Mediator uses technical language or jargon

Mediators who do not use plain English risk losing the attention of the parties who may feel that they would lose face if they asked for the meaning of the terms used. Even when plain English is used by the mediator, it is always wise to ask the parties: "Any questions?" rather than "Do you understand?" If the latter question is asked, it might make the parties feel that they should have understood and they might lose face by indicating that they did not understand.

Mediator asks parties to provide more information to her or him

The mediator might encourage parties to provide more information to the mediator rather than to the other party so that the mediator "can understand better". This is likely to delay or even block communication between the parties. As already stressed, the mediator should encourage the parties to impart information to each other so that they can gain a better understanding of each other's perspectives, past, present or future.

Mediator allows parties to come unprepared, uncertain about their authority to settle

As already highlighted, the mediator should check authority to settle before the mediation starts.

# Chapter 23

The role of interpreters and support persons

INTERPRETERS IN MEDIATION

The need for professional interpreters

The use of interpreters in mediations can double the length of the session and the mediator's work load. It is highly desirable when making use of interpreters in mediation to ensure that they are qualified. The request by one of the parties for use of a friend or family member or legal representative as an interpreter should be declined, particularly when the interpreter would be interpreting for both sides. The danger of bias is obvious.

What is the interpreter's role?

An interpreter's role should be clearly defined to all participants, including the interpreter, prior to the mediation. Experienced court interpreters rarely need instruction on how to do their job, but the mediation forum may be an unfamiliar one and its informality can result in interpreters taking a less strict approach than they would in the courtroom.

In rare cases interpreters can be tempted to see themselves in a de facto mediator role and by-pass the mediator by attempting to conduct the communication between the parties. Where the interpreter and a party are from the same ethnic background, the interpreter has been known to give advice and instructions to the compatriot including furnishing the opinion that "you can't do that in this country".

Interpreters should be discouraged from offering an opinion on a party's attitude or state of mind unless asked to do so. Their role is strictly that of language translation.

It is an absolute mistake to consider the idea of a party being the interpreter. Nor is it useful for mediators to act also as interpreters even though they may have the appropriate language skills. Doing so would almost certainly jeopardise the other party's perception of the mediator's impartiality and heighten the level of suspicion and mistrust.

Guidelines for the effective use of interpreters in mediation

Explaining the process to the interpreter

The mediator should have a short private meeting with the interpreter before the session commences. The mediator may need to briefly outline the mediation process, explain the nature of the meeting and, with a court interpreter, explain the differences in the two forums, particularly the less structured way in which discussions can arise. The interpreter should be required to sign a third-party confidentiality statement.

Agreeing on the method of interpreting

The interpreter should be asked what is her or his preferred interpreting technique: simultaneous or consecutive. In the latter case the mediator needs to pause for a translation of two or three sentences. In the former the mediator will not need to pause at all. The mediator will need to communicate the agreed interpretation method to the parties. The mediator can suggest to the interpreter that he or she can call for time out if the dialogue is becoming too prolonged to accurately translate. Preferably the translation should be as verbatim as possible, rather than an overview being offered, although in some cases a verbatim report may prove to be impractical.

In the interests of efficiency, the mediator should consider omitting the step of reading back the parties' opening statements. This is because interpretation of the parties' statements is so slow that listening requires more effort and the doubt creating rationale for hearing the statements twice is not so vital. Interpreters should be forewarned that they may need to translate the written agreement into the language of the party before the party signs the terms.

In some cases, the party does have a working understanding of the English language and may prefer to ask for the interpreter's help when needed rather than have everything interpreted. The mediator should give the party that choice.

Seating arrangements

Mediators have different preferences for seating arrangements. Some mediators prefer to have the interpreter sit beside them or slightly behind them rather than next to the party they are interpreting for. This is in order to emphasise the interpreter's role as a neutral and technical one. However, this might make instantaneous interpreting problematic.

Other mediators ask the interpreter to sit opposite them at an equal distance from the parties. If that arrangement is adopted it is preferable for a round table to be used so that the parties do not have to turn their backs on the mediator. Round tables also avoid any perception of the interpreter being granted special standing.

How to proceed

When interpreters are present, there are two basic approaches to communicating with the parties, either through the interpreter or directly with the parties — even though the responses will be given by the interpreter. Even when the first approach is adopted, it is still possible for the mediator to maintain eye contact with each party where a round table is used.

Whatever the approach, the mediator needs to explain the communication method to all present. With the first approach the mediator needs to tell the interpreter:

> It's now time for the opening statements. Could you ask X if he would like to start now?

With the second approach, the mediator speaks directly to the party saying:

> X, it is your turn to tell us what brought you here today.

The second approach is not appropriate with simultaneous interpreting, while the first approach might be more natural with consecutive interpreting.

Where the party has some knowledge of English, the second approach, that of direct communication, can be applied whether the interpreting is carried out simultaneously or consecutively.

The parties should be encouraged to communicate directly in the same manner as they would if they were speaking the same language. However, the parties may at times find this difficult to maintain.

Mediators may need to take more notes than usual in this situation because they are not able to rely as much on their own active listening skills to pick up the little nuances as they would normally be able to do. The intervention of the interpretation itself can actually be helpful during the parties' opening statements because the pauses between translations give the mediator time to catch up on what is being said and the opportunity for more eye contact than normal.

If the mediator suspects that the interpretation is not being accurately conveyed because the ethnic dialogue appears to be much more prolonged than the translation which is being offered, then the mediator should intervene and request an explanation, or request that the interpreter cut in on the dialogue and translate more frequently.

The mediator should also intervene if the interpretation is contracted in case the interpreter is engaging in over-summarising. However, some languages are much more expansive than English and some English words and expressions are not able to be succinctly translated. There should be a quick intervention by the mediator where the interpreter and a party are engaging in an ongoing one-to-one conversation.

In such a situation the interpreter is stepping out of role and may indeed be counselling the party or at least taking on a clarifying role. The mediator needs to step in and remind the interpreter of the interpretation "ground rules". Another occasion which called for a reminder was where an interpreter attempted to tell the mediator not to explore a domestic violence issue which had been raised in a child custody dispute because it was perfectly acceptable for a man to hit his wife in that particular culture.

Case Note

The mediator asked a question of a party. The interpreter then spoke to this party who responded with an ongoing monologue addressed to the interpreter without any translation being offered by the latter. The mediator broke in and requested a translation of this conversation. The interpreter's response was: "She said 'Yes'."

SUPPORT PERSONS IN MEDIATION

The presence of support persons in mediation has always been a common feature though some mediation service providers have discouraged it. There is no valid reason for excluding parties from having a support person accompanying them in the mediation session. However, there are three important conditions that need to be applied:

1. The other party's consent needs to be obtained.
2. The role of the support person needs to be agreed upon by all parties.
3. The support person must sign a confidentiality agreement.

It is rare for the other party to decline to consent to the presence of a support person. If, however, one of the parties does not consent, the mediator could suggest that although it will not be possible to include a support person in the mediation, the support person could sit in the waiting room. The party who had requested the support person's presence could seek an occasional brief adjournment to speak to her or him. The party should, however, be reminded that what occurs in the mediation remains confidential.

What role should support persons play in mediation?

The role support persons should play in mediation is to provide personal and emotional support to the party. They should not be asked questions by the mediator, help generate options or join in any discussion. However, the party might turn to the support person to confirm feelings or emotions, for example:

> You remember how badly it affected me when I was told by him that I could no longer have unlimited contact with my daughter?
>
> Yes I do.

The support person may also participate in the private session. The role of the support person in private session may be a more active one as the session is confidential. However, it would still be wise for the mediator not to encourage the support person to take part in the decision-making process.

There are, of course exceptions. For example, in a recent mediation the parents of two young women had paid for the mediation session and both of the parties felt at ease in the private session when their parents (the father of one party and the mother of the other) took a more active role by offering their opinions on options generated by the women and occasionally generating some of their own. The women themselves sought their parents' advice. As each of the parties had a support person present there was not as much danger of a perception of imbalance by either of the parties.

Appendix

PRELIMINARY CONFERENCE PRO-FORMA LETTER

[DATE]

Ms Mary Smith,   Mr Bob Jones,
BY FAX No. 9XXX YYYY   BY FAX No. 8AAA BBBB

No of pages: 9

Dear Ms Smith and Mr Jones,

Mediation of
Smith and Jones

I refer to our telephone conversation and confirm that I have been appointed to mediate the above matter.

I also confirm that the preliminary conference for the mediation will be held on [AT LOCATION] [BY TELECONFERENCE. I WILL ORGANISE THE TELECONFERENCE.] Normally one hour should be set aside for the conference. Participating will be [SMITH TEAM] on the one hand and [JONES TEAM] on the other.

Enclosed please find an Agenda of the matters for discussion. Please consider before the preliminary conference what information you will require from the other party in order to be in a position at the Mediation to negotiate settlement from a position of knowledge.

I enclose a copy of the Agreement to Mediate that I propose be signed at the [CONFERENCE/MEDIATION]. Please raise any comments [PRIOR TO/DURING] the preliminary conference.

Should you have any queries, please do not hesitate to telephone me.

I look forward to [MEETING/TALKING WITH] each of you. Thank you for agreeing to my appointment as Mediator.

Yours sincerely,

Mediator

AGENDA: PRELIMINARY CONFERENCE

1. Explanation of mediation features and the process to be followed on the day.

2. Discussion on the Agreement to Mediate, including:
   # description of parties and dispute;
   # mediator's fees and costs, including payment;
   # arrangements for signing of the Agreement to Mediate; and
   # undertakings on confidentiality until signing.

3. Broadly, what are the matter(s) at issue?

4. Pre-mediation exchange between the parties of information and/or documents. Setting a timetable for any such exchange.

5. Pre-mediation preparation by each party:
   # What is the party's **prime need** that is sought to be met through any mediated settlement;

   # Consideration of **realistic** maximum and minimum outcomes from mediation;

   Within such outcomes, consideration of **options for a compromise agreement**, with which that party can live, *and* the other party is likely to accept; and

   # **Best, and worst, alternatives** to a mediated settlement, including time delays, costs and other consequences for each party, if the dispute is not resolved at Mediation.

6. Who will be attending the Mediation, and what will be the role of any adviser?

7. Preparation of each Party's opening verbal statement, **giving a broad (5-minute) overview** of what led to mediation and that Party's current perspective.

8. **Full authority** required by representatives to settle "within any range that can reasonably be anticipated" without the need to refer to another person for decision.

9. Confirmation of the date, time and place for the Mediation.

Mediator

POST-PRELIMINARY CONFERENCE PRO-FORMA LETTER

[DATE]

Ms Mary Smith,   Mr Bob Jones,
BY FAX No. 9XXX YYYY   BY FAX No. 8AAA BBBB

No of pages: 3

Dear Ms Smith and Mr Jones,

Mediation of
Smith and Jones

I refer to the Preliminary Conference held yesterday and confirm several matters we discussed.

Mediation is essentially a facilitated negotiation involving clarification of the past and exploration of ideas for resolving present difficulties. I emphasise my neutral role as mediator and that mediators do not advise any party nor decide the outcome. As discussed, reaching agreement is a matter for the parties and this is best achieved when mediation's underlying philosophy of co-operative non-adversarial problem solving is observed.

Whilst it is valid for each party to come to mediation with a preferred settlement result in mind, it is useful to consider any fall-back options available and options which may be raised by the other side, bearing in mind that each side is generally seeking to achieve the most satisfactory result for themselves. In this regard, please consider before the Mediation, the items in paragraph 6 of the Agenda sent to you for the Preliminary Conference.

It was agreed that the following information would be exchanged between the parties as soon as possible and in any case by [DATE]:

For and on behalf of Smith:

◆

For and on behalf of Jones:

◆

2.

I confirm that the Mediation has been arranged for [DAY, DATE] at [VENUE].

I note that attending at the mediation for each party will be:
!   [NAMES for SMITH TEAM]
!   [NAMES for JONES TEAM]
As a courtesy to all Parties, any changes in, or additions to, the stated participants should be notified in advance.

I acknowledge the confirmation that one of the representatives of [NAME OF PARTY] will have full and complete authority to settle this matter at the mediation, "within any range that can reasonably be anticipated", without the need to check with any other person for decision.

Your attention is drawn to item 2 of the enclosed Agenda for the Mediation. Please prepare a **brief (5-minute)** verbal opening statement of what led to mediation and your current perspective. This need only be a broad overview from which we shall compile a list of matters for subsequent discussion in as much detail as the parties wish.

I note that, whilst the Agreement to Mediate will not be signed until the start of the mediation session, you have each agreed and undertaken that the provisions relating to confidentiality and privilege will apply as of yesterday and the Agreement will be dated as of that date.

Should you have any queries, please do not hesitate to telephone me.

I look forward to meeting each of you at the Mediation.

Yours sincerely,

Mediator

MEDIATION AGENDA

1. Mediator's opening remarks.

2. Each Party's opening verbal statement, **giving a broad (5-minute) overview** of what led to mediation and that party's current perspective.

3. Mediator's summary of the opening statements.

4. Identification of matters for discussion.

5. Discussion of each matter, identification of options, and the making of offers for possible agreement:

    #   in joint session(s); and

    #   as needed, in confidential private session(s).

6. Settling terms and signing Settlement Agreement, if agreement is reached.

Mediator

Agreement to Mediate

THIS AGREEMENT is made as of   (day)   (month) 200

BETWEEN THE FOLLOWING PARTIES (in this Agreement called "the parties")

Name of party (please print): _____

Address: _____

Name of party (please print): _____

Address: _____

AND THE MEDIATOR (called "the Mediator")

[NAME & ADDRESS]

Appointment of Mediator

1. The parties appoint the Mediator to mediate the dispute between them in accordance with the terms of this Agreement. The dispute is briefly described in Schedule 1 to this Agreement (the "Dispute"). The Mediator accepts the appointment to mediate the Dispute at such time(s) and place(s) as agreed to by the parties and the Mediator.

Role of the Mediator

2. The Mediator will conduct the Mediation in such manner as the Mediator determines.

3. The Mediator will assist the parties to attempt to resolve the dispute by helping them to:

    - systematically isolate the issues in dispute;
    - develop options for the resolution of these issues;
    - explore the usefulness of these options; and
    - achieve a resolution that is acceptable to them.

4. The Mediator may meet with the parties together or separately as the Mediator determines.

5. The Mediator will be neutral and impartial and will not:

   - give legal or other professional advice to any party;
   - impose a result on any party; or
   - make decisions for any party.

6. The Mediator will not accept an appointment or act for any party in relation to any proceedings concerning the Dispute. Neither party will take action to cause the Mediator to breach this Clause 6.

Conflicts of Interest

7. The Mediator must, prior to the commencement of the mediation, disclose to the parties to the best of the Mediator's knowledge any prior dealings with any of the parties as well as any interest in the Dispute.

8. If in the course of the mediation, the Mediator becomes aware of any circumstances that might reasonably be considered to affect the Mediator's capacity to act impartially, the Mediator must immediately inform the parties of these circumstances. The parties will then decide whether the mediation will continue with that Mediator or with a new Mediator appointed by the parties.

Co-operation by the Parties

9. The parties must co-operate with the Mediator during the mediation and will comply with the reasonable requests and directions of the Mediator in relation to the conduct of the mediation and any preliminary steps.

Preliminary Conference

10. As part of the mediation, the Mediator may schedule a preliminary conference at a time and manner suitable to the parties and the Mediator. The purposes of the conference include establishing a timetable for exchange of information and the arrangements for the mediation. The conference may be held face-to-face or by telephone or by other means.

11. The parties and their representatives and advisers who are to attend the mediation session, must attend the preliminary conference with the Mediator.

Authority to Settle and Representation at the Mediation Session

12. The representative of any party must attend the mediation with authority to settle within any range that can reasonably be anticipated.

13. At the mediation, each party may have one or more other persons, including legally qualified persons, to assist, advise or support them, subject to any such person signing the Attachment to this Agreement and the relevant party ensuring that any such person observes Clauses 14 to 16. The number of support persons for a party will not exceed two without the agreement of the mediator.

Confidentiality of the Mediation and Privilege

14. Any information disclosed to a Mediator in private is to be treated as confidential by the Mediator unless the party making the disclosure states otherwise. Anything said to a party by a Mediator in private will not be disclosed by that party to the other party.

15. The parties and the Mediator will not disclose to anyone not involved in the mediation any information or document given to them during the mediation unless required by law to make such a disclosure or except for the purpose of obtaining professional advice or where the person is within that party's household. In the latter two exceptions, the party must advise the adviser or person that the information or document is confidential and will ensure that such adviser or person will observe this clause and Clause 16.

16. The parties and the Mediator agree that subject to Clauses 20 and 21, the following will be privileged and will not be disclosed in, or be the subject of, a subpoena to give evidence or to produce documents, in any proceedings in respect of the Dispute:

    16.1 Any settlement proposal whether made by a party or the Mediator;

    16.2 The willingness of a party to consider any such proposal;

    16.3 Any statement made by a party or the Mediator during the mediation; or

    16.4 Any information prepared for the mediation.

17. If a party produces a document for the purposes of the mediation that is, or otherwise would be, privileged from production or admission into evidence, that party will not be taken to have waived that privilege by producing the document.

Termination of the Mediation

18. A party may terminate the mediation at any time after consultation with the Mediator.

19. The Mediator may terminate the Mediator's involvement in the mediation if, after consultation with the parties, the Mediator feels unable to assist the parties to achieve resolution of the Dispute.

Settlement of the Dispute

20. If agreement is reached at the mediation, the terms of the agreement must be written down and signed by the parties before they leave the mediation.

Enforcement of the Settlement Agreement

21. Any party may enforce the terms of the settlement agreement by judicial proceedings.

22. For the purposes of Clause 21, any party may call evidence of the settlement agreement including evidence from the Mediator and any other person engaged in the mediation as to the meaning or intent of the settlement agreement, but not otherwise any of the matters listed in Clause 16. The party calling the Mediator to give evidence will pay to the Mediator professional fees calculated at the hourly rate stated in Schedule 2, for the time required for preparation and attendance to give evidence and will pay any costs associated therewith.

Exclusion of Liability and Indemnity

23. The Mediator will not be liable to a party for any act or omission in the performance of the Mediator's obligations under this agreement unless the act or omission is fraudulent.

24. The parties separately release and indemnify the Mediator against any claim for any act or omission in the performance of the Mediator's obligations under this agreement unless the act or omission is fraudulent.

The Cost of the Mediation

24. The parties separately will be liable to the Mediator for its share of the Mediator's fees and costs described in Schedule 2.

25. Unless the parties to the mediation agree otherwise, the fees and cost of the mediation will be borne by the parties in equal shares.

26. Each party will be liable to pay such fees and costs in the manner set forth in Schedule 2.

Schedule 1: Description of the Dispute

The Dispute is the subject of proceedings:

No: _____ of _____ in the _____ Court

(Insert brief description of the Dispute)

_____

_____

_____

_____

Schedule 2: Costs of the Mediation

1. **Mediator's Fees:**
    For the preliminary conference, reading material and all preparation time:
    $ per hour

    For the first 4 hours of the mediation session: $

    For each hour beyond the first 4 hours: $ per hour up to a maximum daily fee of $

2. **Room Hire, Travel & Other Expenses:**

    At cost.

3. **Payment Arrangements**

    Each party will pay its share of fees and costs [by cheque at the conclusion of the mediation/within 14 days of the receipt of a tax invoice].

SIGNING OF THE AGREEMENT TO MEDIATE

The parties and the Mediator have signed this Agreement to Mediate as follows:

Date: _____ (day)_____ (month) 200

_____   _____

(Name of party or representative. Please print)   *(Signature)*

_____   _____

(Name of party or representative. Please print)   *(Signature)*

_____   _____

(Name of Mediator. Please print)   *(Signature)*

CONFIDENTIALITY AGREEMENT – ADVISERS AND THIRD PARTIES

In consideration of my being permitted to be involved in the mediation of the Dispute described in the Agreement to Mediate to which this Agreement is attached, I,

_____(name & address)

_____(name & address)

_____(name & address)

_____(name & address)

independently and separately agree with each of the parties and the Mediator that:

1. I will not disclose to anyone any information disclosed to, or received by, me during the mediation, unless required by law to make such a disclosure.

2. I will not disclose to anyone involved in the mediation any document received by me in relation to the mediation from a party to the mediation unless expressly authorised to do so by the party producing the document.

AGREED this   (day)   (month)   200

Name: _____

Name: _____

Name: _____

Name: _____

Mediator: _____

Index

Absent audience, face-saving, 218–219

Acknowledgment, apology
isolating, 245
visual aids, 265–266

Action plan, mutual, issue identification and agenda setting, 46, 50, 61

Active listening
communication skills, 193, 195–197
making use of, 197
mediator's summaries of parties' statements, 32
need for accurate hearing, 195–196
need for appropriate physical environment, 196
neutrality, retaining perception of, 202–203
objectives, 196–197
progressive summarising, 197
reframing, 195
strategic mediator intervention, 211
using parties' language, 197

Adjournment
agreement outcome, 5–7
range of mediation outcomes, 123–124, 129

Adolescents, children, shuttle mediation, 170

Advice, advising
advising parties, 83, 112
delivery of offers, 111–112, 120
giving advice, 88
legal, professional advice, 13
mediator offers advice to party, 320–321
preliminary conference, advisers, 180

Advocate/adviser, mediator acts as, 320–322

Agenda
effective use of, 224
items, topics, 55, 171
post-preliminary conference, pro-forma letter, 335–336
preliminary conference, pro forma letter, 333–334
telephone mediations, 148, 151

Agenda, mediator's private – see Mediator's agenda

Agenda setting
co-mediation, 140
heading, type of, 49
joint session implications, 58–60
mediation model, 4–5
mediator's opening statement, 13–14, 16
mediator's role, 68